William Cullen Bryant, Martha Noyes Williams

A Year in China

A Narrative of Capture and Imprisonment

William Cullen Bryant, Martha Noyes Williams

A Year in China
A Narrative of Capture and Imprisonment

ISBN/EAN: 9783744795128

Printed in Europe, USA, Canada, Australia, Japan

Cover: Foto ©Thomas Meinert / pixelio.de

More available books at **www.hansebooks.com**

A YEAR IN CHINA;

AND A

NARRATIVE OF CAPTURE AND IMPRISONMENT, WHEN HOMEWARD BOUND, ON BOARD THE REBEL PIRATE FLORIDA.

BY

Mrs. H. DWIGHT WILLIAMS,

AUTHOR OF " VOICES FROM THE SILENT LAND."

WITH AN

INTRODUCTORY NOTE

By WILLIAM CULLEN BRYANT.

NEW YORK:

PUBLISHED BY HURD AND HOUGHTON,

401 BROADWAY, COR. WALKER STREET.

1864.

This Volume,

MUCH OF WHICH WAS ORIGINALLY WRITTEN IN LETTERS TO MY MOTHER,

IS AFFECTIONATELY AND TEARFULLY

Dedicated

TO HER MEMORY.

CONTENTS.

CHAPTER I.

CHAPTER II.

CHAPTER III.

CHAPTER VII.

CHAPTER VIII.

CHAPTER IX.

CHAPTER X.

CHAPTER XI.

CHAPTER XII.

CHAPTER XIII.

CHAPTER XIV.

CHAPTER XV.

INTRODUCTORY NOTE.

———◆———

THE Empire of China, with its immense population, its peculiar customs and arts, the character of its people, so unlike that of the nations of Western Europe, and the imperfect stage of civilization at which it has halted for many centuries, if, indeed, it has not somewhat receded towards barbarism, presents an interesting subject of inquiry and speculation to all who concern themselves with the welfare and future destiny of the human race. The settlement of the Pacific coast of the United States, and the navigation of the ocean by steam, have made China our immediate neighbor, and will bring us into relations with her people far closer and more fruitful, either of good or evil, than the subjects of any European power can have. Emigrants from that populous land have already made a descent upon our Pacific States, and with whatever jealousy or aversion their arrival may be regarded, they will probably from henceforth form a part of the stock from which that region is to be peopled.

The great rebellion which, for fourteen years past, has raged in China with such prodigious waste of human life, is now brought to an end. The empire, delivered from this danger and this drain upon its resources, may now turn its attention solely to the arts of peace. Report ascribes to the present Government a disposition to allow entrance to the ideas and improvements of European civilization. The country has been opened to the teachers of Christianity, and there are signs of a willingness to adopt new and better modes of intellectual and moral training.

All these circumstances concur to make China and the Chinese objects of an enlightened curiosity to our countrymen. Scarce anything relating to that country and its people is destitute of interest to the inhabitants of the United States. In the little work to which this note is prefixed will be found accounts of Chinese manners and modes of life derived from a personal observation, for which the author possessed rather peculiar advantages. She is the wife of an American gentleman holding an official station under the Chinese Government, the nature of which I will briefly explain.

By the treaties which have opened the trade of the empire to foreigners, the Chinese Government engages to employ, at each of the five ports mentioned in the treaties, an American, English, or French Commissioner of Customs, with the necessary subordinate officers, and with a Superintendent at their head, who resides at Peking, near the Court. These Commissioners act only between the Government and foreigners; they are appointed and paid by the Imperial Court, which possesses descriptions of their personal appearance so minute and exact that they are easily recognized, and they make to that Court monthly returns of their official acts, solemnly attested. Vastly more revenue is gathered into the Chinese treasury since foreigners were thus employed than before. The native officers were easily bribed, and the Government received but meagre returns from ports which now yield a large income. So well has the change worked, that nothing would induce the Chinese Government to return to the old system.

The author of the pages which follow is the wife of the Commissioner at Swatow, one of the five ports through which the commerce of foreign lands is admitted into the kingdom. Inasmuch as the Commissioners may be sent, by an order from Peking through the Superintendent, from one port to another, it happens that their residence is often changed; and, as they are treated with great consideration by the Chinese, both they and the persons composing their families have peculiar opportunities for acquiring a knowledge of the country and its people.

Of that advantage the author of the present work availed herself. Her accounts of Chinese manners and habits of life bear tokens of the greatest sincerity and conscientiousness. They are manifestly the precise relation of what was presented to her observation, and are given without the slightest attempt at embellishment, and without even any unconscious coloring. Those parts of the work which relate to the domestic life of the Chinese women will, in a particular manner, engage the attention of the reader.

The closing part of the narrative is varied by an adventure very different from what ordinarily falls to the lot of the traveller. On her return to the United States, for the sake of her health, she was so unfortunate as to fall into the hands of the pirate Maffit, who seems to have taken a particular fancy to her personal effects, and included them among his other robberies. The narrative of her captivity illustrates the indiscriminating spirit of plunder with which this new class of freebooters exercise their profession.

W. C. BRYANT.

A YEAR IN CHINA.

CHAPTER I.

A VOYAGE to China in a sailing vessel is an every-day occurrence, and its monotonous sea-life usually barren of interesting incidents ; but taking a steamer, and making a sort of yachting trip of it, as it was our good fortune to do, renders it one of the most enjoyable pieces of sea-travel one can make.

We took passage for Hong-Kong in the *Poyang*, — a new steamer belonging to the mercantile house of Messrs. Olyphant & Co., and designed for navigating the Yangtsz-Kiang, one of the largest rivers of China. Although in appearance greatly like one of our river steamers, she was constructed, — in respect to strength and durability, — more on the model of our best sea-going vessels. She was also most ably commanded by Captain George Briggs, and left the dock at the foot of Tenth Street, East River, on the afternoon of October 26, 1861. Two

1

or three steamers, built and intended for the river navigation of China, had, previous to this time, sailed from New York; but we believe none of them had carried passengers, while the *Poyang* had, with the women and children, sixteen. On going aboard the vessel we found her deck and cabins quite thronged with people, few of whom were incited by curiosity, but were attracted thither from affectionate interest, to make their final adieus, and to cheer with good wishes those of their friends who were about to leave for that far off land, —

> "Beyond where Ceylon lifts her spicy breast,
> And waves the woods above the watery waste
> To the fair kingdoms of the rising day."

The morning had been cloudy, and a slight drizzling rain, which set in a little before the warning bell summoned our friends to leave the vessel, did not tend to make our last farewells the more cheerful. A steam-tug was to accompany us down the Narrows, and the Messrs. Olyphant, with a party of friends, together with several clergymen and some friends of the passengers, remaining on board, we enjoyed their companionship for two or three hours longer, during which time a cold collation was served; and having some missionaries among our passengers, interesting religious services were had in the cabin, when, with much earnest prayer, we were com-

mended to the care of our heavenly Father. The
time for the return of these friends having at length
arrived, the steamer was stopped, and with many
adieus they were safely transferred from the vessel to
the tug. Then amid loud cheers and the waving of
handkerchiefs we separated ; and as the distance was
fast widening between us, the colors of each vessel
were constantly dipping, and making their last signals of farewell. There was also a general waving
of handkerchiefs from the silent group on our quarter-deck, and a straining of moistened eyes to get a
last look of the little vessel, whose final disappear-
ance, upon the far-off horizon, told us that we had bidden a long farewell to dear friends and Fatherland.

Our good steamer ploughed swiftly through the
billows, and in a short time we were well out at sea,
having ample opportunity, before reaching the rough
Gulf Stream, to look about and note our surroundings as they affected our prospects for a comfortable
or an uncomfortable voyage. The kind and stirring
character of our stewardess soon satisfied us as to
our cabin prospects, nor did she in the least disap-
point our expectations. In all respects we were
well cared for, and everything was arranged to make
us as comfortable as we could be during so long a
voyage. The next morning we were in the Gulf
Stream, where we had very rough weather for three

days, — during which time, as we expected, sea-
sickness made its appearance, but fortunately, in
nearly every case, to be of only brief duration. It
soon left us to the full and uninterrupted enjoyment
of sea-life; but our early recovery we attribute chiefly to remaining much of the time upon deck, and to
constant regularity at meals; — the sensible advice,
as it proved to be, of a friend experienced in voyaging, and which we commend to all others who may
at any time be similarly circumstanced with ourselves. A few of the passengers, however, suffered
greatly; and the state-rooms becoming uncomfortable
as we entered the warm latitudes, the half-way invalids arranged themselves at their ease in the cabin;
some lying down, and others in a variety of attitudes,
sitting and bracing themselves against the sides of
the cabin, with lugubriously distressed faces, presented pictures of a life on the ocean wave which
embodied far more of the grotesque than the picturesque.

We had entered the tropics, and the heat increasing, although we were almost constantly favored
with a fine cool sea-breeze, our dining-saloon was becoming too warm for comfort. This was somewhat
remedied by resorting to the *punka-frame*, — being a
frame, as its name implies, covered with muslin
and placed over the table, where at meal-time it was

put in motion by the machinery of the vessel, and served all the purposes of a fan. The weather was charming, and we steamed along as quietly as though on a placid river. We had a kind and polite company of passengers, and there being clergymen among the number, prayers were had in the cabin morning and evening, and religious services were held in the dining-saloon every Sunday, to which all were invited. Our experienced and gentlemanly captain and his officers were men to inspire confidence; and the rough passage through the Gulf Stream had fully satisfied us that our vessel was a stanch and firm sailing craft, and also that whatever experience and skill could do for our safety during the voyage, would be done.

On the morning of the 9th of November we sighted St. Antonio, the northernmost of the Cape de Verd Islands. The atmosphere was hazy, and at a distance of twenty miles the island had the appearance of a bank of clouds resting upon the horizon. On closer observation, however, we saw the rugged sides of the mountain steeps; and what had appeared to be a heavy, dark cloud, became the well-defined crest of a mountain, which loomed up in the centre of the island to the height of seven thousand four hundred feet above the level of the sea. We coasted for some time within four or five

miles of its rocky, precipitous sides, finding it sublime in lofty peaks, deep gorges, and barren wastes,
which, with its shadowy ravines, presented a series
of grandly unique pictures.   The sea was of the
purest aqua-marine hue, — a lovely, tropical sea,
— and so clear that one could easily follow the
movements of the finny tribe far down in what
seemed to be the deepest deep.

The Cape de Verd Islands belong to Portugal,
and are of volcanic formation, many of them being
nothing more than masses of barren rocks and
mountains.   They are three hundred miles distant
from the coast of Africa, and have a hot and un-
healthy climate.

We were to stop for coals at Porte au Grande, the
chief port of the island of St. Vincent, and, leaving
the shores of St. Antonio, a sail of thirteen miles
brought us to the entrance of the fine bay which
forms the harbor of this island.   On nearing the
shore we found the scenery more wildly picturesque
in jagged rocks, and wonderful mountain peaks, than
at St. Antonio ; and it did not require any very great
effort of the imagination to transform the singularly
castellated and battlemented cliffs into ruined castles
and fortresses of the olden time.

The little town or village of Port au Grande, — a
miserably squalid nook of houses, — lies on the bor-

ders of a beautiful bay which is shut in on the south, east, and west by mountains, one of which, directly in the rear of the settlement, appears like an old fortress, and has a cloud continually resting upon its summit. The bay itself opens to the north, from which quarter one gets a cool sea-breeze; and in the distance, through a yellowish gray, dusty atmosphere are seen the mountains of St. Antonio. It is said that this peculiar atmosphere is produced by an impalpable sand blown by the wind from the African coast.

There are but few white people in this colony, but the African race are quite numerous. We were coaled by these people, who are not slaves, but, in common with the whites, are always spoken of as Portuguese. There are slaves on some of these islands, but the Portuguese Government some two or three years ago passed a law manumitting them in fourteen years. They speak a *patois* of Portuguese, English, and French, mingled with their African dialect. Little boats lying just under the stern of our vessel were filled with these people, all chatting glibly, and most curiously interlarding their conversation with an occasional word of English or French, which only made their unintelligible jargon seem the more rude and barbarous. The houses had a most miserable appearance, and were stuccoed in the Oriental style with a kind of dirty yellow or cream-colored chunam. The place boasts of one Romish church, the priests of which are Africans, who have been educated and prepared for the position which they occupy by Portuguese missionaries. Some of our passengers visited this church for the purpose of witnessing a marriage ceremony; but their account of it, together with the other services performed there, did not impress us very favorably either in regard to the priests or the people. The weather was very warm, — the mercury rising as high as 87° in the shade on reaching the islands. There is very little vegetation here; but we observed the palm growing before one or two houses in the town, and we also found some tropical fruits, but they were grown on the more fertile and productive islands. This island is mostly sterile, while St. Antonio has some fruitful valleys.

There were two wells a little back of the shores of the bay, — one of them an Oriental-like fountain, which, with its shrubs and overhanging trees, was a very attractive object. The life-picture which this fountain presented at evening, when resorted to by the young women of the place, — who, filling their water-jars, and placing them on their heads stepped lightly homeward, — reminded us that we were fast journeying towards the East.

We displayed the American flag and fired two guns on entering the harbor; but, although there were two United States vessels, besides some English and French, lying at anchor within the bay, none of them noticed us. This, however, was satisfactorily explained when the English Consul boarded the steamer; for we then learned that we had been mistaken for the Rebel pirate Sumter, and that our approach, and entrance into the port, had caused a good deal of commotion in the little colony, the Home Government of which had but a short time before sent instructions to the Governor that no privateers, of the so-called Southern Confederacy, should be permitted to stop in those waters for coals or other supplies; and the officials, being determined to carry out these instructions, were already on the point of bringing some guns from a little fort, perched on the steep mountain-side, and placing them in a position where they could be brought to bear upon our vessel. The masters of the United States ships were also, for a short time, in great trepidation; and one captain of a whaler made ready to slip his cable as we steamed towards the bay. He hailed from New Bedford; but, instead of being obliged to run away from us, came on board with evident pleasure, bringing a boat-load of his men to attend our Sunday religious services. Before reaching these islands we fell in with several vessels, but in almost every instance, when our colors were unfurled, there was no recognition of the civility until the distance between us was fast increasing; and one vessel in particular we thought exceedingly ill-bred, in not at all noticing our salutations. It seemed now to us very evident that we had all along been mistaken for a Rebel pirate. Our vessel was long, low, and dark-looking; but with all these suspicious circumstances against us, it seemed as though, whenever we sighted a strange ship, or were entering a strange port, that a single glance through a glass at the women and children on our quarter-deck, would have satisfied any one that our mission was anything but piratical.

The heat had so increased that on the twelfth day of November the mercury stood at 89°; but although we were to steam directly into a region of much fiercer heat, we were glad to hear, at noon, that our vessel was coaled and nearly ready for sea. Towards evening we took a last look of the beautiful harbor of Porte au Grande, with its remarkable surroundings; and steaming out of the bay, found ourselves the next morning coasting along the island of Fuego,[1] and near to the foot of a mountain by that name, which is a volcanic peak, and has given its appellation to the island. It was a matter of re-

---

[1] *Fuego* is the Portuguese word for fire.

gret that this volcano was not in a state of eruption, as we were not more than twelve miles from it, and could distinctly trace the rough and jagged edge of the crater, and the deep seams down which the lava had formerly flowed to the sea. Another lofty mountain, reminding us, in its outline, of the best pictures we have of Mount Ararat, loomed up by the side of Fuego; but no mountain on any of the islands can compare with the latter either in height or grandeur of appearance.

We passed the southernmost point of Fuego, having the island of St. Jago, the largest, most populous, and productive of the Cape de Verd group, cn our left. We were too far distant, however, to see the land distinctly, and before the 15th of the month had left the whole group far behind, and were nearing the African coast. Shortly after leaving the islands we were spoken by an English merchantman; and it was quite interesting to observe (although we were several miles distant from each other) how easily our captain and his first officer, with the aid of a glass, translated the nautical signs by means of Marryatt's well-devised code of signals. The ship in question was the *Ocean Gem*, bound for Cape Coast Castle; and the captain wished us to report her at the first port we entered. Cape Coast Castle brought painfully to mind the sad fate of L. E. L., — the gifted Miss Landon ; and her own words, —

"But thou dost leave thy memory like a ghost," —

seemed sadly in keeping while sailing so near the spot where her sudden death, still somewhat involved in mystery, occurred.

When in the latitude of Sierra Leone and Liberia, we were fifty miles off the coast of Africa, and our first view of this continent was near Cape Mesurado. It was a very warm, although a bright and beautiful tropical morning; and after passing a little south of the Cape we coasted within eight or ten miles of the shore, having in full view a region of country most luxuriant in rich tropical verdure. The land is low near the sea, but rises with gentle undulations in the distance ; and with the aid of a glass the thatched huts of the natives could be distinctly seen, sprinkled among what seemed to be extensive and beautiful groves of the palm. Many of these groves stretched back as far as the eye could reach; and the trees being of magnificent growth, the landscape presented a scene of the most surpassing beauty. The sea-shore was dotted with fishermen's huts; and wherever the eye turned, vegetation wore an aspect rich and luxurious beyond description.

While admiring one of these lovely landscapes a little after mid-day, opposite the Grain Coast, several small and frail-looking canoes suddenly made their appearance upon the waters around us, each one being paddled by a stout man, and a boy of not more than twelve or fifteen years. When first seen one of the little craft was making every effort to reach us; and her sable navigators were, by signs, trying to induce us to stop and barter with them for fish; but paddle for dear life, as both old and young Africa seemed to do, they were disappointed; yet nothing daunted they still persevered in the chase, their little shuttle-shaped canoe darting beautifully over and between the waves; until, in the end, they were compelled to give us up and return. In ten or fifteen minutes, however, another canoe appeared, as if by magic, still nearer to the vessel; whereupon we were so importuned that our captain finally gave orders for stopping the engine, and then called stoutly for Africa to come alongside. This graceful little bark, like the first, was manned by two persons, whom we thought to be father and son; and they evidently understood the full force of the phrases, — " Now come on as fast as you can," " pull away," " paddle hard," &c. They sat in the bottom of the canoe, and their paddles, which were made of bamboo, were plied without their moving the body; being first thrust into the water on one side, and then on the other, with an extraordinary ease, dexterity, and grace, while they were approaching us with marvellous speed; now with prow and half her length in air, then sinking behind a wave we nearly lost sight of her, but directly would appear the heads and shoulders of these athletic, dusky people, giving unmistakable proof of possessing some skill, with much vigorous bone and muscle. On nearing the ship they made us understand by signs that another of their boats, directly in the rear, contained a man capable of speaking English; and just then another canoe was seen coming, if possible, with greater swiftness, the men paddling and propelling her like athletes, while she darted through the water with the celerity of an arrow from a well-strung bow; and being in a moment alongside our vessel the occupants lost no time in endeavoring to barter their fish for bread and clothes. During the progress of these negotiations some sea-biscuit was given them, which they devoured with evident relish.

These fishermen did not have stupid faces, but their countenances beamed with an intelligent and eager interest when nearing us; not merely an animal eagerness, nor was it that dull and brutified expression which some maintain to be a predominant characteristic of the African in a state of nature.

The vessel being once more under way, one of our Anglo-African friends complacently waved his hand, and, bowing, said "Adieu!" and when responded to by some one on board ship, seemed much delighted, and, as if proud of his knowledge of the English language, animatingly rejoined, — "Good-night!" A good-night salutation from such a source, and addressed to us, a company of voyagers from the far-off occident, who at that moment were in danger of *coup de soleil* from the mid-day heat of a blazing tropical sun, afforded us great merriment; and altogether, our falling in with this strangely unfortunate race broke pleasantly into the monotony of our sea-life, and gave us new and interesting topics of thought and conversation. The coast opposite was about fifty miles from Monrovia, and these fishermen had probably obtained the little knowledge of English, which they possessed, in process of intercourse with that settlement. The next night we passed Cape Palmas, — a point we greatly wished to see, — but the sky was dark, and no land visible. Before morning, however, we had reached the Gulf of Guinea, and on the 21st of November passed the most eastern meridian of Greenwich, crossing the equator the same night.

Our entrance into the South Atlantic was disagreeable in the extreme. It was the rainy season,

which one must experience in order to have any
idea of the discomforts of its damp, chilly, and yet
sultry atmosphere.   Everything becomes saturated
with moisture, and "the damp, the mould, the rain,"
penetrates into one's bone and marrow, as well as
into all of one's personal effects.   We found it necessary to put on woollen garments, although the mercury indicated a temperature of 84° and upwards, —
one day reaching even to 93°.   Accustomed as all
of us were to great extremes of heat, this weather
proved most trying and debilitating, — the chilly
dampness giving us aching limbs ; nor was the
blazing tropical sun, which shone forth with its withering heat, after every shower, less to be dreaded.

The night of the 26th of November was very
dark and rainy ; and as we were nearing the port
of St. Paul de Loando there was a constant heaving of the lead, and ringing of the bell for the engine to be put at half speed, until after midnight;
when, not having any pilot, and it not being sufficiently light to admit of steaming into the bay
with safety, we laid to.   At eight bells, the day-
light beginning to appear, we were again on the
move, with the shores of Western Africa in full
view ; and before breakfast, turning a high, sandy
bluff, entered and anchored within the harbor.   We
were directly boarded by our Consul, Mr. Cunning-

ham, and some Portuguese officials; the former of
whom remained to breakfast with us, and was evidently pleased at our arrival. He is a New Eng-
lander, and has lived here, altogether, nine years;
having visited the United States only once during
that period. From him we learned many interesting particulars in regard to this colony and its
inhabitants; but a life here must be disagreeable
and solitary in the extreme, for an Anglo-Saxon,
and we only wonder how any of our race can ever
become accustomed to the fierce heat and disagreeable character of the climate.

We anchored in a spacious and beautiful bay,
the shores of which were very bold and barren.
Iron and copper abound in this and the adjacent regions of country; and the bluffs are composed of a
coarse ferruginous sand, having very dark surfaces,
in consequence of the liberal admixture of iron in
the soil. At one point, below the bluff formation, in
a part of a curve of the bay near the sea, this *cuir*-
colored sand is heaped in small pyramids, in shape
not unlike those of Upper Egypt. Little is known
of their formation, but every year they become
smaller, and are imperceptibly wasting away. They
are four-sided, and the outer edges of their angles
are as smooth and regular as though constructed
of masonry. This, together with their uniformity of

position, on the curve line of the bay, gives them
every appearance of having been formed by the hand
of man.

Loando is a well-known Portuguese colony, formerly one of the greatest slave marts on the coast,
and no friend of humanity can enter the port without indulging in the most painful reminiscences of
the sad wrongs and cruelties formerly perpetrated in
these waters. In consequence of the strict *espionage*,
however, which the English Government now main-
tains on the high seas, the slave-trade cannot be
carried on successfully; and an English Commissioner, whose presence is not overmuch relished, is
also stationed here, in order to see that the treaty
stipulations are properly regarded. But for this
precaution, it is feared that the Portuguese Government would endeavor to revive their horrible traffic
in human beings at the first favorable opportunity.

The town of Loando is situated on a high, sandy
bluff, sloping quite down to the water, and the
houses of the European residents, which are constructed of sun-dried bricks, with very thick walls,
are of two stories, and furnished with verandas.
They are located along the curve of the bay, so as
to command the cool sea-breezes, and are finished
externally with pale yellow chunam. The roofs are
flat and tiled, while those of the natives are thatched.

The windows are not glazed, but are draped with some kind of curtain fabric instead, and in some instances with a fine matting made by the natives.

There are four churches in the place, one of which — an old cathedral, but now falling into ruins — was built more than two hundred years ago. We were informed, however, by a Portuguese officer, that no one but the priests attend at the morning service of mass; and that only a few negro women were to be seen at church at any time during the day; and yet but a few weeks before our arrival there was an importation into this colony of a bishop and thirty priests, from the mother country. There is a large, low, and substantially built Custom-house near the beach, where most of the commercial business is transacted, and nearly all the importations are sold at auction. The town is lighted with oil, and as seen of an evening from the quarter-deck of the *Poyang*, presented quite a brilliant and imposing appearance. It is, however, fast going to decay, — the slave-trade, which enriched and built it up, being nearly destroyed; this mart, that once flourished, and was supported by the ill-gotten gains of cruelty and oppression, has now lost nearly all outward appearance of thrift and prosperity.

Our attention was particularly arrested, on first

entering the harbor, by the situation of the three
forts whose battlements frown over its waters. One,
— the San Pedro, built on the bluff point around
which we sailed on entering the bay, — is in a most
commanding position to guard the channel through
which vessels enter from the north. It is built of
brick, with an exterior finish of chunam, like that of
the private houses in the town. The San Francisco
stands three quarters of a mile farther down in the
curve of the bay, on a low, sandy point or beach,
extending quite out into the water. This fortification is also of brick, and is finished with a chunam
mixture, which gives it the appearance of being
constructed of a light gray limestone. The last of
these three fortifications — the San Miguel — is
built on the extreme and highest point of the bluff
on which the town is situated, and is a much larger
and more formidable structure than either of the
other two; and commanding, as it does, the entire
sweep of the bay, can be made a sure defence for
the place from any attacks of vessels of war.

The native population of Loando and the adjacent
villages is said to be 40,000, with only three thousand Portuguese; and of the latter four hundred are
convicts, sent here by the Home Government to garrison the forts, protect the people, and sustain the
laws. (?) There certainly can be but little confi-

dence inspired by the presence of soldiers made up of such characters; nor can a colony defended by them be a very desirable retreat. The Portuguese ladies appear on the promenade only towards evening, and are then carried in palanquins by their slaves. The extreme heat did not permit of our making an excursion in the vicinity of the town, and we saw but little, therefore, of its natural attractions. The tamarind tree was flourishing, and in full bloom, a little back on the shores of the bay, — its delicate foliage of exquisite green contrasting beautifully with the surrounding landscape.

Only a few of the whites speak pure Portuguese, nor can one directly from the mother country understand the *patois* in use. It is a mixture of Portuguese and Congo, but made up more of the latter than the former. The Portuguese themselves fall into the habit of using it, and are compelled to do so from necessity, as all their servants, — slaves, — as well as the rest of the people about them, speak either this *lingo* or the pure Congo.

Two vessels bearing the American flag were lying at anchor as we entered the harbor, one of which, — the *J. T. Dodd*, — a large American bark, was towed from up the coast a few days previous, by an English gun-boat that fell in with her while cruising in search of slavers. She was first seen near Cape

Palmas, and her commander (professing to be the
first mate) said that the captain and some of the
crew had gone into the interior to bargain for palm
oil and ivory, of which they proposed taking a
cargo. The vessel had formerly been a slaver, and had
already taken two cargoes of slaves from this coast,
with the last of which she was herself taken and
sold as a slaver. Her appearance now was very suspicious; but nothing could be done, as her papers
were all right, and her clearance dated from Cadiz,
although her crew were Portuguese. Having, however, all the appliances for shipping a cargo of slaves,
the gun-boat hovered about her for many days. She
was old, decayed, and in a leaky condition; and her
self-styled mate finding that he could not elude the
vigilance of John Bull, finally made a virtue of necessity, and wisely concluding that his old craft was
unseaworthy, engaged the captain of the gun-boat
to tow her into this port, where she was sold the day
after our arrival for $2500.

Here, as at Rio, in South America, the slave boatmen always sing at their work, and their strangely ir-
regular and monotonous refrains are heard from early
morn until late at night. The coaling of our ship was
done by these men in the following manner: The
coals to be shipped were lying on the shore directly opposite where we were at anchor, and a gang of slaves

rowed lighters to the beach, where there was another gang of men and women, with native baskets, shaped much like our New England wooden bowls, and holding nearly half a bushel. These they filled with coals, and placing them on their heads waded out to the lighters, into which they deposited their contents. At the ship the coals were hoisted from the boats in large tubs, by means of a pulley and tackle; and at the head of the gang doing this work was a tall Congo, of fine physique and great muscular strength, who, full of animation, cheered on the men, and acting as a sort of fugleman for the party, was the first to pull at the tackle and the first to stop, each time giving the word of command to the rest of the gang. He also led them in singing their wild and mournful refrains, pulling at the rope, and keeping excellent time; now assuming the most fantastic and comical attitudes, and now with the head, body, and hands in motion, keeping up a sort of half dancing, half stepping movement of the feet, at once very grotesque and amusing. If at any time a pause in their labors chanced to occur, this man, waving his hand and throwing back his head, with delighted expression and a broad grin on his features, began the singing and dancing with renewed energy, which quickly communicated itself to the whole gang, and for a few minutes the scene before us was startlingly wild and wierd-like. These people work slowly, and an overseer was constantly moving about among the shore-gang, with a whip in one hand, ready, as one of our passengers remarked, to stir them up the moment they showed any disposition to flag in their labors. We trust that the day is not far distant when, in our intercourse and dealings with this unfortunate race, there will be some recognition of the principle taught by our Saviour's golden rule, — "As ye would that men should do to you, do ye also to them likewise." The most valuable of these slaves can be purchased on the coast for twelve or fourteen dollars a head, while at the island of Cuba, and also in most of the Southern Slave States, previous to the rebellion, they would have brought as many hundreds, — and one of our party thought that the leaders of the gang would there be valued as high as two thousand dollars! None of this unfortunate race that came under our observation appeared weak either in mind or body, nor did their faces indicate a vicious and hardened character. Several grades of them visited the vessel, most of whom were tall, well-formed men, arrayed in all kinds of African costume — some more or less grotesque in appearance — and many wearing only the *cummerbund;* while others, bearing themselves with a manly and reserved air, were elaborately and picturesquely draped in cotton prints of large figures, and strikingly brilliant colors. We had two subordinate Custom-house officers on board, night and day, as long as we remained in port, who were also pure Africans, but dressed in the European style. All the high officials were Portuguese of gentlemanly bearing, and wearing the showy uniform of Southern Europe.

We received an early visit from the English Consul, Sir Henry Hartley, a Post-Captain in the Royal Navy. He is a man quite advanced in years, having been in the naval service at the time of the fall of Napoleon, and was also on board the ship that carried him a prisoner to St. Helena. There was no English mail steamer from this dark, out-of-the-way corner of the earth, and we were greatly indebted to Sir Henry for his thoughtful and kind politeness in offering to send our home mail, with his despatches, to the English Consul at Lisbon, where they would be forwarded to England, and thence to the United States.

CHAPTER II.

On the afternoon of the 29th of November, after having passed four days of terrific heat in full view, if not "amid Afric's burning sands," we were finally coaled, and had the steam up ready for sea, when our captain discovered, much to his chagrin and disappointment, that the "red-tape" regulations of this dilapidated, out-of-the-world colony would not permit him to sail until the next morning. It seems that the harbor-master, — called by the Portuguese *commandante,* — a sort of official wearing a military cap with bright buttons, and a uniform ornamented with gold lace, and having a bearing decidedly of the Spanish hidalgo style, — would not give the *Poyang* a clearance nor pilot us out of the harbor until the next morning, because Captain Briggs had not informed him twenty-four hours previous, as was the rule, that he designed sailing that evening. The captain, not being aware of this necessary preliminary, sent a message to the officer ; and, pleading his want of information on the point as an excuse, requested him to overlook the unintentional disregard of his port rules, and to permit him to leave. But the Loando port rules, like the laws of the Medes and Persians, were not to be altered to suit our convenience, and we were obliged to succumb to the necessity of remaining another night in the harbor. Our hearts did not go out very kindly to this grandiloquent *commandante*, for keeping us one more night than was necessary in the stifling heat and malaria of the African coast; and on boarding us the next morning, although our officers received him with the most reserved civility, it did not seem to disturb his pride, or to diminish in the least degree his imperturbable reticence and lordliness, which was well worth the imitation of the most skilful diplomate. The boat of this dignified functionary, manned by six stalwart Congo slaves, was towed astern the vessel as we steamed out of the harbor; and although we moved slowly, still the boat had rough sailing in the swell, and it required no little skill and strength for her steersman to keep his little craft afloat. When, however, we began to move more rapidly, it was both comical and painful to witness the affrighted faces and attitudes of our swarthy friends in the boat; nor less ludicrously serious were their beseeching tones, as again and again they cried out " Capitan! Capitan!" There was one poor fellow, in particular, who did not regain his composure until long after his master, the " Capitan," had spoken to him from the quarter-deck of the vessel, reassuring him of his safety. The boat and paddles were painted white, and the Congos were also neatly dressed in white, with little white linen caps upon their heads; and when this pompous official left us with his slaves facing the bow of the boat, and paddled swiftly landward, the spectacle was uniquely picturesque.

On sailing out of the harbor we passed an outer point of the high bluff on which a portion of the city is built, and at the extremity of which is situated the fortress of San Miguel, already mentioned. South of this elevation there runs out a tongue of land, or sandy beach, where our *"commandante"* lived; his house, with its verandas and Eastern style of architecture, placed in a little patch of tropical green, and surrounded with palm-trees, presenting, as we steamed past, quite an attractive Oriental picture.

The change from the close and heated air of Loando to the fresh, pure, and bracing sea-breeze, as we sailed down the coast, had a most magical effect upon all of us. One must exist four days and nights in a stifling furnace heat, such as we endured, in order to fully appreciate the life-giving influences of the change. While in port the average temperature was 96° according to our thermometer; but had the mercury marked ten degrees higher it is doubtful if we could have suffered more. We were all of us accustomed to a high degree of temperature at home during the " heated term," as it is called; but the peculiarity about the heat which we experienced at Loando was that it produced an atmosphere distressing to the brain, paralyzing to the limbs, and prostrating to the whole system. There is no heat in the world more withering and baleful in its influence upon strangers, — particularly the Saxon race; and exposure to it, and the night air, is soon followed by an attack of the African fever. The fact that we were leaving an atmosphere so deadly, and were in such excellent health, (although at the island of St. Vincent we were told that the yellow fever had appeared among the garrison at Loando,) inclined our hearts to a sentiment of profound gratitude for our continued preservation, and the mercies we were still enjoying.

We had a quiet sea, and continuing to sail near the coast, were on the morning of the 2d of December off Port Alexander, — a settlement near Great Fish Bay, — which is at the mouth of the Nourse River, between the sixteenth and seventeenth degree of south latitude, and a little north of the latitude of the island of St. Helena. Directly on passing this port we steamed near the shore of Cimbeba, — a barren and sandy desert, which stretches along the entire coast, reaching below the tropic of Capricorn,

— or from Great Fish Bay to Santa Cruz, a place on the coast of Damara ; making a distance of nine hundred miles, where neither fresh water, nor any vegetation can be found.   The shores are very bold, and their sandy banks deeply and peculiarly seamed, as though gullied by heavy rains.

On the 4th we outstripped the sun ; passing that luminary in twenty-two degrees and fifty-eight minutes of south latitude.   A little before twelve o'clock of that day, our kind and courteous captain, always ready and happy to add to our comfort, pleasure, and stock of information, called us to come on the quarter-deck and see how thoroughly attenuated and shadowless we had become.   Readily obeying the summons, we were directly walking under the full rays of a mid-day sun unattended by our life-long shadows ; and although aware of the reason for the absence of our old companions, the thing seemed so strangely peculiar that we could not resist the continual impulse to look searchingly, first on one side, and then on the other, and finally down to our feet, in order to see if there was not a little remnant or line of our old friends still remaining.   Not being successful in this endeavor, we were obliged to confess to some little sympathy with poor Peter Schlemyhl, and a readiness to borrow his seven-leagued boots, that we might go quickly in pursuit of our lost umbras.

While nearing the sun the weather was much cooler, — the mercury falling to 72°, — and, from experience, we became agreeably aware that his perpendicular rays are less powerful than when they are cast somewhat obliquely upon the earth. We now encountered head winds, together with a very rough sea, — the effect of a gale which had just prevailed along the coast; and again old Neptune made faces at some of us, while at others he actually pulled his beard and shook his trident, disagreeably reminding us that he was still ruler of the ocean, and did not mean to be forgotten.

Soon after encountering the heavy sea up the coast the weather became cloudy, and the cold increased until the mercury fell to 62°, rendering the atmosphere not unlike that in the vicinity of icebergs, and causing some of our timid ones to feel not a little apprehension. In addition to this, a dense fog closed in about us, so that we could see but little farther than a ship's length; and the light being obscured at the entrance of the port which we were nearing, we were obliged to lay to until the morning dawned, and the sun, rising in a clear sky, had dispersed the fogs and vapors.

The morning was serene and beautiful; but although we were early on deck we found that our vessel had already passed Robin's Island, lying at the entrance to Table Bay, and dividing it into two channels, at either of which ships may safely enter. Nor were we in time to get the best view of the mountains composing the head, rump, and tail of the couchant lion; but Table Mountain was clearly defined, and as we rounded Green Point and steamed up the bay, passing the shipping at anchor, the villa-like country residences, with their lawns and gardens, were seen in the distance, stretching along the mountain slopes by the sea, and soon the African, but, to us, home-like, city of Cape Town rose upon our view.

The city of Cape Town lies at a curve of the bay, almost directly at the base of Table Mountain and the Lion's Head; the first of which, rising 3500 feet above the level of the sea, had its square, table-like top covered with clouds of fleecy whiteness.[1] The latter rears its proud head sublimely; and we thought as we gazed upon this scene, combining so much of the grand and beautiful, that no fairer landscape could be presented to the eye than the magnificent array of ocean and mountain scenery with which we were surrounded. Doubtless our respite from the monotony of sea-life rendered this feeling more appreciable than it would otherwise have been, and prepared us to enjoy this never-to-

---

[1] This is called, at Cape Town, the " Table-cloth."

be-forgotten scene with the most intense relish and gratification.

We anchored in Table Bay on Sunday morning, the 8th of December, having been but ten days out from Loando. Directly on our arrival we learned from the Custom-house officials who boarded the vessel that a severe gale, which had raged here and along the coast for ten days previous, had just passed away, and that we might felicitate ourselves that we had seen it in no worse form than in its last dying swells, which, during the last few days of our passage, had vexed the seas which we traversed.

Although all our surroundings tended to impress us with the fact that we were in a foreign land, there were, also, many pleasant things to remind us that we were still within the pale of Protestant Christendom, and that this Colony, like her mother-land, was under the civilizing and sanctifying influence of the Bible. Again we heard the Sabbath bells, whose tones were touchingly sweet and home-like, and were delighted to array ourselves like shore-people and go to church. Table Bay is subject to frequent visitations of sudden and very severe winds; and a rule of the port makes it obligatory upon all masters of vessels, in taking people to and from the city, to use a boat smaller, but in other respects much like the lighters employed in lading ships, and which is so constructed as not to be liable to capsize in a sudden squall. Taking passage in one of these boats, we were landed at the jetty, (which, with the streets leading to it, was wearing a Sunday-keeping aspect,) and proceeded directly to St. George's Cathedral. On entering the church we were seated by the verger, or beadle, who wore a black serge gown, made after the fashion of the surplices worn by the clergy. The Rev. Mr. Douglas, Dean of the Cathedral, preached from the twenty-first chapter and thirty-third verse of St. Luke's Gospel, and gave us a practical discourse, in a style of writing, and manner of delivery at once polished and elegant. He was assisted in the services by three clergymen, and the entire Cathedral Service of the English Church was intoned by a choir of eighteen colored boys, none of whom were more than twelve or sixteen years of age. They were the sons of Kaffir chiefs, and students of the Kaffir College, of which we shall say more hereafter. They were arrayed in white robes, and their responses were not only melodious, but characterized by a reverential sweetness. The aisles were paved with red tile, and mural tablets adorned the walls. The choir, which was situated on the ground-floor of the Cathedral, at the right of the chancel, had, on one side, a very fine organ, ornamented in front with a row of small Corinthian pillars, and on the other side, stalls for the choir, who were shielded from view, when sitting, by drapery.

The Cathedral is an imposing structure, in the Grecian style of architecture, having a peristyle of Corinthian columns in front, and a lofty spire surmounted with a cross. The exterior is covered with a stucco of the same ochroleucous material used at Loando, — this being the prevailing style in which the buildings and public edifices at Cape Town are finished. The attendants at the Cathedral, we were told, comprised the *élite* and aristocracy of the city, and were mostly refined, as well as stylish and fashionable in their appearance. We observed, however, among them, and occupying the same pews, colored men and women, who also bore unmistakable marks of being educated persons. In the seats occupied by the Sunday-school children the colored and white race sat, indiscriminately, side by side; and as we walked down the centre-aisle, on leaving the church, we observed a very tall and well-dressed Kaffir, with prayer-book in hand, and having a gentlemanly bearing, walking close by our side. Many of the people living out of town drive in to church; and there was quite a display of handsome equipages. The horses of the Colony are superior, and one of an inferior grade is rarely met with. Of vehicles, the English hansom seemed a favorite "turn-out," and much in use in the city; but in such a warm climate it cannot be as comfortable as some other modes of conveyance.

We were anchored just off from the foot of Table Mountain, and the weather continuing serene, on returning from church we found that the table-cloth of cloud had lifted from its top and entirely disappeared. This peaceful serenity, however, only presaged a coming tempest; and at about seven in the evening dark clouds began to gather in the east, and over the top of the mountain, and the roar of the approaching wind sounded like the heavy booming of distant cannon. In a very short space of time the clouds had not only covered the flat top of the mountain, but were rolling and floating with infinite grace and beauty down its side in a cataract, presenting to the eye a sort of aërial Niagara, — an object of sublimity which could not be contemplated without producing in the mind a sensation akin to awe. This gale, which continued with unabated fury for forty-eight hours, blew with increased violence at night, when it howled fearfully through the rigging of our ship, in mad concert with the waves which dashed furiously against us. A large fleet of vessels were riding at anchor in the bay, with their bows landward, and not a stitch of canvas flying, —

forming the foreground of a marine view, which, as seen from our quarter-deck, was wild and grand in the extreme. To describe it, we know to be impossible. We only wished for the pencil and genius of a Church to transfer it to canvas. Instead of decreasing in violence, as we had hoped, the storm assumed a far more terrible and threatening phase; and fearing that it would cause our vessel to drag her anchors, orders were given to get up steam, so that if necessary we could put out to sea in order to avoid foundering in the bay. The stanch little *Poyang*, however, shivered but slightly, and did not change her mooring; although the wind from sundown until midnight was like a hurricane in violence. These southeasterly gales are of frequent occurrence, sweeping not only the bay but the town itself. They are said to blow away all disease, and to render the climate salubrious and healthy; hence the inhabitants are pleased to call the " black southeaster" the Cape Town doctor.

During the prevalence of the gale it was perilous to go on shore, even in the substantial and safe-sailing lighters; and at one time it would have been nothing short of downright madness for any one to have attempted it even in them. The next day, however, was calm, and the bay was again as placid as a river; so, taking advantage of the beauty of the morning, and feeling that if we wished to go sight-seeing we must improve every moment, (as the coaling was to be prosecuted with the utmost vigor, in order to sail with depatch,) we took a boat, and sallied forth to "do" the town.

The streets have a fine business-like appearance, and cross each other at right angles; the jetty at which we landed being at the foot of Aderly Street, which terminates in a beautiful avenue of English oaks near the base of the mountain. Leaving the busy and bustling crowd at the wharf, and passing a short distance up Aderly, we enter Darling Street, which is a fine avenue, crossing the former, and running for some distance parallel with the bay. Here, judging from the extensive haberdashery establishments, the women of Cape Town must do their shopping. The best hotel of the place is also in this street, as well as the " Old Curiosity Shop," kept by Bridges, and a place of interest, as will be seen further on. We shall not disguise the fact, that, true to our womanly instincts and tastes, we were curious to learn everything possible in regard to dress, and the ornamental advantages enjoyed by our Saxon sisters of this out-of-the-way South African Colony ; but found, during the little shopping which we executed, that there was no particular difference between them and our own countrywomen in this respect: the main point with the tradesman being to get hold of their money, and the principal point with them being to spend it when they could get it, — which are, perhaps, two of the most unerring indications of civilization and refinement that can be met with. We next visited the book and print shops in quest of sketches of scenery, and delineations of the different peoples common to the country ; but could find nothing that would be of any service to us, except a few small cards, on which were paintings, in water-colors, of the different native races inhabiting South Africa. These being represented in native costume, and at their particular occupations, as warriors, fishermen, water-carriers, &c., (which, together with their huts and little boats, were well and spiritedly executed,) gave one a tolerably correct idea of the personal appearance of the various tribes coming under the jurisdiction of the Colonial Government, besides portraying many living further to the north, and occupying a region of country beyond their rule.

We have already alluded to the fact that in St. George's Cathedral the white and black worshippers sat side by side, in recognition of the Christian equality of the two races. We found, however, that this principle of equality was not confined to the Church, but that it pervaded all the business classes, — with whom the oppressed African had equal rights, and equal opportunities to elevate himself and his race in the scale of being.

On Plein Street we entered a highly respectable haberdasher-shop which was kept by colored people. The proprietor was absent, but his wife — a woman of excellent address — was behind the counter, and her son, a young man of pleasing manners, was also acting as clerk. The tradespeople of Cape Town, like the tradesmen of England, have their dwellings in the same building with their shops; and on perceiving that we were strangers and Americans, the mother and son invited us to walk into their parlor, where it was cooler, and we could refresh ourselves after our long walk. The son led the way, and greatly entertained us by showing some rare African curiosities, and telling us of the interior of the country and its people. He was what would be called a well-educated young tradesman, and we fancied had passed a portion of his youthful days in England. His use of our vernacular was with a taste and skill more like that of a well-read professional student than a business clerk. We were told of another son who was in England, but made no further inquiries, although we were much interested in the family, and wished to know more of their history.

From what we could observe, these people occupied a position in the community corresponding in all respects with that of the whites in the same business; and no one appeared to feel that this state of things was any other than it should be.

At No. 9 Darling Street we found the " Old Curiosity Shop" to be a place of singular interest; where the skins of animals, the plumage of birds, all kinds of Kaffir curiosities, and many other of the natural productions of Africa could be procured ; while Mr. Bridges, the keeper of the shop, entertained us highly with his enthusiastic conversation in regard to his treasures, and communicated some of his personal reminiscences of Dr. Livingstone, and Sir Gordon Cumming, both of whom were frequenters of his shop during their visits to Cape Town. The old man, however, inclined to the opinion that the narrative of the latter must be taken *cum grano salis.* Soon after entering this shop the keeper appeared at the door of a room in the rear, with the head of a gemsbok in his hand, which he kindly showed us. It had just been sent to him from the interior, and being a very superb specimen of that animal, he was about preparing it for preservation. In looking about for the wonderful in this extensive collection, we noticed some exceedingly delicate shells, which were kept in a glass vessel ; and on making some inquiries in reference to them learned that they were found in the year 1856, on the sandy beach at Kalk Bay, — a bight in Simon's Bay, —

which is situated between the naval station and Cape Town. The old man told us that, as far as he could learn, they had never been found in any other locality; and also that they had appeared but once at Kalk Bay, and then were visible but for a short time. He had sent some of them to Mr. Layard at the British Museum, who informed him that he had never before met with, nor heard of them, and that they were nameless, not being mentioned or described in any works treating on conchology. We purchased a few of them, hoping to place them in the hands of some naturalist; but, with all the rest of our Oriental curiosities, they were destroyed on our homeward voyage by the officers of the pirate Florida.

While out sight-seeing we learned that there was a Museum, Public Library, and a Botanical or Public Garden, besides two Colleges, which were desirable places to visit. We accordingly went direct from the Old Curiosity Shop to Widdow's Hotel, — a comfortable English inn on the same street, — and after refreshing ourselves with a generous *tiffin*, (a term used at the Cape, and at the East generally, for lunch,) took a carriage, and drove to the Kaffir College. This institution is designed for the education of the sons of Kaffir chiefs; and at the time of our visit had been established but two years.

It is, to a certain extent, under Government patronage; and the parents only pay for the instruction of their sons a nominal sum in cattle.

Mr. Glover, the Principal, (who is a nephew of Sir George Grey, the former Governor of the Colony, but now Governor of New Zealand,) was absent, having gone to England to solicit further aid for the Institution. The establishment is handsomely situated in the curve of the bay; and, occupying a fine slope of land at the southwesterly foot of Table Mountain, commands an excellent view of the shipping. It is over a mile from town, and is well furnished with shrubbery and shade-trees; and having belonged to one of the early Dutch settlers, came under cultivation at the time of the first occupation of the Colony. The house and out-buildings were also erected by the first proprietors.

Some years ago this place fell into the hands of the Colonial Government, and at the time of the Sepoy Rebellion was used as a depot for horses, one thousand of which were purchased in the Colony for the use of Her Majesty's forces in India, and kept here, in an immense Dutch barn, until they could be shipped to Calcutta.

This building is constructed of brick, and is provided with very high, thick walls, and pointed gables, having a roof supported by bamboo rafters, and covered with the Cape rush. It is now being put to good uses, having under its spacious roof the chapel, school-room, dining-hall, and most of the workshops occupied by the Kaffir students. The house, which faces seaward, is also built of brick, having two antiquely pointed gables roofed with tile, and is surrounded with picturesquely fashioned Oriental verandas. We regretted to learn that the clergyman in charge, during Mr Glover's visit to England, was also absent, having gone to town; but on being introduced to Mr. Hewitt, the Chief Warden, as strangers and Americans, who wished to see the Institution, and learn something of its history, plans, and prospects, this gentleman received us very kindly, and ushering us into the parlor, said he was sorry it was their half-holiday, as a number of their boys had just left for town, and we could not see them at their studies; but remarking that he would show us the establishment with pleasure, directly led the way to the principal building, of which we have already spoken, and which, in spite of its enormous proportions, was nearly hidden by trees and shrubbery.

We first entered the carpenter's shop, where we found a number of boys at work, under the instruction of an English mechanic. Here Mr. Hewitt pointed out a lad of twelve or fifteen years of age,

as a son of Umhala, one of the most distinguished
Kaffir chiefs. The boy's name was Condele, and he
was in fact a prince of the blood royal. They all
appeared cheerful and happy, although seemingly
shy of strangers, and were diligently at work, making lecturns and other church furniture. Mr. Hewitt
remarked that they worked chiefly on such articles,
which were made of teak-wood and finished in a
nice manner. We also visited the other workshops,
which presented about the same appearance, excepting the tailoring-room, which was under the supervision of an English woman, whose sewing-class
numbered but seven boys. The school-room was a
large and airy apartment, floored with red tile, and
well furnished with the necessary fixtures. Upon its
walls were suspended maps and cards, and on the
latter were printed texts of Scripture.

The chapel, a spacious and well-proportioned
room, was appropriately fitted up with seats, having an altar, chancel, and reading-desk of teak-wood,
all made by the students. It was used only for the
daily Church Service, as on Sunday the officers and
students attend worship at St. George's Cathedral;
and the choir of boys we heard there, as already
stated, was composed of the students from this
College. The walls were prettily painted in a sort
of fresco, and were done *con amore* by some amateur

lady-artists of Cape Town. Over the altar and between the two windows back of the chancel, there was a large illuminated cross, about which was entwined a vine; while over and at each side of it was traced in illuminated letters the text, " I am the true vine, and my Father is the husbandman." The stone-colored, or shaded ground of the walls was flecked with what seemed to us a representation of the *fleur-de-lis*, although it may have been intended for the plume of the Prince of Wales. This was done in a tint of maroon. The floor was of wood, and carpeted, and the building was well ventilated, — the ceiling of all the apartments rising to the pointed roof, from which height a rustic chandelier was suspended, constructed of some dark wood, in the form of a cross, and furnished with sockets for candles.

The dining-room was long, ample, and furnished in a plain but comfortable manner; and the walls were ornamented with large engraved portraits of Queen Victoria, the Prince Consort, and their children, all in gilt frames. Prince Alfred, during his recent visit to the Cape, became greatly interested in this College, and on returning to England presented it with these pictures. The boys have a thoroughly religious and useful education, but at the same time each one is obliged to learn some trade. They are allowed to choose whatever handicraft they may fancy, and almost all trades were popular among them except that of the tailor, which is regarded as a menial service, and in their own country is always performed by women, who, wherever the light of the blessed gospel has not shone, to the practical illumination of the heart, are looked upon as a degraded and inferior class of beings. Gardening, for the same reason, is also in bad odor; and the pursuit of agriculture has yet to gain even a respectable position among these royal Kaffirs, who rarely work in the garden attached to the College, excepting when, as a slight form of punishment, they are adjudged to serve at that employment for a certain time.

The design of the Institution is preparatory, — the cleverest of the boys, as they advance in their studies, being sent to England for a more thorough education, after which they usually return to their native country as missionaries and teachers. One had already been sent there, and was pursuing his literary course at Oxford.

In the same building with the tailoring-room there was an English missionary lady, who had a class of six Kaffir girls. Three of them had been with her fifteen months; the rest a much shorter time. All of the former were quite proficient in reading, and one little creature, in particular, pronounced her words with an accent and voice of inimitable sweetness.

After walking through the garden, and the small vineyard adjoining, we returned to the parlor, where a very nice cup of tea awaited us; and our first introduction to this Eastern custom reminded us that we had already reached the neighborhood of the Orient. While we were refreshing ourselves, a large music-box (also the gift of Prince Alfred) discoursed some charming music; after which the gentlemanly warden gave each of the ladies a bouquet from the garden, and we left with agreeable impressions of that enlarged and noble Christian benevolence which had established the Institution, and was still steadily working for its advancement.

Mr. Hewitt had formerly been a missionary, and one of our party asking him if the Kaffir were more stupid and difficult of cultivation than other heathen, he replied that they were less so, and learned more readily. He also remarked that the boys possessed great facility in learning, and were quick and ready at all kinds of handicraft. The next morning a part of the missionary party on board our vessel also paid a visit to this College, and meeting the acting Principal, who had formerly been a missionary to the Kaffirs in the interior, had an interesting conversation with him about that race, together with their present religious condition and prospects. He regarded them as the descendants of Ishmael, and in proof of this pointed to one of the boys whom he thought of a decidedly Arab physiognomy. What further ground he had for such a theory we did not learn. The Kaffirs are readily distinguished from the other African tribes, and are considered more courageous, determined, and independent than the Hottentots, or Bechuanas, who, with the former, constitute the chief races of South Africa. Their skin is of a brownish black tint, while the Congos of the western coast are of a shining jet-black color.

On returning to the wharf we found that a light southeaster was again disturbing the waters of the bay; and setting sail for our ship, drove with so much violence before the wind that we not only *shipped* seas, but *un*shipped our rudder, — a circumstance which placed us, for the time being, in a position of more danger than we had been in since leaving New York.

As the *Poyang* was to be ready for sea the next afternoon, the early morning found us again in the streets of Cape Town, — it being our design to visit the Museum and Library, together with the Industrial Schools belonging to St. George's Cathedral, and also, if possible, to take a peep at the Botanical Garden. All these, together with the Government buildings and the African College, — an institution open to the youth of the city, — are in the same

4

neighborhood, and, situated on either side of the avenue of oaks mentioned as a continuation of Aderly Street, are enclosed by a brick wall. Over the entrance-gate leading from the street into the avenue, an inscription on the wall gives the year 1848 as the date of the foundation of the Library and Museum. The building appropriated to these institutions is a brick edifice of Grecian architecture, having a peristyle of Corinthian columns, and stands directly at the right of the entrance to the grounds above mentioned. At the time of our visit the exterior was not completed, but the building within was finished throughout in a substantial English style.

In the entrance-hall, or saloon, were a few pieces of statuary and some pictures; and on the right was a door leading to the Library, which is a commodious room with well-filled alcoves. We could not learn the number of volumes it contained, but the arrangements and fixtures were excellent,—each department and language having its separate alcove, and a desk for the use of visitors. There were also handsome and finely arranged library-tables placed at each end of the room, which, with the other fixtures, were made of the rich dark teak-wood; and suspended on the wall, at the head of this apartment, was a full-length portrait of Queen Victoria, arrayed in her royal robes. When Prince Alfred visited the Library, this painting was covered with drapery until the band struck up " God save the Queen!" then the son, on getting his first glimpse of this excellent picture, — a very life-like representation of Her Majesty, — was so overcome that he burst into tears.

Leading out of the Library we entered an apartment called the Educational Room, in which were all kinds of philosophical and chemical apparatus, — the last of which was particularly extensive. The walls of this room were literally covered with diagrams, paintings of botanical specimens, maps, and charts.

On the other side of the entrance-hall is the Museum, to which the public have access only for one day during the week. Our visit had fallen upon a day when it was closed; but the obliging librarian, being informed that we were Americans, and were to sail in the evening, went at once in search of the person in charge, who, on making his appearance, said he would admit us with pleasure, but must lock us in. Then showing us where we could touch a bell when we desired to go, he closed the door, and we found ourselves in a large apartment containing an extensive collection of well-preserved animals, birds, and reptiles, as well as geological and fossil specimens, and many curious and rare

articles connected with the early history of the Colony. Our attention was particularly attracted by
a large representation of the *mammalia, ruminantia,*
and *quadrumana;* and the groups of hunting tigers
and hyenas were so life-like in attitude and appearance as to disagreeably startle one on turning suddenly upon them. It did not require any great effort
of the imagination to give these animals all the
forms and features of life, or to fancy the savagely
grinning creatures really regarding us as a very tooth-
some morsel ready for their enjoyment. There were
very large collections of the *ophidia* and *batrachia,*
preserved in spirits and stuffed. If the expression
can be considered allowable, South Africa is certainly rich in reptiles. We noticed two remarkable
skeletons of a python and a yellow cobra, with
all their bones perfect and of an ivory whiteness.
These were under glass cases, so arranged as to exhibit the reptiles in their natural attitudes; and with
heads erect, lying half-straight and half-sinuous, the
terrible beasts impressed us as frightfully hideous
and life-like. The representations of the deer family
were also numerous, comprising a stuffed specimen
of nearly every buck mentioned by Sir Gordon Cumming; and a beautiful little animal called the clip-
springer, which stood in the same group with the
latter, was a very attractive and interesting object.

There was also a fine collection of coral, and the specimens of *radiata madrepora* were very beautiful. Among the minerals we noticed several large and superb specimens of crystallized malachite.

The birds were very numerous, and were preserved in fine order, being arranged after the usual mode in glass cases, which entirely covered one side of the large room. The beauty of their plumage I shall not attempt to describe. Some of the most numerous were of the orders *palmipedes, grallatores,* and *rasores;* — the collection comprised specimens of nearly all the birds of South Africa, from the little humming-bird, with its exquisite rainbow tints, to the large, coarse, and sinewy ostrich, — with every variety of plumage, from the most gorgeous to the gravest hues. The bright and gay, however, predominated; and the red of the flamingo, the yellow and bright salmon of the parrot species, together with various green and orange-colored shades, were most numerous. Our admiration was greatly excited by a bird, as large perhaps as our common woodpecker, but in form very like our finest barnyard cocks. He was a spirited-looking creature, of true lordly port, with a handsomely shaped comb delicately edged with red, which formed a beautiful contrast with his rich, orange-colored plumage. The tips of his wings and tail were flecked with black, and he rejoiced in a name admirably in keeping with his bearing, being called the "cock of the rocks."

A group of Kaffirs, composed of two men and a woman, done in plaster, and painted black, strikingly represented the contrast in social position of the two sexes among that people. The men, who were arrayed as native warriors, stood proudly looking up, in attitudes denoting independence, manly bearing, and self-reliance; while the woman, kneeling between them, having a downcast and servile expression of countenance and posture, with her infant fastened on her back, and in her hands a stone, significant of her readiness to perform the menial labor of grinding the corn, looked the impersonation of patient endurance and meek submission. The whole was spiritedly executed, and its faithful embodiment of the degrading influence of heathenism upon woman led us to feel more devoutly grateful, than we had ever before, for the blessed influences of Bible Christianity, which places our sex upon a secure religious and social equality with man.

We found here several interesting relics connected with the history of the old Dutch Colony, among which was an oaken chair covered with quaint carvings, upon which was fastened a card, setting forth that " Piet Gysbert Nood, Governor of the Colony of Good Hope, died in this chair in 1728."

The Botanical Garden, which fronts the Library and Museum building, is rich in tropical trees, shrubs, and plants, and remarkable for containing a great variety of the cactus family. The arbors were covered with beautiful creepers, among which we noticed the passion-vine growing in much luxuriance.

The Industrial Schools are on the other side of the street, and occupy two buildings of gray stone. The one appropriated to the Infant School is a pretty little Gothic structure, and was established in 1850, under the patronage of the wife of Sir George Grey, being now called Lady Grey's School. The advanced department was established by Lady Charlotte Bell, of England, in 1820. Although under government patronage, these schools are not entirely charitable institutions, a small sum being usually paid for tuition. The school-rooms are large and well supplied with fixtures, including a philosophical apparatus, which the managers of the advanced school have recently introduced at a great expense, for the purpose of extending the usefulness of the institution, and affording the advantages of a superior English education to all. The principal and several of the teachers now employed are from

England, each having stipulated, before leaving home, to teach five years. In both schools the white and black children sit together, and are in the same classes. We found the principal (or rather preceptress) to be a gentle, intelligent, and lady-like person; and deeply regretted that we had not more time to remain, and learn something further of her particular experience in the education of colored children.

There are 32,000 people in the city of Cape Town, of whom 10,000 are Mohammedans, who have their priests, mosques, and schools. We met one of their priests in the streets, in full costume, with his Mecca-blessed *comboloio*, or rosary of beads, in his hand. A learned Oriental traveller once told us that a Mohammedan priest is rarely seen conversing without his beads, with which he toys much as a Spanish lady does with her fan.

There are five churches in Cape Town, one of which — the old Dutch Reformed Church in Aderly Street — was first built in 1713. The fort and city hospital, as well as all the other buildings and public works, are of a thoroughly substantial character; and a breakwater, the corner-stone of which was laid by Prince Alfred during his visit, and which is to extend from Green Point two miles out into the bay, was in process of construction while we were there. This great work, which will cost several millions of pounds, is built by casting large pieces of stone into the water until high enough to erect a stone-masonry upon them. At the time of our visit there had already been expended upon this enterprise the sum of one million of pounds sterling. Wharves, also, like those at Liverpool, are to be built. Every day our ears were greeted with the familiar screech of the steam-whistle, — as fifty miles of the railroad, which is to terminate at Port Elizabeth, on the eastern coast, were already completed and in running order. The whole work was to be finished during the autumn of 1862. The Custom-house is an extensive brick building, standing not far from the wooden jetty at the foot of Aderly Street.

The market is held in a large square, from four to six o'clock in the morning, when the vegetables and fruits remaining unsold are disposed of at auction. The cattle and sheep are much superior to those of St. Paul de Loando, — the sheep brought on board at that port bearing a strong resemblance to goats, and the wool (if it could be called wool) was much like the hair of that animal. The face of the creature was the only thing that looked *sheepish.* The different breeds of long-tailed sheep, for which the Cape was at one time so celebrated, are said to be almost extinct, the crosses of the Merinos and Lei-cesters having superseded them, as being more prof-itable, both on account of the quality of mutton and the fineness as well as the yield of wool. This arti-cle is exported to England in large quantities every year, and some of it, also, finds its way to America; but the staple and quality of the Cape wool has of late years greatly improved.

CHAPTER III.

Fully aware that we were leaving the most home-like port we should make during the voyage, our adieus to Cape Town were with mingled feelings of gratification and regret. Thrift met us there at every step; and the place had a substantial and prosperous, as well as a quiet and comfortable, English air, which one could not fail to notice after visiting the miserable, tumble-down Portuguese settlements of Porte au Grande and Loando. To visit Cape Town directly after stopping at the last-named places made us feel profoundly grateful for our descent from the Anglo-Saxon stock, and impressed us with the truth of the oft-repeated remark that " the English are the best colonists." This is undoubtedly owing, in a great degree, to their persistent energy and industry, and also to the fact, that, wherever they go, the spirit of enterprise and the elevating influences and comforts of our Protestant religion goes with them.

At three o'clock on the afternoon of the 12th of December we weighed anchor, and our good ship being turned once more seaward, we steamed out of

Table Bay. Taking our seats on the quarter-deck, just under the bridge connecting the wheel-houses, and facing the stern, we prepared to note the points of interest as they passed before us while sailing out of the bay. First the city, with its background of mountains, receded in the distance; then the shipping; and passing the breakwater, the fortress, the city hospital, and light-house, we rounded Green Point, with Bird's Island on our left, and were soon fairly out at sea. We had a stiff head-wind to encounter; but our good ship ploughed her way swiftly through the dark-green billows, and soon were seen in outline the other side of the Lion's Back and Head,—the former greatly lengthened, but the latter bearing itself as loftily as ever,—and in the valley between the two a fine road wound its way over the country, with large and fertile farms on either hand.

At this point we made a *détour* along the coast, and obtained a fine view of the other side of Table Mountain, the coast formation reminding us strongly of the Highlands of the Hudson. Then came a succession of the same high and rugged elevations, which, like Table Mountain, were oblong in form and flat at their summits, having their squared ends abutting directly upon the sea, whose waves were dashing against their rocky sides. Directly after these we passed two lofty peaks which were

united at the base, having a gradual slope covered
with soil made of the *débris* which had washed down
from their barren and almost perpendicular steeps.
As we sailed along the coast we saw much mountain scenery of a similar character, although occasionally a conical peak appeared, reminding us of
the Cape de Verd Islands. Some, also, were in form
not unlike the pyramidal sand-hills on the shore of
the bay of Loando; and on rounding a huge mountain of this description, which stood boldly out
towards the sea, Table Mountain disappeared from
view. The strata of these summits are peculiar
in their formation, being nearly horizontal, and
are evidently of volcanic origin. After meeting a
small coasting propeller, which rode the waves
beautifully, notwithstanding the heavy swell, we
lost sight of the Lion's Head, which had so long
towered on high in gloomy grandeur, and came to
a descending range, over whose slope old Table
Mountain again reared its head, forming the background to a splendid landscape, with the sea in the
foreground, and a little cove hard by, in which was
nestled a small hamlet. Further on we passed a
more regular range, which was perpendicular from
the base; and then, turning, had a lateral view of
the huge, square range we had first passed, now
stretching as far back as the eye could follow its

dim outline into the interior. Then came a narrow and verdant tongue of land, which widened as we approached, but which was soon lost in another range of mountains very different in appearance from any of the former, being more rounded, and greener near the base, although their tops wore a barren and sterile aspect. Until reaching this point we had kept within three or four miles of the land; but now, although we still sailed due south, the coast-line was receding, and being summoned to tea, our panoramic picture of all that is wild and wonderful in romantic and sublime mountain scenery was suddenly broken.

On returning upon deck, we found our course much the same, and the distance which we were making from the shore increased very little; but the coast tier of mountains was lower, and we had a fair view of two distinct parallel ranges, with light, fleecy clouds resting between them, and glistening in the rays of the setting sun. We were also fast approaching the southernmost point of the Cape of Good Hope, which is here about five miles wide, and going below, kept our watch at the stern of the vessel until eight o'clock in the evening, when on the smaller of two mountain-peaks near the sea appeared the revolving light of the Cape. In the foreground of these mountains a long tongue of land extends far

out into the sea, and upon its extreme point stands
another Pharos, to guide the mariner along the coast
in safety. We had now a heavy sea, with the darkness increasing; and, anxious to get a view of the
revolving light from the quarter-deck, we ascended,
but had barely gained what we deemed a sheltered
position, when a great sea broke over the deck, and
sweeping the place where we stood, gave us a most
thorough and unexpected *douche*-bath, which sent us
below *instanter*, where we were glad to remain for
the night.

The next morning there was comparatively little
sea, and at eleven o'clock we were off Cape Lagul-
lus, — the southernmost point of the African continent, — and with the aid of a glass could see the
light-house, and a small bay or cove near at hand,
where vessels were riding at anchor. In the afternoon we met a fine clipper ship under full sail, and
speeding through the water like a bird before the
wind. On nearing her we displayed the American
flag, when she promptly ran up the Union Jack ; and
the signals being again put in requisition, we learned
that she was the *Lord of the Isles*, from Hong Kong.

Steaming onward in a northeasterly direction,
Africa gradually receded from our view, and we had
barely sighted and passed the southeastern point of
Algoa Bay, when we met with another sea, whose

swell continued with unabated violence for three days, and greatly impeded our progress. Soon afterwards, when very nearly in the latitude of twenty-six degrees south, and in longitude thirty-seven degrees east, we sailed through many miles of what is termed " the whale's feed," which, by the action of the currents, was floating in streams to the southeast. It is said to be an animalcule, and its appearance is not unlike oak saw-dust; while underlying, and mingling with it, is usually found an abundance of craw-fish. Whales, being very fond of this food, are frequently found in its vicinity, and the next day we were spoken by an American whaler, and stopped, while her boat was sent off for news. She proved to be the *Young Phœnix*, of New Bedford, and had been out fourteen months without any tidings from the United States, having taken during that time eleven hundred barrels of oil. It is impossible for one inexperienced in the hardships of sea-life to properly appreciate the feelings of a ship's crew thus isolated, on meeting with a vessel so recently from home. The interest with which they perused the supply of papers which we gave them must have been of that absorbing character for which the English language affords no adequate expression.

The weather was becoming very warm, and the mercury, which had already risen to 85°, was fast

seeking a higher elevation. We had passed the
"whale's feed," and were voyaging along with but
little that was noticeable to break the monotony of
sea-life, or to add to our stock of information. We
observed, however, that the waters assumed a tint
of blue deeper than we had noticed in the Atlantic
tropics. While sailing there we were particularly
charmed with the extreme brilliancy of the stars;
often beguiling the hours until late at night, in
watching the rising of the planets, and the appearance of the glorious Southern Cross. Never, however, were we so enchanted with the splendor of the
starry vault as when tracing our quiet course upon
the Indian Ocean, particularly while on our passage
from Port Louis, in Mauritius, to Singapore. Venus,
which even in our Northern clime is a planet of
extraordinary beauty, shines here with such regal
splendor as to cast a shadow, and, with the other
heavenly bodies, stands out, as it were, in bold relief;
thus fully realizing the strange conceit of the an-
cients that the stars were "fixed," or riveted like
nails to a solid super-mundane sphere.

No description can convey to the mind the fascinating, poetic charm of the lovely Southern Cross,
or the hopeful and religious thoughts which it in-
spires, as it is seen sparkling and glistening while
floating through the deeply clear, and transparent

ether of the tropical heavens. The serenity of the
evening, the balmy weather, and cloudless sky,
wooed us to the open air, where, hour after hour, we
watched the rising of this, and kindred constellations that never illuminate our Northern sky ; together with the curious Magellanic clouds, which
are supposed to be other planetary systems. The
superb lustre of Aldebaran, and the increased brilliancy of the Pleiades, in Taurus, together with the
surpassing effulgence of the stars composing Orion,
— the largest and brightest of the Southern constellations, — often held us spellbound for hours ;
and most reverently impressed us with the truth of
the Psalmist, that "the heavens declare the glory of
God, and the firmament showeth His handiwork."
We also caught something more than a faint glim-
mer of the meaning of the Almighty, who, when
addressing Job, said : — "Canst thou bind the sweet
influences of Pleiades, or loose the bands of Orion?"

On the afternoon of the 20th of December we
were nearing the southeastern shore of the "Island
of the Moon,"[1] and before night were within eight or
ten miles of the land, with the shadowy outlines of
two large mountains distinctly visible. We coasted
for several hours along the low shore of this comparatively unexplored country ; but,

[1] Madagascar was formerly thus called by the natives.

" Green Madagascar's flowery dales,
  Her vernal lawns, and numerous peaceful bays,"

were enveloped in a hazy, dreamy, tropical atmosphere that hung over the mountains like a veil, and
floated across the lowlands, soon to be dissipated by
the glorious sun, even as the shades of heathenism
and the darkness of superstition, which once entirely
enveloped in tenfold night this beautiful country,
are beginning to be dissipated by the glorious light
of the Sun of Righteousness. We sighted Fort
Dauphin in the bright tropical moonlight, which
also brought to view the mountain ranges and the
coast, that here assumed a bolder outline. We
were heading, however, for the Isle of Bourbon and
the Mauritius; and the morning found us once more
where the clear cerulean of the horizon met only the
darker blue of the ocean. We had looked our last
upon a land combining in its romantic mountain-
scenery much that is grand and sublime in Nature,
— a land whose flora is unequalled, being particularly rich in rare and superb orchids, and remarkable
for its traveller's-tree, from whose leaf-stalk, when
pierced, pure water gushes to refresh the thirsty way-
farer.

Early on the morning of the 23d of December
we were sailing along the coast of Bourbon, which
we first made at its southwest point, and were

watching the day, then just breaking beyond its lofty volcanic mountains, the tops of which became radiant as the early light played upon their summits. This island lays considerably higher than Mauritius, but its scenery is said to be less beautiful. The shore-base of the coast-line formed by the mountains is square and precipitous, and in one place extended out into the sea for a mile or more, like an immense breakwater. We were now off St. Denis, which is the chief port of the island, although a very insecure one during the prevalence of high winds. Ships lying in this harbor are always kept in readiness to sail at a moment's warning; and we counted a fleet of fourteen sail, with all their canvas set, lying in the offing, and ready to slip out to sea at the first intimation of foul weather. At a sort of wharf, or jetty, a flag is hoisted whenever boats from the ships can land in safety. There were remarkably deep gorges between the mountains in the rear of the town, which one of our missionary party, who had lived for some years in Northern India, compared to those he had seen among the Himalaya Mountains, through which ran living streams of water. Passing other mountains whose steeps were cultivated, and covered with a rich verdure half way up their sides, we sailed a little to the east, and St. Denis disappeared.

As we coasted along the island the mountains gradually receded from our view, and we were soon off a more extensive slope of country reaching far back from the sea, with finely cultivated plantations whose fields teemed with a rich tropical luxuriance, and picturesquely situated houses dotting the landscape in every direction.

We had scarcely lost sight of Bourbon, when at mid-day of the 23d of December we discerned the broad-shouldered mountains of Mauritius, sixty miles in the distance, and at five o'clock in the afternoon were coasting near their base, intending to make the harbor of Port Louis. These mountains presented an almost infinite variety of forms. At one point an old castle-like looking peak passed before us, followed by several smaller ones, all rising directly out of an extensive plain; while another cone-shaped mountain that attracted our attention seemed as if surrounded by natural lawns, which were covered with a luxuriant herbage of the richest green. The country seemed to be in as high a state of cultivation as at the Isle of Bourbon, and the plantations, with their neat residences, gave every indication of thrift and prosperity.

While admiring the rarely equalled beauty of the scenery there came very suddenly upon us a slight tropical shower, which passing away rapidly, as the sun reappeared, the arch of a beautiful rainbow sprang from behind the mountains, giving to the varied landscape an air of surpassing beauty and enchantment. This scene, however magnificent, was but the prelude to another equally grand and beautiful. A tropical sunset is always a splendid spectacle, but a tropical sunset after a storm is an event in one's lifetime, — one of those few phases of Nature, in fact, which cannot be described any more than the impressions which they create. A scene like this it fell to our lot to witness on that memorable evening, as the shower moved off, — its dark skirts tinged with brilliant sapphire by the setting sun. Then there were the white and fleecy clouds that lagged in the wake of the storm, exquisitely tinted with the pale red of the opal and the delicate violet of the amethyst, — so beautiful as almost to vie with the hues of the rainbow, whose broken arch gleamed just over the distant mountains.

We fired our guns, and rounding a lofty peak, (which, with a signal-station upon its top, loomed up at our right,) entered the harbor of Port Louis. We did not wait to take on board a pilot, for although it was our Captain's first visit to this island he was too accomplished a navigator to require any such aid. With the vessel at half speed, we felt our way up the channel by continued soundings, until we reached the quarantine ground, our quarter-deck filled with a happy group, whose hearts seemed over-running with delight at the beauty of the scenes around them, to say nothing of our anticipated pleasure in "doing" the town and environs of Port Louis.

The warning advice of an English ship-captain whose vessel we passed while coming up the harbor, — "not to attempt going to the wharf," — fell like a discordant note upon our ears; and on reaching the anchorage a burly English pilot came alongside, but would not touch his foot to the gangway-stairs until well assured that there was no sickness on board, and that no death had occurred since our leaving the Cape. He was a bustling, loquacious man, and when ascending to the quarter-deck said, in a very brusque and loud tone of voice, " Well, we have the cholera thick in this port!"— the effect of which announcement was electrical, and, mute with sudden fear and disappointment, one by one, we withdrew to the cabin below.

But "the art of our necessity is strange;" and although the *chateaux en Espagne*, reared upon the pleasure and satisfaction we were to receive in look-ing up the lions of the city, and its neighborhood, had vanished like the beautiful clouds of the tropi-cal sunset, and in the fearful summer heat, (the mer-

cury ranging at 90° and upwards,) we were about
to meet a dreadful pestilence, no one seemed panic-
stricken, and very little was said on the subject.
It was, however, interesting to notice the similar
effect this entire change in our prospects had upon
all on board, — each one seeming more inclined to
commune with his own thoughts than to commu-
nicate them to others. At this time the words of
Isaiah came very forcibly to mind : " In quietness
and confidence shall be your strength"; and none
seemed to doubt, that, to be fortified with the Christian's hope and trust in such an emergency, was of
infinitely more value than a display of senseless bra-
vado, or yielding, on the other hand, to a weak and
unmanly fear. We learned afterwards that the pilot
had somewhat exaggerated the extent of the disease,
not being in the most "melting mood" imaginable
in consequence of the rapidity of our movements,
which prevented his boarding us in time to place
us in quarantine. For many weeks previous, all
vessels from the Cape of Good Hope had been
compelled to pass this ordeal, on account of the
prevalence of the small-pox at the latter port during the autumn.

No one was permitted to go on shore until the
port physician had visited the ship, and satisfied
himself as to our general good health. We were

already somewhat reassured of the safety of our position, and Captain Briggs, after visiting the city, returned with an account so different from the pilot's statement, that we were satisfied the disease had more of the endemic than epidemic character, and was confined, as near as we could learn, to a locality on Grand River, two miles from Port Louis. In 1854 the cholera raged fearfully in the city of Port Louis, and the most stringent measures were now being taken to prevent a similar calamity. It had been brought to the port by a vessel from Calcutta; and the ship which we spoke at the entrance of the harbor was also from that city, being loaded with India Coolies, among whom the cholera had appeared while on the passage. On her arrival, of course, the vessel was promptly quarantined.

The island of Mauritius was discovered in the sixteenth century by Pedro Mascarenhas, a Portuguese, by whom it was called *Ilha do Cerno;* but Van Neck, a Dutch navigator, who touched at the island in 1598, finding it still uninhabited, called it Mauritius, in honor of Maurice, the Prince of Orange. It was, however, abandoned by the Dutch, and we were told by a citizen of Port Louis, that the story in regard to their having been driven out of the island on account of the great multitude of rats that infested it, was universally received as an historical fact.

In 1721 the French took possession of the island, and much of its present prosperity is due to the ability, and good management of its French Governor, the celebrated M. de la Bourdonnais. It was afterwards, however, taken by the English in 1810,— to whom it was definitively ceded by the peace of 1814. The island is said now to contain 350,000 inhabitants, of which number only ten or twelve thousand are Europeans. The country is very mountainous, and the soil is of a reddish cast; but the land is generally fertile, well-watered, and rich in tropical productions, — the trees, fruits, and plants common to the Eastern tropics growing here in great perfection.

Notwithstanding the island produces excellent coffee and spices, sugar is cultivated to the exclusion of almost every other staple commodity, — three hundred millions of pounds being exported annually, most of which goes to France. The blackwood, or ebony, grown on the island is said to be the most solid, close, and shining of any in the world, and if all of it is like that which was brought on board our vessel, it has a well deserved reputation. Very little corn, or grain of any kind, is raised; most articles of provision, and other supplies, being imported from the Cape of Good Hope, Madagascar, India, and Bourbon. The extensive grazing lands of Madagascar produce fine cattle; and from that island, where, Camoens says, —

"The lowing herds adorn the vales of green," —

the Mauritians are supplied with beef.

African slavery, which formerly existed here, was abolished more than twenty years ago; but some of the most remarkable and attractive natural points of scenery on the island are said to be connected with the injustice and misery experienced by that unfortunate race, who, although guilty of a blacker skin than the races of Asia, are now daring to look up and claim an equal brotherhood with the family of man. On becoming freemen, they stood comparatively little chance of bettering their condition, or of remaining as they were. It is said that, amid the toil and moil of the more privileged and advanced Asiatic races with whom they came in competition, — none of whom were under the unrelenting ban of prejudice that everywhere meets the African, — these poor people have mostly passed away. It is, however, acknowledged that some who are left have succeeded in making themselves comfortable homes, and in gathering together some wealth; and those who have attained such positions of comfort, and respectability, have done so in the face of difficulties, which, to have been overcome by one of our own race, would have caused him to be regarded as an indomitable, and very clever Saxon.

The city of Port Louis is the chief port, and capital of the island, and lies in latitude 20° 9′ 56″ south, and in longitude 57° 28′ 41″ east. It is situated at the head of a triangular bay, and is partly built on the slopes of the mountains, which enclose it on three sides. The highest of these is the Pouce, which rises directly in the rear of the town, to the height of 2800 feet, and from which another range of mountains extends to the sea in a southwesterly direction. The mountain range, which encloses the town and its beautiful suburbs, extends to the northeast ; and back of them, towering high above his compeers, is the summit of the celebrated Peterboth. The town, as seen from the harbor, has rather an imposing aspect. The Creoles, Coolies, and the descendants of the former slave population, occupy different localities, and an occasional minaret of a mosque is seen in the Coolie quarter of the city.

Port Louis was first settled by the better class of French families, many of whom were of the old *noblesse ;* and their descendants, still keeping up the old ancestral dignity, have given to the society in which they live, a tone of superior cultivation and polish, rarely met with even in countries nearer the centre of civilization. The population is said to be between fifty and sixty thousand, and comprises representatives from nearly every nation on the face of the earth. It is considered one of the most cosmopolitan places in the world, all the foreign trade of the island being transacted there; and at early morning, during the business hours, the bustling crowd of English and French merchants, military, and policemen, sailors, and Chinese, Arabs, Bengalese, and Parsees, together with natives "to the manor born," all seen in their different national costumes, present to the eye of an untravelled American a scene at once novel and interesting.

There are large warehouses on the wharves; and a few steps from the landing an entrance, through a spacious gateway, leads into a large, open space, called the Place d'Armes, which is planted on each side with trees. The Governor's house is situated farther beyond, towards the mountains.

Previous to 1845, sugars and other articles sent from the Mauritius to Great Britain were charged with the same duties as the like articles from India; but during that year the custom rules and regulations were changed, and the duties being fixed the same "as on like goods of the same growth, produce, or manufacture of the British Colonies in the West Indies," the trade was thus placed on the same footing.

The fort, which commands the town and harbor, stands on a spur of the mountain we rounded on entering, and the passage being difficult, every vessel on approaching is required to hoist her flag and fire two guns; and at night a light must be shown, when a pilot goes on board and steers the ship safely into port.

For the first three months of the year the island is subject to terrible hurricanes, or *cyclones*, and during that time the weather is unsettled. Squalls of wind and rain precede these tempests; and their advent being near at the time of our visit, heavy rain-clouds were every day seen to expend themselves on the tops, or down the sides of the mountains, and sometimes a slight sprinkling was received on board our vessel. We watched these never-failing precursors of the gales that were to follow, with fearful interest, after hearing the English seamen's chaplain, the Rev. Mr. Richards, relate his perilous experience during the year previous, when he and his entire family came very near being destroyed by remaining on board the Bethel ship through the hurricane season. His remarkable escape did not have the effect of calming our anxiety, and we were more than ever anxious to be at sea again in order to get out of their latitude.

We were told that on account of these winds the

dwellings in the town are only of one story, having, for security, strong outside shutters, called hurricane-shutters, and doors of unusual strength. When the barometer indicates the coming of the hurricane, a gun is fired from the citadel as a signal for all vessels to take down their upper masts and yards; and at the same time a flag is hoisted at the port-office, as a warning to all ships lying outside the inner harbor to put out to sea. If a vessel hesitates, or refuses to move from the outer anchorage when thus warned, a gun is fired upon her from the fortress, and she is compelled to leave. Absolute necessity requires such a course, as no ship can remain in the outer harbor, during the prevalence of these winds, without being driven upon the rocks and destroyed. The inner harbor can accommodate but a few vessels at a time, which are moored in rows, side by side, and in some way fastened together, with a small clear space of water between them. Each vessel is anchored both at the bow and stern, which reminded us of St. Paul's shipwreck, when they "cast four anchors out at the stern, and wished for the day."

It is well known that Mauritius is the scene of St. Pierre's little romance of " Paul and Virginia," and that their tombs are in a garden at Pamplemeuses. The *St. Geran* was wrecked on the neighboring

coast, in 1745, and a bight adjoining it is called the
Bay of Tombs, — Paul and Virginia, according to
the old legend, having been buried there. Pamplemeuses is reached after a charming drive of seven
miles in a northerly direction, and no one visits Port
Louis without going there. Therefore, hoping for
the best in regard to the sickness in the city, we
also made a pilgrimage to that classic region.

It was Christmas Day, and the heat very oppressive, — the mercury rising to ninety-six degrees and
upwards in the shade ; but we did not set forth on
our excursion until late in the afternoon, when the
fierceness of the sun's rays was upon the wane, and
the air somewhat tempered by the evening breeze
from the ocean. Leaving the ship and landing at
the wharf, we encountered a group made up of
nearly every nation of the East, from the jet-black
African to the light Arab, who, squatting on the
ground, were intently engaged in gambling with
cowries ; and passing on, we walked through the
arched gateway, already mentioned, to the Place
d'Armes, where the gentlemen of our party, after
some chaffering with a group of voluble drivers, and
owners of open barouche-like carriages, succeeded
in obtaining two vehicles, and we drove off. The
streets of Port Louis, and the roads leading from it,
are macadamized in the best manner, and the gut-

ters, as well as the sidewalks in the town, are paved with stone. Many parts of it are ornamented with shade-trees, and an ample supply of excellent water is brought from the mountains, over deep gorges, in aqueducts built of stone masonry. One, in particular, near which we passed, was constructed in the Romanesque style, and had a very antique and imposing appearance.

The drive was delightful, the road being lined on either side with hedges of the aloe and cactus, interspersed with various other tropical shrubs, flowers, and trees. The curiously tasselled flowers of the aloe, borne upon a foot-stalk fifteen or twenty feet in height, was a particularly attractive object; and along the road were seen extensive sugar-plantations bordered with hedge-rows, together with the houses of the planters, and the thatched cottages of the Coolies. The palings enclosing the yards of private residences were in many instances hidden by a species of convolvulus, — a creeper more beautiful in flower and verdure than any of our Western varieties, — and some were surrounded with hedges of exquisite flowers, while within were beautiful little parterres filled with many kinds of flowering shrubs and plants.

Mauritius is literally an Eden of flowers; and on Christmas morning, besides having our cabin-table

6

resplendent with their beautiful tropical tints, some of our Christmas greetings came accompanied with beautifully arranged bouquets. To us the Oriental *sylva* seemed to partake of a no less remarkable character. There was the banyan, bamboo, fig, almond, mango, banana, cocoanut, and different varieties of the palm, together with the pomegranate, unfolding its beautiful flowers; while at every turn, large flowering trees, in full bloom, displayed the richest tints of yellow, purple, and red. One of these trees, in particular, we shall always remember for its stately and gorgeous beauty. It was growing by the road-side, at Pamplemeuses, and was at least forty feet in height, having a full acacia foliage of delicate green, amid which were large clusters of brilliant scarlet flowers. We afterwards learned that it was the *Poinciana regia*, commonly called *mille fleurs*, or *flamboyant*, and that the time of its blossoming is from December to April.

Everything combined to make our drive so like enchantment that we almost questioned within ourselves whether we were there *in propria persona*, or only dreaming. It being Christmas, all classes had a holiday, and the Coolie population, as well as the Creole, were out arrayed in their best. The whole length of our way, both on going to and returning from Pamplemeuses, was thronged with these people.

There was the Bengalee woman, who had donned her brightest red, yellow, or purple *sari;* — a garment made of one long piece of cotton cloth, or some other light fabric, that gracefully covered the head and person ; and walking beside her was her Hindoostanee sister, with her dress composed of three garments; viz. the *kurti,* which we should term a jacket; the *saya,* answering to our skirt; and the *chudar,* — a piece of white muslin, or calico print, of one yard and a half or two yards in length, which is thrown lightly and often jauntily over the head. The men, resplendent in holiday garbs of white and red, — their loose robes flowing gracefully, — were walking, or riding in donkey-carts ; and well-to-do Mussulmans drove past in carriages, or sauntered leisurely along the road in groups; some of whom, when overtaken by their hour of prayer, prostrated themselves as we passed. Everywhere mingled with the moving crowd were Coolies occupied in their various callings : some we observed with large circular flat baskets on their heads, not unfrequently filled with chickens ; and others, with heavily laden panniers of fruit and vegetables, were troting along at a brisk pace, to and from the city. Both sexes had lithe figures, and were exceedingly erect and well proportioned. Both also showed their fondness for ornaments, — wearing rings not only on their fingers, and hanging to their ears, but also pendent from the nose. It was a common practice, also, to fasten an ornament of some kind on the forehead, and they abounded in bracelets.

Arriving at Pamplemeuses, we were met by a Bengalee Coolie who lived in a cottage near by, and who, after acting as cicerone, asked for *bukshish.* Following this man, we were led into the garden, and a few steps brought us to a small oval pond of sluggish water, passing which, a short distance along its right bank, we were directly standing near the tomb of Virginia, — that of Paul being directly opposite, on the other side of the muddy pool. Both tombs were much dilapidated, all that remained of them being two square masses of brick masonry stuccoed with plaster, each of which had a delicate iron shaft passing down through its centre from the top. The masonry formerly served as a pedestal, the iron shafts acting as supports for the clay, or coarse terra-cotta urns that stood upon them; and both monuments were originally enclosed with light iron railings. No vestige, however, either of the railings or the urns is now remaining; but over each the pliant and graceful bamboo rustles mournfully in the wind, and a species of vine-like mimosa trails closely at their base. The alley of bamboos, the shaddock-groves, as well as the cocoanut-trees, and the mango

and orange-groves, if they ever embellished that
particular spot, have passed away. Many years ago
a house of entertainment was kept in the vicinity,
and the place was much frequented by the French
residents of Port Louis.

It seems a pity to spoil so affecting a story as that
of the lives and loves of Paul and Virginia, but we
were assured by an English Protestant clergyman
of Mauritius that nearly the whole narrative was a
myth. Not but that some such persons might have
existed and been shipwrecked on the coast; but
this was merely the *incident* which St. Pierre worked
up into a touchingly affecting tale; none, excepting
a few French, believing it to be a real life-narrative.
Some of our *compagnons du voyage*, who were in full
belief of the story, were greatly disturbed because
we laughed at the idea; and yet we were quite as
intent as they in plucking flowers and sprigs of the
bamboo and mimosa, to preserve as mementos of
our visit, while we thought with renewed pleasure
of the days when we first conned the pages of St.
Pierre's interesting little book.

Pamplemeuses and its environs are exceedingly
charming and attractive. A fine old Cathedral, in
the Gothic style, stands at a little distance from the
Tombs, with a cemetery near by, whose graves and
monuments were adorned with fresh floral offerings;

and the abundant display of beautiful Christmas bouquets and wreaths, placed by loving hands upon the last resting-places of the dead, gave a very cheerful aspect to the enclosure. Most of the bouquets were in vases of handsome design and workmanship, and were fixtures to the monuments and tombs.

The Zoölogical, or Royal Gardens, in the same neighborhood, cover about fifty acres of land, and are laid out on a grand scale, — both sides of the avenue being bordered with the rarest and most valuable trees in the world. At certain intervals there are stone seats, which serve as resting-places for visitors; and we observed little gutters, on either side of the spacious walls, through which water is conducted for irrigation. Our time did not permit us to examine the ground as thoroughly as we wished; but we took a hasty glance at the avenue of superb palms, which is said to be scarcely equalled in extent and beauty in the world, and saw, for the first time, the Jack-fruit-tree, with its singular fruit, which hung at a distance of thirty feet from the ground and had already attained a great size, but was not ripe. There was, also, among the shrubbery, a fine *echite,* from which we took a few of its strangely variegated leaves.

The last evening of our stay in Mauritius was devoted to visiting the Christian Cemetery, which

interested all of us, but had peculiar attractions for
our missionary party, from the fact that Mrs. Harriet Newell, one of the earliest American missionary
women, lies buried there. Although separately enclosed, it is contiguous to the burial-place of the
Mussulmans of India, and also to those of the Parsees and Chinese; occupying with them a low portion of ground lying at the southeastern side of the
harbor.

A spacious winding avenue along the sea-shore
— which seemed to be a favorite place for the Europeans to exhibit their dashing turn-outs — conducted us to its gate, the avenue being bordered on
either side with tall filao-trees, which are very like
the cypress. The action of the wind from the sea
has inclined these trees slightly in the direction of
the cemetery, to which they lead; and the fitful sigh-
ing of the breeze, as it rustles sadly in the foliage,
makes it a strikingly mournful entrance-way to the
resting place of the dead.

The grounds contained many tombs and monuments, — some of the latter being ornate and expensive, although most of them were plainly and substantially made of the coarse native granite, which
admits of a fair polish, and is readily procured from
the mountains which overshadow the place. Evergreens, shrubs, and flowers were abundant, and the

Coolie water-carriers were busily engaged in watering them for the evening, as we wandered in various directions in search of Mrs. Newell's grave. We were without a guide, and consequently encountered some little difficulty in finding it, but finally succeeded in our endeavors, after a patient and persevering search among the monuments. The grave is enclosed by a low tomb of native stone, and on its top rests a white marble slab, having upon it, at the head, an urn in bas-relief, under which is inscribed the following : —

Sacred
to the memory of
MRS. HARRIET ATWOOD,
Wife of Rev. Samuel Newell,
Missionary at Bombay.
Born at Haverhill, Mass., U. S. A., Oct. 10, 1793.
Died, after a distressing voyage from India to this place,
Nov. 30, 1812.

Early devoted to Christ, her heart turned towards the heathen.
For them she left her kindred, and her native land,
and welcomed dangers and sufferings.
Of excellent understanding, rich in accomplishments and virtues,
she was the delight of her friends, a crown to her husband,
and an ornament to the Missionary cause.

This humble monument to her memory
is erected by the
American Board of Commissioners for Foreign Missions.

The tomb and marble slab were kept clean and in good condition, and we were told that the spot was every year properly cared for by religious Americans and Englishmen, who gladly availed themselves of the opportunity of performing this work, simply as a labor of love.

The brief life of one so beloved and accomplished has doubtless been regarded, by many of those who see and judge after the manner of men, as having been uselessly sacrificed, if not absolutely thrown away. To those, however, who know something of the workings of Protestant Christian missions in heathen lands, and can speak from observation of the great need of such women in the missionary field, the dedication of Mrs. Newell to the work, her patient sufferings, and short career, have yielded much fruit, and been of infinite service to the cause. Her example has also actuated so many of her countrywomen to cheerfully and gladly devote themselves to the same noble purpose, and has had such an effect in inclining others to become earnest and diligent workers at home, for the advancement of the Redeemer's kingdom, that, on standing at the side of her humble grave, one can feel with truth that "though dead, she yet speaketh." If there is a spot on earth where this sentiment can be truly felt, it is at the grave of one so young, and self-devoted, and accomplished, who shrank from no hardships, and halted at no sacrifice, as long as the cause of Christ and the good of souls was the end in view. With her, Christian duty was paramount to every other consideration ; and although her early death was an irreparable loss to the cause in which her soul seemed to have expended its best energies, still it was fitting that the " Lord of the harvest" should call her thus early home, for it may well be said of her, in the eloquent language of Tasso, —

> " These birds of Paradise but long to flee
> Back to their native mansions."

Beside a gigantic stone-cross which we encountered while in quest of Mrs. Newell's grave, there were two or three similar ones in other parts of the cemetery, all of which were well proportioned and handsomely finished shafts, round in form, and made of the native granite, about twenty feet in height, with cross-pieces six or seven feet long. The effect of this symbol of our Christian faith, as it was seen at different points above the graves and monuments, was religiously sublime, and seemed to us to be not only a token of Christ's love for us, but also an earnest of the Christian's final rest in heaven.

A Mahommedan funeral, which we met in the avenue of filao-trees on our return, was a wild, strange, and mournful scene. The coffin, which was placed on a sort of bier, and carried on the shoulders of men, who were walking at a brisk pace, was shaped like the roof of a house, with a ridge-pole-like top. It was draped with calico of a pale ochreous yellow, and wreaths of pink roses were hanging down on either side. A turbaned priest walked at the head of the bier, but the motley throng of men accompanying the remains, paid little heed either to order or propriety. They looked far more like the ordinary street crowds in the East than a funeral procession, and were talking with great volubility. Occasionally the voice of the priest was heard above the din, gravely chanting in a half monotonous tone; but the main feature of the scene, and that which the most painfully impressed us, was the thoroughly indifferent air of all composing the procession, their conversation evidently being upon business and other worldly matters. This was the first heathen funeral we had ever witnessed; but we can conceive of no circumstance that could have led us to more sincere and hearty self-gratulation that we had been born and educated in a land of Bible religion and Christian influences.

CHAPTER IV.

THERE is no lovelier spot in the world than Mauritius, nor can any other land boast of mountain scenery more sublime or picturesque; but it seemed to us while we remained there that the heat vied in fierceness with that which we had experienced at Loando, although it was by no means as balefully withering in its influence. We were told, however, that the summer heat would not attain its full force until the months of January and February; and this, together with the burning atmosphere, and the alarming nearness of the hurricane season, — to say nothing of the prevalence of the cholera at Port Louis, — inclined us to bid a cheerful farewell to the island.

We had already passed the citadel and bell-buoy, and, having discharged our pilot, were watching the fast receding shores, when we met the English mail-steamer from Point de Galle, in the island of Ceylon. We saluted each other, and then learned — what was given to us as reliable news — that war had been declared between America and some other power, but the name of the nation with which our

Government had come in collision, our officers, from some defect in the signal, could not interpret. This created, at first, some painful doubts and misgivings; but the belief finally gained ground that so long as the Southern Rebellion remained unquelled the United States would not embroil herself in a foreign war, unless it was forced upon her by the most imperious necessity.

The weather continued quiet and the sea was still undisturbed, although for three or four days after leaving Port Louis there were times when dark, lurid, and portentous clouds hung heavily upon the horizon and floated over us, and one evening there was also a dead calm, when everything excepting the glass indicated a coming tempest; but we steamed out of its neighborhood before it burst upon us, and all breathed more freely when getting ten or twelve degrees north of Mauritius, for we were then tolerably certain of a safe and quiet voyage. Some months afterwards we learned that we had not miscalculated in regard to the coming of the *cyclones*, or wind-storms, but that, in a few days after we had sailed through that region, it was visited by one of these terrible hurricanes.

We weighed anchor at the harbor of Port Louis on the afternoon of the 27th of December, and on the morning of the 30th, at eleven o'clock, our wheels had completed one million of revolutions since leaving New York. On the 2d of January we passed the Chagos Archipelago, the largest island of which group (Diego Garcia) belongs to England. It is fourteen miles long and eight in width, and is of coral formation, having a fine harbor, in the form of a crescent, setting into the island like the cavity of a shell. Good water is found by digging eight feet. It is covered with cocoanut-trees, and the Mauritians inhabit it mainly to engage in the cocoanut-oil manufacture.

Day after day, while in the Southern Indian Ocean, the mercury rose nearly to 100° in our cabin, and the sea was as placid as a river; but after passing the Chagos Islands, the heat, at one time, sensibly decreased to about 85°, making a delightful change. Again we crossed the equator, and steering for the northwest point of the island of Sumatra, on the morning of the 9th we had sighted her verdant shores, and were making for the Surat Pass. This narrow passage, which Hosburgh says "is called by the natives Selat Anoos, is formed between the east end of Stony Island and Acheen Head. It is about one hundred and fifty yards wide, with twelve or fourteen fathoms of water. The passage itself is not more than one hundred yards in width, and owing to the strong eddies on each side of its entrance, it is not very safe without a commanding breeze, excepting when the tide is just turning."

The day on which we made the passage was one of those perfect ones when the blue ether above us was of the same clear and deep color as that through which the stars floated at night, and the brilliant sunlight fell with soft and gentle sheen upon land and water. Entering from the west, Acheen Head, a high, verdant slope, looms up to the right; but after making the Straits of Malacca on its north-east side, it is a steep and rough cliff-land. Pulo[1] Chin-chin rises to the left, and her mountain-sides and fertile land skirting the shore were covered with evergreens, and cocoanut-groves. Acheen Head, as we sailed through the Pass, towered high above all; and its sides being superbly dressed with rank grass, tropical trees, shrubs and vines, among which were nestled the picturesque huts of the Malays, presented a most charming appearance. At one point we sailed so near as to enable us to count the overhanging trees, and were seized with an involuntary desire to attempt reaching the vines that hung trailing over the water. We had seen much of the beautiful, the wildly grand, and the sublime in scenery during our voyage, but nothing comparable in

[1] *Pulo* is the Malay for island.

attractive loveliness to that which met our eyes as
we entered the Surat Pass and sailed into the Straits
of Malacca.　This was the crowning glory of all, —
"a thing of beauty, and a joy forever."

The shoal water on the left, as we entered the
Strait, was dotted with the little fishing-boats of the
natives, which are something like a canoe in shape,
and while fishing are made secure and stationary
by being fastened at stem and stern, in clusters of
five or six.　Hosburgh remarks that "if the fishing
canoes are not seen out at this place before seven or
eight o'clock in the morning, a fresh breeze may be
expected during the day."　Little sail-boats were
also gliding in every direction, constructed with
a narrow framework about their gunwales, which
served as a balance to prevent them from being
capsized if struck by a sudden squall of wind.

On rounding Acheen Head we passed the mouth
of a river bearing the same name, two miles from
whose outlet, in the interior, is the town of Acheen,
where there is a Mahommedan chief, and a daily
market is held between two and three o'clock in
the afternoon, at which eggs, fowls, and fruits can be
procured, and if a day's notice be given, ships can
also get bullocks and goats.　A little beyond the
mouth of the Acheen River there is an anchorage for
vessels; and three ships, two English and one Turk-

ish, were lying there as we passed. Pepper, which is the chief article of produce, is obtained in large quantities in traffic with the natives.

Coasting for two days along the shores of this beautiful island, we occasionally had an excellent view of a native village, situated in what seemed to be a fine grazing country or well-cultivated fields. Doubtless the apparent cultivation was mostly wild, tropical luxuriance; for nature in every phase was attractive and lovely as seen from our stand-point; but where every man carries a savage knife, called a creese, at his girdle, and is not to be trusted if any temptation comes in his way, distance not only "lends enchantment to the view," but also produces a feeling of decided security, which, under the circumstances, cannot for a moment admit of wishing for a nearer acquaintance.

Great care and skill are necessary in navigating this strait, on account of the dangerous shoals and numerous small rocky islands which are met with in making the passage. Fortunately, however, we had moonlight nights, and Captain Briggs, fully equal to every emergency, never shirked any of his duties or responsibilities, but night after night remained upon deck directing the soundings, which were made with extreme caution as we proceeded through the channel. During one of those nights

7

we passed a very extensive and dangerous shoal, on which, not long before, a steamer had struck and been wrecked.   There was formerly no light upon, or near it, but sometime before our passage a vessel was moored near the shoal, which displays a light every night as a beacon to mariners.

We caught our first glimpse of the continent of Asia on the morning of the 11th of January, and during the day kept our eyes almost constantly turned towards those extensive countries, between India and China, where, an old writer tells us, "Ptolemy places his man-eaters, and Mandevylle found men without heads, who saw and spoke through holes in their breasts."   In the afternoon we were off the city of Malacca, which presented, upon the depressed or flat coast, an extended line of low buildings, with a high flag-staff near the water, from which we were signalled.   There was quite a show of shipping in the harbor, and a lofty mountain range loomed in the distance; while beyond lay the Central Flowery Kingdom to which our steps were hastening.

Those fortunate ones who never leave Fatherland with the prospect of living abroad, can know little of the emotions with which one approaches, and looks upon the strange country that is to be his home for years, perhaps for life; then, the blood and thoughts flow quickly, and however cool one's nature, for the time quietude and repose vanish.

We arrived at Singapore in the morning of January 12, 1862, after having navigated for several hours through the intricacies of an archipelago of small rocky islets. We heard the heaving of the lead during most of the night; and this, together with the fact that the steamer had been put at half speed, caused some of the more wakeful of cur passengers to be on the *qui vive* until the morning appeared, and we were safely at our moorings.

Singapore has a very fine and commodious harbor, which is in the form of a crescent; and the town is built partly on, and partly at the foot of a chain of hills, that rise with picturesque effect a little back from the shore. The most conspicuous of these hills is surmounted by a fort, and occupied by the Government buildings; and on the others are the finely built bungalow residences of the foreigners. The business quarter of the place is near the water, and a substantial stone wall skirts the shore, at about the centre of which there is another strong fortification, mounted with heavy guns, that, pointing towards, sweep the bay with a decidedly *noli me tangere* aspect. To the right of this fort, and following the shore, there is a fine drive and promenade, called the Bund, where foreigners, at early morning and evening, walk and drive to enjoy the cool sea-breeze. At the time of our visit there was a great deal of shipping in port, and an extraordinary multitude of boats were moving in every direction. Here we met, for the first time, with Eastern boat-life,—the Chinese boatmen being very numerous, and living, according to the custom of their country, in their own boats.

We had scarcely reached our moorings in the harbor when the water teemed with Oriental life, and we were surrounded with boats of nearly every Eastern nation, filled with motley groups of all shapes, sizes, and colors, who made the air resonant with the clatter of their various tongues. These people were all engaged either in selling fruit or small wares, and were earnestly ejaculating and begging of us to buy, — some even presenting themselves on board with recommendations for the purpose of "doing" our laundry. The East Indians are a most interesting people; and Ramasamy,[1] our Dubash, — i. e. interpreter, — a man who furnished supplies for our ship, — was a fine specimen of the race, with a quiet, unperturbed, and dignified mien, which is characteristic of the people.

Coming from the fierce summer heat of Mauritius,

[1] Almost all Hindus bear the name of some one of their gods. *Samy* means god, or lord.

and the Southern Indian Ocean, some of our company were much debilitated, and to such the more moderate temperature of Singapore was gently, but delightfully bracing. We hoped, on getting into port, to find letters and news from home; but having travelled at so rapid a rate as to outstrip the overland mail, we found that no news had been received from the United States, excepting a vague rumor, by telegraph, of a threatened war with England, on account of the Mason-Slidell difficulty, — which report both the American and English residents at Singapore feared would be confirmed on the arrival of the mail-steamer, then hourly expected. This explained the purport of the news designed to be communicated to us by the steamer which we passed on leaving Mauritius, and which caused us at the time some little anxiety, not only on behalf of our country, but also on our own account. Had the report proved true, we should have been obliged to surrender our vessel into the hands of the English, on our arrival at Singapore; any attempt to escape to sea from under the guns of the fortifications being an act of folly, if not downright madness. But having faced unscathed the yellow-fever at St. Paul de Loando, the small-pox at Cape Town, and the cholera at the Mauritius, besides passing safely through the hurricane latitudes without even meeting with a severe squall, we were inclined to hope that the ominous cloud just rising in the western horizon would also disperse, and that no such thing as a serious collision would occur between the two countries. Trusting, therefore, that Providence would permit us to finish the remainder of our voyage unmolested, we decided to enjoy our stay at Singapore, and look after the "lions" as usual.

Our captain determining, if possible, to sail for Hong Kong before the arrival of the English mail-steamer, made greater despatch in coaling than it had been customary for him to do at any other port on our route, and our time, therefore; did not admit of a very thorough "doing," either of the place or its environs. Rising, however, betimes on the following morning, we were sipping a cup of tea and eating a biscuit while on our way to town in one of Ramasamy's covered boats. Near the landing, according to arrangement, the Dubash had a Malay garee — a small coach, or cab-like vehicle, drawn by a little Malay pony — awaiting us. The carriage was built and finished with an eye to tropical comfort, — the cushions of the seats being covered with a fine and cool fabric made of the Manilla grass ; and between the body of the carriage and the top there was an open space, of one or two inches, left for ventilation. Our Malay *syce*, or driver, was neatly dressed, after the fashion of his caste, with a turban and upper garments of pure white; and pending from both the upper and lower lobes of his ears were gold rings, set either with emerald or an excellent imitation of that precious stone. Sometimes he rode, but more frequently ran beside his horse, urging the animal on, and looking the picturesque to perfection.

We first took the public drive upon the Bund, which is a beautiful, broad, and well-made macadamized road, having an enclosed public ground on the left, where the sight of a rich growth of grass gladdened our eyes and reminded us of home, it being the most verdant turf we had seen since leaving the United States. The hill-sides of Singapore are green and beautiful with grass, which is doubtless owing to the rains that, we were told, visited the place nearly every day. The town is built over a large surface, and the cultivation of trees, shrubs, and flowers, in the large grounds surrounding the bungalow residences, receives so much attention that the place seems as much like the country as the city, with all the advantages of both.

On the Bund, a little beyond the public grounds, there are three spacious bungalows standing near each other, which are used as a hotel, and kept in the European style for the convenience of foreigners. We passed, during our drive on the Bund, European ladies and gentlemen on foot, and on horseback, nearly all of whom were looking thin and pale, showing how difficult it was for Western exotics to thrive in the East. We drove through the Malay and Chinese quarters of the town, where the bay has so much of a curve that the Chinese boatmen safely moor their little floating cabins for the night, and at that early hour found them occupied in eating or preparing their morning meal. We also visited the market, and saw the Chinese gardeners, just in from the country, briskly trotting along with their panniers so heavily laden with fruits and vegetables that their shoulder-pieces of flexible bamboo vibrated at every step. There was also the native cart, drawn by buffalo-oxen, which reminded us of Sunday-school days, when, in the Rev. Dr. Barnes's " Notes on the Gospels," we first saw a picture of the same sort of vehicle. The harness and whole establishment looked the same as that said to be used in the Holy Land in the days of our Saviour. There were the same contrivances, the same kind of cart, and the same manner of arranging the yoke and the oxen, which, taken together with the driver, made the old picture *in loco*, and assured us, far stronger than our feelings could do, that we were far away from home. In the vicinity of the market we passed a cluster of Malay huts, which were built in the bungalow-style, over a salt marsh, and supported by stilts, or piles, with thatched roofs of plantain-leaves.

In the course of our drive we took the circuit of the hill on which are situated the bungalow houses of the foreigners, and around which winds a fine macadamized road. They were bordered with shrubs, flowers, and tropical trees, — the cocoanut-palm, the nutmeg-tree, bearing its beautiful pendant fruit, the bread-fruit-tree, the graceful bamboo, and many others. In the grass, also, by the road-side, we observed mimosas of exquisite tints. We took in our way the Christian Cemetery, the Episcopal Cathedral, and Police Station-house, with its wicked-looking and treacherous-eyed Sepoy sentinels, in full British uniforms, and had a profound Oriental salaam from an overseer of a gang of hard-looking convicts, comprising Malays, Chinese, and Indians, who were at work on the road.

The town is supplied with spring water, which is brought from the hills; and the neatly constructed circular stone fountains, in well shaded and picturesque situations, are much frequented. They are seen to much the best advantage in the early morning, when the bronzed, and grotesquely-dressed groups of people around them give one a good idea of Oriental fountains. But the picture presented by the native washermen and women, on the banks of the Singapore River, was, if possible, still more unique and remarkable. The little stream was fairly alive with them; and our Western ideas of care, economy, and thrift were outraged, as we saw them thrash the stones with the garments they were cleansing, so that we were ready to exclaim, — What fabrics can live through such mauling!

Having "done" the town as thoroughly as our limited time would permit, we drove to the bank of the Singapore River, not far from the Bund, where our boat had been ordered to wait for us; and, on passing from our carriage to the wharf, met two grand-looking Parsees, one of whom was a priest, who wore his peculiarly striking costume with a bearing more suggestive of *hauteur* than it is possible for words to describe. Once more seated in our boat we sailed along the business wharves, on which were large warehouses, or *go-downs,* as they are called in the East; and, passing through the mouth of the river into the bay, were soon again on board ship, much delighted with our excursion, besides having appetites sharp-set for breakfast.

Most of our missionary party left us at this port; three of whom[1] were to proceed to Calcutta, *en route*

[1] Among these was the Rev. Levi Janvier, D. D., of the Presbyterian mission of Lodiana, — a place in the Punjaub province, — the recent news of whose sudden and lamented death has saddened the heart of every one who had the pleasure of knowing him.

to Northern India, and two to Bankok, where they were to be stationed. We parted from them with the kindest wishes for their future usefulness, and months afterwards were happy to hear of their being safely settled in their respective fields of labor.

Some of the most delicious fruits in the world are grown at Singapore. At the Cape we procured very nice oranges, apricots, and pears, but were too early in the season for their excellent grapes. At Mauritius the luscious mango and appetizing lichi were in their prime; but here two or three different kinds of oranges were ripe, among which was the delicate mandarin; and the pine-apples, freshly cut from the plants, were abundant and in full-grown perfection. Here, also, we first met with the dainty mangosteen, which is superior to all the fruits of the East; being of such delicacy and exquisite flavor that it is said some one, on first partaking of it, declared it must be the nectar of the gods. The mango of Mauritius is a large and beautiful fruit, having a color on one side like the blush of a peach, and, with those obtained at Manilla, are said to be as fine as any in the East.

On the afternoon of January 14th, just as we were getting up steam to leave for Hong Kong, the guns of the English mail-steamer were heard, and she was soon sailing into the harbor. We acknowledge to having been a little anxious on her arrival, but it was soon ascertained that she brought no confirmation of the rumors which had reached us. She announced, however, the news of the death of Prince Albert, at the receipt of which not only the English, but the foreign residents generally, seemed much saddened, as well they might be, in sympathy for the widowed queen ; regretting that he who truly magnified his high position, and was a blessing to his kind, had so suddenly passed away. Our colors were among the first seen floating at half-mast for the illustrious dead; and with this sign of our respectful regard and sympathy, at five o'clock in the afternoon, we sailed out of the bay, and into the Straits of Singapore, feeling truly thankful that actual war had not thrown us into the hands of our affectionate English cousins. Ramasamy was the last to leave our ship. As we moved off he took his stand in the centre of his boat, and while making his graceful salaams, his tall and dignified figure, neatly arrayed in white and set off with a red sash and turban, made up, together with his Eastern boat and boat's crew, a fine picture.

The northeast monsoon, a wind that blows down the China Sea from October to April, had been unusually severe during the winter, and while lying in the harbor of Singapore we were much of the

time in motion, on account of the swell produced by
the tempestuous state of the sea at the North. It
was also reported that the previous mail-steamer
from Singapore to Hong Kong had been lost; and
altogether we had the prospect of a rough passage
before us, and a severe handling from old Boreas
for all the quiet seas and sunny skies which had
thus far accompanied us. To say that we dreaded
the passage to Hong Kong would convey but little
idea of the fears experienced by timid travellers
when compelled to meet such emergencies. There
is great enjoyment to such delicately constituted
people in a quiet sea, and a fair breeze; but let the
reverse happen and the change is fearful, nay, we
might say well-nigh appalling, but for the thought
that our heavenly Father can protect us as well in
the hour of peril as in times of safety. There is
no place where the awful grandeur of God's power
is so strikingly manifested as at sea, and no perils
like those of the great deep can so humble the heart,
or make one feel more thoroughly bereft of all available earthly aid. The same eye, however, that had
watched over us in our days of calm and sunshine,
slumbered not when the tempest overtook us, but,
following us to the end, we finally were landed in
safety at the desired haven.

In a few hours we had threaded the Straits of

Singapore, and were on the China Sea facing the monsoon. For two days it was not as rough as we had expected it would be ; but after that, the wind increased to such a degree of violence that it became necessary to take down our top-masts. Still our vessel rode the waves like a duck, and notwithstanding both wind and current were against us, she labored so little in the sea that our feeling of security became proportionably stronger, and we felt both hopeful and confident.

When in about the ninth degree of north latitude, we passed the Condore Islands. One of the largest of this group belongs to the French, who have a small colony on the island ; and on the western side there is a very good bay, where a man-of-war was lying at anchor for the protection of the little settlement. The French Government have selected the island for a coal depot, although the English formerly held possession of it, and some forty years ago had a garrison stationed there. This, however, was finally destroyed by the Malays, who fell upon it and put the soldiers to the sword.

On the night of the 17th of January the stiff breeze which had been blowing ever since we left Singapore culminated into a fearful gale, and the next day (Saturday) was one full of anxiety to all on board. It was not deemed advisable to apply more steam-power to the machinery, and the force against us was so tremendous that for twenty-four hours, — during which time the gale seemed to do its worst, — the same amount of steam which had usually propelled us at the rate of two hundred miles per day, advanced us only at the rate of ninety-three miles. The sky assumed the dull, metallic blue shade which usually characterizes it at sea during a fierce gale of wind, and our vessel was in some danger from the short and heavy waves that lashed her sides most furiously.

Being unwilling to remain below we sought a dry place on the quarter-deck, where, facing the stern, we quietly watched the storm. There was little conversation; but once during the day, our friend, Mr. S——, coming from the bow of the ship, — the scene at which point was too much for our weak courage to face, — sat down near us, and for some time cruelly whistled the air of "Home, sweet home!" while he kept time with his fingers upon the woodwork of one of the skylights on the quarter-deck. I could not trust myself to say a word by way of remonstrance, knowing that his thoughts were busy with the wife and little ones he had left in his own happy home; but was glad when he ceased, and hope never again to hear that sweet melody under the pressure of such painful apprehensions.

Thanks to a kind Providence, the wind fell at about midnight of Saturday; and on Sunday morning — having still one of our missionary clergymen on board — we assembled as usual for religious services, and gratefully rendered thanks for our merciful preservation.

A few hours after the worst of the gale had abated we made Cape Padaran; passing which we found more quiet waters, and were soon near that shore where

"Cochin China's cultivated land ascends."

During the remainder of the day we were sailing within three quarters of a mile of the bold, rocky coast, which is lined with high mountains, sometimes running in two parallel coast ranges, then three, and at one time I counted four distinct tiers rising one back of the other. In form and slope they reminded me of the Green Mountains of Vermont, and were entirely different from any we had seen during the voyage. The verdure of their sides was of a deep green; and the shade cast by the clouds that rested upon them, giving their surfaces a still darker hue, made their appearance a remarkable combination of the grand, the gloomy, and the picturesque. We were now passing localities that were formerly infested with Malay pirates; and were told that even now any vessel which is so unfortunate as to be lost on the coast is soon surrounded by the same piratical, grasping, and treacherous race.

The bracing and deliciously cool atmosphere of the northeast monsoon had a grateful effect upon all on board our vessel, and was delightful after the many weeks of depressing heat that we had endured. After leaving the coast of Cochin China the weather became more favorable, and we moved onward with more rapidity, until, on the morning of the 23d of January, after threading our way among the small islands in the neighborhood of Hong Kong, we sighted Victoria Peak, and, firing our guns as we sailed around its base, entered the harbor.

Before the *Poyang* had reached her anchorage we were boarded by two gentlemen belonging to the house of Olyphant & Co., who, surprised and delighted with our safe and speedy passage, welcomed Captain Briggs with great warmth, while they complimented him on having made the quickest voyage on record. At 12 o'clock we were moored before the city of Victoria, after having been at sea only eighty-six days, seventeen of which were passed in the ports where we touched for coals.

8

CHAPTER V.

The harbor of Hong Kong — which is said to be one of the finest in the world — is elliptical in form, and completely landlocked by mountains and bold rocks, which give it an exceedingly picturesque appearance; while the large amount of shipping, and great number of boats, that always throng its waters, present a scene full of life and bustling activity. My destination was Whampoa, but arriving at Hong Kong in advance of our time, the friend who was to meet me there had not yet reached the colony. I was, however, warmly welcomed by my friend and countryman, Mr. S——, the United States Naval Agent at Hong Kong, — at whose house I was most hospitably entertained, and kindly cared for.

When in a foreign land, the love of country, like one's religion, becomes a sacred emotion; and as I had learned, while on my voyage, to regard our national flag with increased affection, I was pleased to find it floating at the stern of Mr. S——'s gig, and to be taken to the landing under its protecting folds. The Chinese boatmen at the oars, who were arrayed in the blue and white uniform of our navy sailors, also caused my thoughts to turn anxiously homeward, where thousands of our noble soldiers and sailors were sacrificing their lives in order to sustain the free institutions of our fathers.

All Hong Kong was agog with the excitement caused by the rumors of a war between the United States and England; and many of the colonists believed that a serious collision was inevitable. Among our own countrymen there was a variety of opinions, and an anxious looking for the result, which was expected by the next mail.

Mr. S——, who magnified his office, and whose patriotism had the ring of the true metal, had in his "compound"[1] a high flag-staff, at the head of which, in fine weather, the "Star-spangled Banner" was always flying. One day, when speaking of the possibility of a confirmation of the war news, he remarked that he should not, under any circumstances, lower his colors, nor order any of his people to take them down. He added, however, that the moment the Colonial Government were certain of their right to do so, they would undoubtedly remove them, and take possession of his establishment; but that they would find very little property to seize, as he had already taken the precaution

---

[1] A general term for the enclosed grounds about the houses of foreigners.

to dispose of, and send home, his most valuable stores.

The summary manner in which our war-steamer, the *Saginaw*, was ordered out of the harbor of Hong Kong, created some indignant feeling among the loyal American residents; as it was a well-known fact at the time, that, in her disabled condition, had a storm occurred during her short voyage to the Macao Roads, her safety must have been endangered. I was at Whampoa the May following, when Captain Watkins, who was sent from California to take charge of the *Saginaw*, brought her into that port for repairs, and heard that officer allude, with some spirit, to the unhandsome and ungenerous management of that affair; while, at the same time, he expressed the hope that our naval depot would finally be removed from Hong Kong to one of the ports farther up the coast.

The winter having been unusually cool and bracing, all the human exotics from the West were rejoicing under its recuperating influences, the invigorating effects of which would supply them with renewed strength for the long tropical summer that was to follow. There had not been such cold weather for many years; and the sudden transition from the fierce heat of the torrid zone to a climate of such comparatively low temperature, not only made the warmest of garments acceptable, but inclined one to seek the friendly warmth of cheerful coal fires.

The island of Hong Kong is separated from the mainland by a strait from one and a half to five miles in width. The peninsula of Kowlung forms the opposite shore; and on its extreme point, which directly commands the entrance to the English town, there formerly stood two Chinese forts. The bay affords ample room to float a large fleet, and has both deep water and a good anchorage for vessels. Mariners have always been attracted to the island on account of the facilities for procuring a ready supply of the purest water, which is seen falling from the tops of the *Leong-teong*, or "two summits," in a series of cascades, the last of which glides with a graceful fall into a rocky basin on the beach. It is from this fountain, called the *Hiang-kiang*, — the "fragrant stream," — or the *Hoang-kiang*, — the "red, or bright torrent," — that the island is supposed to have derived its name. It was ceded to England in 1849. Its trap-rock mountains are conical, very precipitous, and sterile, but the valleys are sheltered and fertile. There is a large exportation of granite from the island. In its geological structure the trap-rock has the highest position, and the granite is found in immense blocks all over the island.

That part of the bay of Hong Kong which skirts the city of Victoria is faced with a substantial sea-wall of stone. The city is built at the foot of the mountains, which, in some places, have been graded to make room for the buildings on the principal street, which winds along the shore of the bay, and is called the " Queen's Road." Streets leading from this avenue wind around the declivities of the mountains, upon whose terraced sides are perched the houses of foreigners. From the highest terraces, where some of the finest residences are situated, there is an extensive view of the harbor, which, with its series of bays, white with shipping, stretches far away in the distance.

The most desirable locations in the city have distinctive names ; and beside the Government House, there is the Carlton Terrace, Spring Gardens, the Hermitage, the Albany, etc. Our friends resided at Spring Gardens, and occupied a large, rambling, stone house, whose apartments and spacious verandas were well arranged for tropical comfort. This place is situated upon the shore of the bay, and the houses, with their pleasant grounds, front the water, — the rear walls of their "compounds" opening upon the Queen's Road by large gateways. The rooms upon the ground-floor of all foreign residences are called " go-downs," and are only used for store-rooms, and for the accommodation of the servants of the household.

The climate of China is so enervating to people from the Western hemisphere that they rarely take long walks, and in all cases where much locomotion is required they employ Coolies to carry them in sedan chairs. Every family has at least one or two of these chairs, and a couple of chair Coolies; and there are also establishments where strangers can at any time procure, at a very moderate rate, both the chairs and bearers. Some of the private chairs are covered with black or deep-blue broadcloth, and have a lining of silk, with outer trimmings of heavy fringe. These, when ornamented with bright buttons, are very handsome. Among the latter we observed the chair of Lady Robinson, — the wife of the Governor of the colony, — and also that of Mrs. Smith, — the wife of the English Bishop. Mr. S—— being in the United States service, and his father-in-law having been one of our most respected and loyal commodores, I was glad to find his wife's chairs very appropriately covered with blue navy cloth, and ornamented with our naval button. Sedan chairs are carried by means of poles made of bamboo or wood, which the Coolies bear upon their shoulders, and are so arranged that, when lifted from the ground, the elevation of the

lower part of the chair is at least three feet, and
sometimes more.   Any accident, therefore, involving its fall,— particularly in passing over steep and
uneven surfaces, — may occasion very serious con-
sequences.

The day after my kind reception by Mr. and Mrs.
S——, I attended, in company with the latter, an
examination of a school of Chinese girls.   In order
to reach the Albany, where this school was located,
we were obliged to clamber some distance up the
mountain; and extra bearers and chairs being procured, we sallied forth from the great gateway leading into the Queen's Road, and were directly passing
the houses and shops of the European and Chinese
residents, — our bearers threading their way through
crowds of people.   Here and there we met an English officer, and occasionally one of the city police;
while, in passing the barracks, we again encountered
the Seapoy soldiery, — the fearfully wicked expression of whose eyes, as they impressed us when first
seen at Singapore, can never be mistaken or forgotten.   Near the Royal Theatre we turned into a
street that led up the slope of the mountain, and for
a time our stalwart bearers trotted briskly on with
ease and steadiness.   When, however, about half-
way up the ascent, the man walking in front of my
chair began to pant and waver in his movements,

until finally he labored for breath like one very ill. My pace being lessened, I was already greatly in the rear of my friend; and, becoming alarmed at the idea of a possible fall and tumble down the side of the mountain, begged earnestly, both in words and pantomime, to have my chair set down. Having at length made myself understood, the chair was put down in the middle of the road; and the Coolie, who had excited my pity and sympathy, although still panting, was quietly standing, and looking on with that grave and apparently uncon- scious air which a Chinaman knows so well how to affect, when he is intent upon gaining some undue advantage over you. My friend, however, on ap- proaching, read him at a glance. He was only per- forming an old *ruse* upon a newly arrived outside barbarian, — for it seems that the man expected to work upon my feelings until I should, out of pity, pay and dismiss him. Poor man! he had melted me into the pathetic, but the sudden change to the ludicrous was irresistible, when my friend, under- standing the case, exclaimed, in Canton English,[1] "How fashion that! — what for you no carry that chair?" Not a word was uttered by the Coolie,

---

[1] Foreigners, not speaking the Chinese language, in their inter- course with the natives make use of a *patois*, called Canton, or pigeon (business) English.

who, apparently oblivious of what was passing, seemed neither to hear, nor to be conscious that anything was wrong. After a short pause, my friend, accompanying her words with spirited little gestures, continued : — "Fightee la,[1] — I tellee Massee of you, and he no givee you one cash ![2] Takee up that chair, chop-chop ! no can carry alla proper, — no can catchee that cash ! I say you no carry — Massee no givee one single cash !" My bearers, who readily understood what was meant by " Massee no givee one single cash," unless they performed their contract, thereupon took up the chair, and carried it with apparent ease to the end.

On reaching the school we found Bishop Smith, with his wife and many others, already there ; but the Governor's wife not having made her appearance, there was a little delay. This school, which is under the patronage of the Bishop, numbered sixteen girls, from four to fourteen years of age, and was in charge of Miss Wilson, an Englishwoman.

Her Ladyship having at length arrived, after some religious exercises were had, the children were

---

[1] "Fightee," and "chop-chop," both mean quick, directly, immediately.

[2] A single *cash*, which is equal to one farthing, is the smallest fractional part of the Chinese currency.

examined by their teacher. The Bishop, with the aid of a Chinese student, then interrogated them for some time, and after making a few remarks to the audience dismissed them.

The girls of this school, besides receiving a useful education, are taught and thoroughly trained in the precepts of the Bible. Two of them, who were twelve or fourteen years of age, and were from the better class of Chinese families, had quite a prepossessing appearance as they toddled about on their little feet. They were also candidates for confirmation, and were at this time examined preparatory to receiving that rite. The Chinaman who assisted in the examination was a teacher from an institution which Bishop Smith had established at Hong Kong for the benefit of Chinese youths. There were also at Hong Kong other missionaries and schools, supported by different denominations, but my stay in the colony was too brief to enable me to become acquainted with them.

The English mail-steamer, which we left at Singapore, did not reach Hong Kong until thirty hours after the *Poyang* had anchored in the bay; and although we brought the news of Prince Albert's death, the official announcement to the Governor, Sir Hercules Robinson, was not received until the arrival of the mail. The sad intelligence had been

so long on the way that there was only a week, or
ten days, of the prescribed Court mourning left; but
for that space of time the Government dignitaries
wore the sable as directed, and the invitations which
had a few days previous been issued by Lady Robinson for a grand reception on the twenty-ninth of
the month, were countermanded. This was done by
sending a servant to those invited, with a note containing the following announcement: —

" In consequence of the melancholy intelligence
of the death of His Royal Highness, the Prince
Consort, Lady Robinson's ' at home,' fixed for the
29th instant, will not take place.

                        " Henry Aikenson, a. D. c.
    "Govt. House, January 25."

Under this a list was given of the names of those
invited; and to be certain that the paper had been
presented to all, each one signed his name directly
opposite where it was already written.

On sending a message or a package by a Chinese
servant, it is always necessary to send a note, which
in the *patois* is called a " chit." Writing notes is in
fact an " institution " among the foreign residents;
and rarely a day passes that one has not more or
less of them to despatch. To be sure that they
reach their destination, the servant also carries a

" chit-book," in which is written the name of the person to whom the note is sent, together with the day of the month; and on the return of the messenger, if the person addressed is found to have signed his name, it is proof positive that the trust has been faithfully fulfilled.

Having been joined by Mr. W——, who arrived from Whampoa on Saturday, on Sunday we attended service at the Bishop's Cathedral, where we witnessed the solemn ordinance of confirmation administered to a large number of English sailor-boys, from a naval receiving-ship lying in the harbor. There were also one or two English officers who were confirmed, besides several sailors, and the two Chinese girls whom we saw at Miss Wilson's school. The boys had been trained and catechized, preparatory to receiving the rite, by their chaplain, who was present.

Amid these solemn ceremonies it was gratifying to reflect that a thorough knowledge of God's commandments, the Catechism, and the Creed, together with the continued faithfulness of their chaplain, might not only tend to the moral elevation of the boys, but, under the Divine blessing, be the means of making many of them thoroughly religious men.

The English have always much to say of our " nasal twang " and " Puritan snuffle ; " but few Yan-

kees, however, can successfully emulate the Bishop
of Victoria in that doubtful accomplishment. I have
occasionally heard clergymen at home in whom this
defect was fearfully conspicious, but never remember meeting it in a more intensified form.

The camelia japonica, which is indigenous to
China, was in bloom when we were at Hong Kong.
Being generally cultivated in the gardens, it is much
used for bouquets, and the rarest, as well as the most
beautiful, are obtained in as great profusion as roses
are with us. One day, while paying a visit to a
friend, a lovely little girl came in from the garden
and presented me with a bouquet of the most superb
buds and blossoms of the camelia that I ever saw.
Next to the beauty of the gift, what surprised me
the most was its lavish degree of elegance; for having always regarded the possession of one camelia
as a luxury, I could not divest myself of the idea
that the possession of so many was an extravagant
indulgence.

Before Hong Kong was colonized, the various
members of foreign commercial houses in the south
of China resided at Canton, although, for the benefit
of the sea-air, they frequently passed the summer
with their families at Macao. But after the English
had established a more home-like place of residence
at Victoria, they made their principal head-quarters

there, and left the junior partners to transact the business at Canton. Hong Kong has therefore become the centre of attraction to all foreigners, as well as the arbiter of style and fashion in China. Like all English colonial communities, precedence in rank and position is closely adhered to, and rules throughout all cultivated society. As we remained in the place only ten days, I could of course know but little comparatively in reference to these matters; although from our friends, who had the *entrée* to the circle of Lady Robinson, I gained a favorable impression in regard to her ladyship and the society of which she is the centre. Much attention is paid to forms of etiquette among all the foreign communities in China; and the little — but, nevertheless, always agreeable — amenities of life are seldom forgotten. Notwithstanding the great difference in modes of living, — which are totally unlike those of the Western hemisphere, — the structure of society and its conventional rules are thoroughly English. Men of wealth and position live in a very luxurious style, — the East India Company having given a permanent tone to society in general, the effects of which are still manifest in the prevailing habits and customs of the people.

Many of the residents of Hong Kong keep European horses, but the climate is so unfriendly to them they survive but five or six years after being brought into the colony. I observed some handsome turnouts, among which the basket, or " Croyden carriage" appeared to be the vehicle most in use.

The roads are finely macadamized, and in the cool of the day there is a great deal of horseback riding. As in all English communities, the races constitute one of the principal amusements of the people; and in order to have a suitable place for this purpose, the surface of a spacious and level vale, called the " Happy Valley,"— which is near the eastern limits of the town, and lies between two beautifully swelling mountains that open upon Sanpan Bay,[1] — has been reclaimed from a state of saltmarsh, and now forms an extensive race-course. At a convenient point well-adapted buildings are arranged, and fitted up with all the necessary appliances for the accommodation of judges and spectators. During the races this place is thronged with gay and busy crowds of fashionable people ; but to one newly arrived from the occident there is a strangely odd mixture of the grave and gay, in the surroundings and present use of the valley. The Protestant,

---

[1] So called because it is the principal mooring place, and is, in fact, a floating village of little boats, called "sanpans," in which the Chinese fishermen and boat-people live. It is one of the numerous bights with which the coast of Hong Kong is indented.

Roman Catholic, and Parsee cemeteries are situated at the distance of only about three rods directly in the rear of the covered seats for the spectators, and the stands for the judges. These populous "cities of the dead" are in separate enclosures, although contiguous to each other, and are shaded thickly with evergreens and flowering shrubs. In the Protestant ground we observed single camelias in bloom on shrubs eight or ten feet in height. We also noticed, within the Parsee enclosure, several fresh graves already dug, and learned that it was the custom to have such places ready when called for, as it was often necessary in so warm a climate to bury the dead as soon as possible. This close proximity of a race-course to such an array of burial-places impressed us disagreeably; and we could not but think that so incongruous a blending of the gravely solemn with the gay and boisterously jolly, if met by an Englishman anywhere else than among his own countrymen, would call forth severe animadversion not only upon the community, but upon the nation to whom the people belonged. The graves of the Chinese are also scattered nearly to the top of the mountain slope on the opposite side of the valley; but their resting-places are found on all the hillsides, as well as on most of the unoccupied ground in China.

9

On nearing the port of Hong Kong almost the first object that meets the eye are the Chinese graves, and the attention is arrested by the peculiar style of some of their tombs, which are in shape like the Omega (Ω) of the Greek alphabet. The graves on the slope of Victoria Mountain, near the water, are very conspicuous.

Ancestral worship (of which I shall say more hereafter) is a part of the religion of the Chinese which prompts even the poorest people to care for and keep in good condition the graves of their household. Only the better or more wealthy classes, however, put up tombstones to mark the spot; and none but the mandarins, or those well to do in the world, build the elaborate tombs of the Greek-letter form.

On our arrival at Hong Kong the Chinese population were in the midst of their New Year festivities, during which all classes cease their occupations, and for some days indulge in mirth and enjoyment. One day during this festival we witnessed a very extraordinary game of shuttlecock played before some Chinese houses on the Queen's Road, by young men, who, with marvellous skill, used their feet for battledores.

Dr. Williams, in his " Middle Kingdom," says that " the evidences of the approach of this chief fes-

tival appear some weeks previous; when a general
cleaning of houses, boats, and garments takes place,
and all accounts are settled and debts paid. On
its arrival, the whole population throw off the old
year with a shout, and clothe themselves in the new
with their change of garments." At this festive season, also, the boat-people decorate their little floating houses with bright-colored papers, on many of
which are printed prayers addressed to their deities.
These papers, which were arranged so as to flutter
in the wind, together with the bright-colored lanterns and paper-flowers, which are also frequently
used in the decorations, give the boats a very gay
appearance. It was said that a thousand of these
ornamented boats were lying at Sanpan Bay when
we visited it. They were closely moored in tiers,
side by side, reaching far out into the waters, while
papers of brilliant hues were floating from their oars,
helms, and also from the tops of their little mat-
covered cabins.

CHAPTER VI.

A SMALL English steamer, called the *Feema*, or *Flying Horse*, was plying between Hong Kong and Macao, and wishing to visit some friends living at the latter place, instead of directly going to our own home at Whampoa, we took passage on the 2d of February and proceeded thither.

Besides our party of three, there were only five or six foreigners on board, most of whom were English. Among them we observed an English lady, who, notwithstanding the severity of the weather, was travelling with her feet encased in delicate slippers. We probably should not have remarked this fact had we not read some severe criticisms, from the pens of English travellers in the United States, in regard to our own countrywomen imprudently risking their health in the same manner. We do not, however, remember of having met, in our travels at home, a gentlewoman whose feet were so slightly protected for the season. We mention this incident to show that, after all, there is not a very wide difference in the careful or careless habits of our Anglo-Saxon cousins when compared with our own. In our vain boasting, and some other peculiarities, we are greatly alike, which only the more clearly proves our legitimacy to the same stock.

The distance to Macao was only forty miles, yet when off Lintin Bay — which is a part of the delta at the mouth of what is called the Canton River — there was so heavy a sea running that our little cabin reeled, and old Neptune again shook his trident at us. An hour or two, however, brought us to the Macao Roads, and passing in view of the Donna Maria, and Guia forts, which occupy the tops of two rocky hills, we steamed into the inner harbor.

Before we could anchor, our vessel was surrounded by little passenger-boats, managed for the most part by women, who vociferated at the top of their voices; each one, in order to secure passengers, being solely intent upon getting the prow of her boat nearest to the companion-ladder. At the time of the confusion at Babel the Chinese race must have had a large representation there; for the clatter of tongues that greeted us at some of the ports, on our voyage from New York, was as the murmur of a peaceful rill when compared to the great cataract of shrill voices that here well-nigh deafened us. It was impossible to hear the deeper tones of the men in the general uproar; while it was absolutely frightful to see those

of the passengers who had no ladies to care for, leap-
ing, nearly mad with the wild tumult, into the first
tanka-boat[1] they could reach.   Under these circumstances, passing without accident through the peril
of getting into one of these rocking little boats, —
which was skilfully guided and propelled by three
stout tanka-women, — and being safely landed at
the Custom-house jetty, was a matter of sincere
felicitation.

The warm welcome one receives on reaching old
friends in a foreign land goes far towards compen-
sating for the *désagrémens* of travel; and notwithstanding our new surroundings may be strangely
unfamiliar, the presence of beloved faces from the
old home-circle creates a gratefully satisfied feeling
of content.

The peninsula of Macao juts out from the southeastern end of Hiangshan, — a large island near the
mouth of Lintin Bay, — and is connected with it by
a narrow, sandy isthmus. "The town," says ——,
"occupies a position rather of beauty than strength;
for the summits that surround its peninsula side also
command it, and the waters of its inner and outer
harbor are navigable for vessels of considerable burden."   It is an old Portuguese colony, — the penin-

---

[1] *Tanka* means egg ; therefore these boats, being egg-shaped, are
called in the Colony tanka-boats, and the women managing them,
tanka-women.

sula occupied by the city being three miles in length by one in breadth. One side of it is curved into a bay, whose beauty is often compared to the bay of Naples. Along the shore-line of this curve lies the *Praya Grande*, — a grand promenade. The opposite side of the peninsula is high and rocky, with a little curve towards the sea; and the ridge of this eminence, as well as its sloping sides, is covered with houses, churches, and now, nearly deserted convents.

The Portuguese obtained permission to settle here about the year 1537, — not, however, as an independent community, but in association with the native population, and during their good behavior or the Emperor's pleasure. For this privilege they promised, at first, to pay a large sum of money, but their exclusive policy and efforts to secure all the Chinese trade to themselves and the Spaniards, ruined them in their speculations, so that the Emperor, in 1843, agreed to receive from them the small ground-rent of one hundred and fifty pounds sterling per annum. In 1847, according to Doctor Williams, the population of the peninsula was not far from 30,000, of whom 5000 were Portuguese.

Macao was formerly the private residence of the foreigners in Southern China, but since the establishment of an English colony at Hong Kong, it has been nearly deserted, except during the summer months, and even then but few families frequent it for the whole of the warm season. There are, however, foreign consuls there; the United States, at the time of our visit, being represented by Gideon Nye, Jr., Esq., — an American gentleman whose earnest loyalty, elegant hospitality, and kindness, will be pleasantly and gratefully remembered by all his countrymen who visited Macao during his occupation of the consulate.

Some of the largest and most comfortable dwellings occupied by foreign residents at Macao were erected one hundred and fifty years ago, when the colony was the richest mart in Eastern Asia. They are built on the plan common to most other Eastern cities, having walls two or three feet in thickness, which are sufficiently strong to withstand the devastating force of the terrible typhoons that annually visit the country.

The mansion of the Governor of the colony is situated upon the beautiful Praya Grande, and the extensive buildings formerly occupied by the East India Company also front on that lovely promenade. One of the oldest houses in Macao was the home of Dr. Williams, where we were guests. It is two hundred years old, and its spacious apartments — like those of other residences occupied by foreigners —

are admirably arranged, and adapted to the necessities of so warm a climate.

There are several forts, only one of which we visited. This is called the Guia, or Del Monte, and was built in 1638, — one hundred years after Macao was first settled. It stands on a rocky eminence of the same name. In building it the rocky summit was merely cut down so as to form a level surface. Stone battlements, having very thick walls, were then constructed, and upon these guns are mounted. The Guia fort is the highest elevation in the settlement, and as it commands an extensive view of the sea and roads, is used as a signal-station.

In clambering up the hill to the Guia fort we encountered many Chinese graves. These, as we have already mentioned, are never enclosed; but the cattle pasture among them, and footpaths, made by the inhabitants, lead between and around them. Before reaching the hill we passed through a portion of the Government Park,[1] in which a memorial-stone is erected to mark the spot where, two centuries ago, a Dutch admiral was killed while advancing from his boats to attack the colony.

[1] On our excursion to the Guia we traversed a portion of the Praya, and also the Alameda, a public square, which is planted with trees, and passing through one of the two gates, in the northern wall of the city, followed the Campo Road that led to this park.

The temple of Makauk — the first Buddhist monastery which we visited in China — is a very picturesque joss-house, built among the cliffs and granite boulders near the sea-shore. It is sacred to the goddess *Kwanyin*, i. e. the Hearer of Cries; who is also called the Goddess of Mercy, Holy Mother, and Queen of Heaven, — which Dr. Williams says is only another form of " Our Lady." Kwanyin, although more particularly the goddess of the boat-people, fishermen, and sailors, is also a favorite divinity of the Chinese generally. This temple is very old, and is said to have been built by Chinese sailors, who were saved, with their junks, through the perils of a dreadful typhoon, in which a great number of seamen were lost. The main entrance is guarded by two huge, but grotesque lions sculptured in stone, and the tall red flag-staff, in front of the temple, designates its locality to the passer-by.

In one of the volumes of " Allum's Views in the East," there is a very correct picture of this temple as seen from the harbor, — so faithful a copy, indeed, that a careful observer, having once seen the temple from that point, would readily recognize the original. A descriptive writer of scenes in the East has given so minute and excellent an account of this pile, that we cannot do better than to quote his words entire : —

" At the foot of the great stairway are three large monumental slabs closely inscribed with names, titles, and laudatory records. An enclosure, resembling the holy ground that surrounds the ancient sanctuaries of Europe, is formed by means of walls connecting the rude rocks that occur in the circuit, and which are always religiously retained by Chinese artists to decorate. A balustrade, resting on this dwarf wall, is divided by compartments enriched with tracery, and decorated with various representations of instruments of music, implements of art, and weapons of war. A child, seated on a quadruped of a nondescript species, is attended by venerable men, and followed by two females carrying umbrellas; while Satan, adorned with monstrous horns, is fleeing from the party in the utmost dismay.[1]

" Another division is filled with a group representing the dedication of the temple, and the votive act in which it had its foundation. The design of the temple includes five separate structures, — the centre more lofty, the lateral gradually descending from it, and different also in character and decorations.

" A rich cornice supports a highly ornamental

[1] In the religion of the Chinese there is no love of their god, but a great fear of the devil, or of the spirit of evil, which they are always aiming to propitiate.

roof, entirely of porcelain, on which rests a boat or junk, sculptured with representations of various natural scenes and customs.   Beneath the cornice are two oblong panels, enclosed in frames of bright and colored stone, — the higher containing bas-reliefs of grotesque figures and extraordinary combinations, the lower filled with apothegms from the writings of the great founders of the sect of idolaters who come here to worship.   Beneath this latter tablet opens a large circular window, the frame of which appears to have been cut, with incalculable labor, from a single block of stone.   Pilasters, wholly covered with inscriptions, separate the central from the lower divisions ; and these are also adorned with porcelain roofs, massive cornices, and tablets, on which admonitions and wise maxims are emblazoned.

" Each division is pierced by a square window of large dimensions, the carvings on which, although an extraordinary evidence of untiring labor, and unexampled perseverance, are neither beautiful nor intelligible."

It was here that I first met with the banian-tree, which is always found growing in the grounds of Buddhist temples.   These trees had attained a great age, and were so near the buildings that their great gnarled roots grew over and under the rocks, while their branches overshadowed much of the pile.

After examining the establishment we passed into one of the rooms of the cloister, where we were served with some New-Year's confectionary by an old priest who had been an inmate of the temple fifty years.

The temple of Mongha — another Buddhist monastery — is situated about a mile from Makauk, in the village of Wanghai, one of the suburbs of Macao. It is famous from the circumstance that here, in 1844, the treaty made by the United States plenipotentiary, the Hon. Caleb Cushing, with the Imperial commissioner, Kéying, was ratified. Dr. Williams, who visited this temple with us, and who was present at the signing of that treaty, told us that the idols were removed from the chief apartment in order to make room for the occasion.

The presence-chamber of this establishment, which contains large brazen images of the Past, Present, and Future Buddha, is a spacious apartment, decorated with extraordinary tracery and carvings. We observed upon one side of the wall a remarkable specimen of the latter, parts of which were painted in colors, and were told that it represented the Buddhists' idea of the cosmogony of the universe. This confused and grotesque delineation of Oriental wisdom reminded us of Goldsmith's remark, that "the origin of the world has puzzled the philosophers of all ages." Whether this remark could with propriety be applied to the world or not, we were pretty certain that it could be applied to the picture, for a more incongruous and unmeaning design we never remember of having seen. The temple had been renewed at great expense, the year previous to our visit, and the grotesque decorations of the exterior, together with the horrid-looking dragons that ornamented the roof, were as bright and fresh as new paint and gilding could make them. Beyond the chief presence-chamber there is a shrine containing an image of the god Esculapius, and also one of the goddess of mercy, — Kwanyin, — which is guarded on each side by grotesque images. Tanka-boat women, in neat holiday attire, making New-Year's offerings and proffering requests, were prostrating themselves at her shrine. These poor deluded women were kneeling on mats, and throwing little bamboo sticks on the floor before them, in order to ascertain whether the goddess would hear or refuse their petitions. At short intervals, — while they were alternately casting the bits of bamboo, and bowing until their foreheads touched the floor, or, rising, stood burning incense or joss-sticks before the image, — a large bell, placed a little at the right of the idol, was occasionally struck by a young priest, so as to attract the attention of the deity.

These adorations, made to a senseless image, together with the ringing of the bell, called to mind a passage in the First Book of Kings, (xviii. 27,) and we could not but wonder how any person coming from a land blessed with the teachings of the elevating religion of Jesus, could witness such scenes of gross superstition and idolatry, without rejoicing that the Christian missionary had been sent among these people to teach them the truths of the Bible, and a knowledge of the true God. The seemingly paradoxical expression, that "the credulity of unbelief is greater than that of belief," appeared here to have

" A local *habitation* and a *name;* "

and although I remained in China long enough to become, in some degree, accustomed to witnessing idol worship, still I never got rid of the thoughts and impressions produced by the acts of heathen idolatry which here came within my observation.

Three or four years ago the foreign Protestant residents at Macao purchased a part of the large grounds belonging to the temple of Mongha, and laid them out as a cemetery. Magnificent banians, of more than two hundred years growth, ornament and shade the place, making it one of the most charming localities in the suburbs of Macao. The old Protestant burying-ground, located in the heart of the city, is also an interesting and lovely spot. It was purchased of the Portuguese by the old East India Company, and is enclosed within a high stone-wall, having an entrance-gate which opens upon the San Antonio green. The Protestant chapel stands within this enclosure, and the grounds are orna-mented with a variety of trees and shrubs. One little spot, in this burial-place, was to us invested with a tenderly sad and mournful interest, for here the mortal part of one of our own home-circle, who had left us in the strength of his early manhood,

> " Slept that still and placid sleep,
> For which the weary pant in vain."

Here, as at the Protestant grounds at Hong Kong we observed that the majority of the interments were young men. It is natural for most persons to feel a peculiar solemnity on visiting a burial-place, but this emotion on entering a Christian cemetery in a distant heathen land is greatly intensified. Several of the officers of the old East India Company are buried in this enclosure; and the remains of Dr. Mor-risson, the English missionary, who made the first translation of the Bible into the Chinese language, are also entombed here, — which circumstance must always render the spot a place of distinguished interest to the Christian. Other missionaries, — noble men and women, — who worked on cheerfully until the exhausting influence of the climate forced them,

"Weary with the march of life,"

to lie down and die, here "sleep the sleep that knows no waking," until the morning of their bright and glorious resurrection.

Chinnery, the English artist, who during his lifetime became quite famous for his fine delineation of Oriental scenery, and his remarkably life-like sketches of the boat-people and other classes of Chinese, has also a conspicuous tomb within these walls. His pictures not only bear the impress of genius, but are particularly remarkable for their exquisite fidelity to nature, in which respect he is justly entitled to rank as the Teniers of the East.

Romanism is the established religion of the colony; yet, out of thirteen churches, all but three are sequestered. St. Paul's, a grand old stone church, which was built in 1634, was destroyed by fire in 1835. The façade, and high stone steps of this edifice are still standing; and judging from the ruin, which is a conspicuous object, — meeting the eye from every point of view, — it must have been an imposing structure.

One of the chief points of interest in the Casa

Gardens — which we visited — is the grotto where Camoëns, the Portuguese poet, is said to have written most of the Lusiad. Those familiar with that poem are aware that its author was banished to Macao by his Government, and spent five years of his life in that colony. The gardens are now owned by a Portuguese family, who reside in the imposing old mansion within the walls, and from whom visitors must procure permission to enter the enclosure.

The place belonged formerly to the East India Company, and the house was then occupied by the chief officer of that establishment. A grand flight of stone steps leads to the main entrance of the dwelling, and at the time of our visit pots of rare plants, placed on stands, were arranged in a semicircle at their base; while oleanders — whose great growth and tropical luxuriance gave them more the appearance of trees than shrubs — were growing, and in full bloom on each side of the steps. These beautiful grounds are enclosed within a high stone wall, and were originally laid out on a scale of magnificence in keeping with the luxurious style and princely state for which the officers of the old East India Company, in their palmy days, were celebrated. Camoën's Grotto — which is situated in a charming spot — contains a bronze bust of the poet, standing on a pedestal, on which are also traced,

in bronze letters, some stanzas from the " Lusiad."
There is also set in the rock a marble panel, having
engraved upon it a poem in praise of Camoëns.
The poetic inscription is by a Frenchman, who calls
himself the "poete exile." The bust is a rude piece
of art, but we were told that one, finely sculptured
in marble, was about to be sent from Portugal to
replace it. The Portuguese nation have long since
awakened to a just sense of Camoën's merits, but
they can never blot out the severe expressions that
occur in some passages of his great poem, in which
he laments the neglect and injustice which he suffered from his country. Among these the following
is full of the most bitter irony.

> " Ye gentle nymphs of Tago's rosy bowers,
> Ah, see what lettered patron-lords are yours!
> Dull as the herds that graze their flowery dales,
> To them in vain the injured Muse bewails :
> No fostering care their barbarous hands bestow,
> Though to the Muse their fairest fame they owe ! "

Trees overshadow this grotto, and a flight of stone
steps lead to the top, where a large flat surface extends over and beyond it. When Macao was the
principal residence of the families of foreign merchants, picnics were held in these gardens, and the
children performed their little dances upon this rocky
floor.

In most parts of the grounds tropical trees and shrubs are so numerous as to form an almost impenetrable shade; while the tough and gnarled roots of hoary banians have crept up and down some parts of the old walls which enclose the gardens, until they have formed a sort of network which acts as a support for the masonry. In other places the banian, of great age and size, grows from the fissures of high, jagged rocks, and the serpent-like roots bind the rudely broken masses and granite boulders firmly together. In contrast with these are the beautifully graceful clusters of bamboo, some varieties of the palm, and trees of a delicate acacia foliage.

We were indebted to the kindness of our Consul, Mr. Nye, for a charming boat excursion to *Tui-mien-shan*, or Lapa Island, which lies west of Macao. A large surface of ground, at the head of a little valley on this island, is covered with broken rocks, and boulders of every shape and size. Among those there is one of very large dimensions, which, on being struck with an iron instrument gives out a loud, clear, and ringing sound, like that produced by striking sonorous metal. From this circumstance it has received the name of the " Ringing Rock," and persons visiting it always carry iron hammers with them, in order to amuse themselves with the echo which it creates in the valley.

The pleasant rambles on this island are much frequented by foreigners; so leaving the "Ringing Rock," and ascending the hill, we were just bending our steps towards a large boulder, in order to rest under its inviting shade, when we were startled by coming suddenly upon what appeared to be a frightful snake. The seeming reptile, which was coiled around a shrub, proved, however, to be only the old skin that a snake, over eight feet in length, had recently left there. The power of the final effort made by his snakeship, in casting off the old habiliment, was manifest from the great number of involutions left in the skin near the tail. We were assured that the snake was not of a venomous species, but could not be induced to remain in that locality, and gladly returned to the more cultivated parts of the vale, where the water of an enchanting little rivulet was made to turn the rude machinery of a very primitive grist-mill. The hoppers of the mill were turned by an overshot-wheel, on which were bamboo cogs, — water conducted through bamboo canes being used in order to prevent friction. We did not, however, incline to linger by the way, and were glad when we had regained the landing, and were once more on board of Mr. Nye's spacious boat, the *Picnic,* on our return to town.

The Chinese manufacture an excellent lime from fossil oyster-shells, and the people following that business at Macao live in a place called the " Lime-kiln Village." Visiting that locality late in the afternoon, we witnessed a curious exhibition of the economy and management of the people. The weather was unusually cold, and at one place a circular burning kiln filled with shells was surrounded by a crowd of women and children. The diameter of the kiln was about ten feet, and the top surface, which was one mass of fire, was covered with the little stewpans, and tea-water vessels of the women, who were busy cooking their evening meal, while the children were pressing near, in order to warm their thinly clad and shivering little bodies. The savory fumes, with which the place was redolent, were suggestive of ragouts made of certain little animals which are said to be the favorite food of the lower class of Chinese.

CHAPTER VII.

AFTER nine days of great enjoyment at Macao, our passage having been secured in the American steamer *Spark*, that plied between the latter place and Canton, we once more embarked, and were soon on our way to Whampoa.[1] The captain and first officer of the vessel were Americans, and our ensign, floating at the stern, reminded us pleasantly of home and Fatherland.

It was on the 11th of February, a beautifully clear, tropical winter morning, and, passing rapidly the fertile and lovely islands of the great Delta, we were soon at the mouth of the Bocca Tigris, or Bogue River. The islands of this delta were formerly greatly infested with pirates, and as we threaded the intricacies of the little Archipelago our attention was frequently directed to certain points noted as having been their rendezvous. Since the establishment of steam navigation, however, between Canton and Macao, and also between the former place and Hong Kong, travellers have rarely fallen into the hands of the pirates whose junks and fishing-boats were at one

[1] Pronounced Wompoo, *i. e.* the yellow anchorage.

time common in those waters, — although in a few
instances parties of these buccaneers have gone
boldly as passengers on board the steamers with
the intention of trying to take them.   Their designs,
however, have usually been discovered and frus-
trated; but after the disclosure of one of these plots
it is customary to search all Chinese passengers on
their coming on board, in order to see if they have
any weapons concealed about their persons, and an
armed guard is then placed over them until it is ascertained to be perfectly safe again to allow them un-
restrained freedom.   The steamers are armed, and
the officers, as well as most of the foreigners, when
travelling, carry pistols about them, so that there is
now comparatively little to apprehend, for English
authority is feared as well as respected in China.

Before reaching the mouth of the Bocca Tigris we
sailed over a large expanse of water called the Linten
Bay, — a name which it derives from an island situated in the southern part of the bay, and near which
the opium ships used to anchor.   Here we fell in
with numerous trading and fishing-junks, and also
with market and passenger-boats, which, in spite of
their clumsy rigging, and heavy matting sails, moved
with much rapidity through the water.   The forms
of many of these sails were singularly grotesque,
and some of them reminded us very strongly of the

wings of an enormous butterfly. Many of the vessels were painted in brilliant colors, and all had eyes traced on their prows. Indeed, it is a very uncommon thing to find a Chinese boat, or even a larger vessel, unprovided with these eyes; and if you ask a Chinaman the reason for so extraordinary a fashion, he usually replies, — "No got eye, no can see; — how fashion can makee walkee?"

The ruins and remains of the Bogue forts, at the entrance of the Bocca Tigris, are sufficient to give one an idea of the frail defences, — which they proved to be, — when exposed to the fire of European guns; and one of our party, at the first glance, remarked "that they must have made a man-of-war laugh." There were ten of those fortifications, all of which were completely destroyed. One of them, situated on the mainland, was called *hie shoe*, from its resemblance in form to a Chinese lady's shoe. A little further on we passed Tiger Island, so called because its outline, as seen when approaching from the river, is not unlike that of a tiger couchant.

Whampoa, — or the yellow anchorage, — where we arrived early in the afternoon, is a reach extending four miles along the river. It is twelve miles distant from Canton. Ships cannot ascend further than this point, but freight is carried to, and from them by means of large cargo-boats. The old

town of Whampoa, with its tall pagoda, is situated
on an island of the same name, which lies at the
north of the anchorage. The banks of the stream
on that side are very low; and although only the
highest buildings, with an occasional minaret-like
cupola, are visible above the foliage of the trees, it
is strikingly Oriental in appearance. The people of
the town have never been very friendly to foreigners,
and consequently the place is but rarely visited. As
we neared the anchorage, the low flat shores were
far from wearing an inviting look, nor were the two
miserably squalid villages of Bambootown, and
Newtown, — which are occupied by fishermen and
boat-people, — in the least attractive; although acting as foil, they helped to set off the picture, making the green hills and fertile little valleys of the
large islands look all the more agreeable. On
Dane's Island are two extensive dry docks, — one
belonging to an American firm, and the other to an
English company. The latter is a very large stone
structure, where the English mail-steamers and
naval vessels are repaired and refitted. Although
at that time there was less foreign shipping in the
harbor than usual, still a number of vessels from
the United States, as well as from England, and
other European ports, were at anchor in the reach,
and that part of the settlement in the vicinity of the
docks, bore quite a business aspect.

Foreigners, whose business oblige them to re-side at Whampoa, live in floating dwellings, called " chops."[1]   These are built on ships, which, after having seen some service, and their spars and rigging having been taken down, are then used as founda-tions for houses.   They are moored in a part of the reach where the river is very wide, being placed a little on one side of the channel used by the steam-ers and trading vessels in passing and repassing to and from Canton.   The cabins and state-rooms at the stern are converted into store-rooms, pantries, and bath-rooms.   The forecastle is used for ser-vants, and over the entire vessel a story is built, that is divided into large and conveniently ar-ranged apartments, and when fitted up with all the necessary comforts of life, are in many ways far more desirable homes than can safely be made on shore.   The kitchen is at the bow of the vessel; and from there to the centre, — near which is the boundary of the family apartments, — are the busi-

[1] This word has various meanings ; I do not know, however, why it is applied to these floating houses.   The Chinese merchants speak of a " chop" of tea or silk, meaning an amount which bears a cer-tain mark.   They eat with chop-sticks ; and a ship's clearance to go to sea, after she has taken cargo, is called a " grand chop."   Then there is the expression, " chop-chop," meaning, if addressed to a servant, to " be quick," or, " do it immediately."   To say " chop-chop." to your chair-Coolie, means " step faster."

ness offices, and also rooms for foreign clerks. On
one side, a narrow passage-way leads from the
kitchen to the family apartments. There is another
similar passage-way on the other side, which, however, has no connection with the house apartments;
and for the convenience of men of business visiting
the offices, as well as for the servants, steps lead to
the water from both of these passages. The flat
roof of the family apartments is so constructed as
to serve for a promenade. The latter, however, is
not enclosed, but has a covering, the frame of which
rests on stanchions; and in order to exclude the sun,
shades, made of a kind of grass, are arranged so as
to drop from the roof. A table, bamboo settees, and
easy-chairs occupy a portion of this space, yet there
is ample room for the enjoyment of one's afternoon
" constitutional," when the weather does not allow
of boating, or a ramble upon the shore. Some chops
have little verandas, or galleries enclosed with Venetian blinds, which are built on each side of the
family rooms, and resting on braces, extend from the
sides of the ship upward. These are ornamental,
and make the house cooler in summer and warmer
in winter, thus adding greatly to the comfort of the
family.

The low lands and rice-fields in the neighborhood
of Whampoa render the climate malarious; but by

being out in a stream with so swift a current as that of the Pearl, — called by us the Canton River, — the miasma does not readily reach the inmates of the floating houses, neither is the air loaded with the shocking odors that often greet one's olfactories when in the vicinity of Chinese settlements. Although the hills and the pleasant vales, on the islands opposite, have many fine locations for dwellings, the time is not yet arrived when the advantages of shore-life can equal those of "chop"-life; and this manner of living, therefore, is preferred by the consuls, officers of the customs, traders, and foreigners generally.

Our steamer stopped when nearly opposite this floating community, and the passengers were conveyed to their homes in the *sanpans* of the Chinese boatmen. Our chop was a Baltimore clipper which had originally been built for the slave-trade; but not succeeding in that nefarious traffic, she was taken to China, and having been sold to the Imperial Government, a comfortable house was erected on her hull for the accommodation of the chief officer of their customs at Whampoa. Occidentals, who are not acquainted with chop-life in the East, invariably associate it with what they read in reference to the multitudes of poor people living in boats upon the waters of China, and hence imagine it to be a miserably half-civilized mode of existence. To such persons the idea must be accompanied with a pov-

erty-stricken picture of discomfort, and an utter want
of all the comforts of life, and the amenities of a cultivated home.   On the contrary, however, my own
experience in this novel mode of living was not only
agreeable, but the oddity of it, together with our
strange surroundings, gave it a peculiar charm.   Our
chop, comfortable in every arrangement, answered
in exterior to the description already given of those
built with verandas.   There was one exception,
however, as we had the advantage of an extra
flight of steps for family use, which led from our
own apartments to the water.   The rooms were
large and airy, with windows opening to the
floors; and the latter being painted in figures and
highly varnished, had the appearance of being covered with nice oil-cloth.   The furniture,—like that of
all foreign houses in China,—was European in the
style of its manufacture.[1]   Even the beautiful china-
ware of the country,—which we admire so much at
home,—is rarely used by foreigners when living
among the Chinese; the simplest European table
furniture being considered far preferable.   Carpets
are only used during the winter, when they are
found to be very comfortable.   During the year that
I was in China, the winter was colder than usual,

---

[1] If a sample—called by the Chinese a "muster"—of Western
furniture is given to a Cantonese cabinet-maker, he will directly produce a well-made and exact copy of the original.

and we were glad to use the little American stoves with which our rooms were furnished. One of the few disagreeables of this kind of floating life was the constant change of view. We were continually turning with the ebb and flow of the tide, and consequently, if one sat at the same window a whole morning, there was an entire change of scene, and of course a corresponding change in the points of the compass. An inactive person, however, to whom variety is pleasing, might even enjoy this. The river at the anchorage is very broad and deep, and fearfully rapid, — so much so, in fact, that a person falling into it must be an expert swimmer in order to save himself.

The house-servants in China are all men, but Cantonese women are employed as nurses for children, and also as waiting-maids for the ladies. The enervating influence of the climate obliges Western women to take life easily; and being obliged to drop most of their active pursuits, they usually are greatly dependent upon the services of these women. The Chinese *Amahs* — as these nurses and waiting-maids are called — often have bright and genial faces; and when introduced into a household where all the servants wear the grave and stolid faces of Chinamen, are a great relief to the every-day picture of domestic life.

We found the men-servants very respectful and obliging, and not only as conscious of kind and fair dealing, but quite as grateful for it as the human race are generally. The Chinese are a patient, persevering, and industrious people, but they have not the appearance of a cheerful race. The respectable serving-women, with whom I came in contact, seemed more cheerful than the men, but even among them I rarely met with a joyous face. This, however, may in a great measure be owing to there being no day of rest like our Sabbath, and therefore no cessation from their daily toil, except on the occasion of some heathen festival. The children of the boat-people learn to work as soon as they can handle an oar ; and those of the landsmen whenever their little forms have acquired strength sufficient to bear the bamboo shoulder-piece, and the little buckets of water, or small packages that pend from either end. I have rarely seen young children, or even men, bear such heavy burdens as they are accustomed to carry in China. The river at Whampoa, — always teeming with boat-life, — frequently presented sad objects of suffering poverty. I saw, however, among these boat-people many neat, comfortable, and apparently happy families.[1]

[1] The unquestioned obedience which is rendered to Chinese parents by their children, and the respectful reverence that is mani-

The head-servants employed by foreign families speak the "pigeon" English, and act as interpreters for the other domestics. This *patois* is nearly a literal rendering of the Chinese idiom into a dialect which is more like "English baby-talk" than anything else I can compare it to, and foreigners readily acquire it. The particular duties of each servant are regulated by fixed rules, and if one should order his "boy," or head-servant, to sweep his room, or carry his trunk to the boat, the ready answer would be, — "That no my pigeon; my callee house-Coolie." On the other hand, should the house-Coolie be ordered to purchase the supplies, or polish the silver, the grave but respectful answer would be, — "That no my pigeon; my callee boy." A Coolie works for certain wages, and makes his own bargains, nor will he serve unless paid his price. Should a foreigner attempt to impose upon or cheat a Coolie, and the fact be made known to him after he had commenced his services, he would leave him directly. A chair-Coolie, under such circumstances, would set down the sedan, and in the

fested for the aged by all classes of the people, are the most remarkable characteristics of the nation. In fact, the Chinese unwittingly keep that commandment to which is annexed the promise, and it has been questioned by many, whether their great antiquity and long-continued existence as a prosperous nation, may not be owing to the honor they pay their parents.

11

most independent manner refuse to move unless his terms were complied with.

I am thus particular in speaking of this class of the Chinese, because the remark has been made to me that the difference as to their position in relation to foreigners, and the wealthier classes of their own people, must be as great as that of American slaves to their masters. But the difference between a people free to go where they please, — to make their own bargains, and to contend with their employers for right 'and justice, — and the poor enslaved African of the South, is as wide as that between light and darkness. As servants, I found the Coolies very systematic and willing, as well as quick at learning to perform their duties according to our ideas, or, as they would say, "America fashion." A lady rarely, if ever, enters the kitchen, and all orders are given to the butler or head-servant. On ordering a dish in which the cook is unskilled, he brings his little furnace to a large pantry, where the lady of the house, with the aid of a waiting-man's "pigeon" English, and an occasional use of unmistakable pantomime, succeeds in giving the grave and stolid-looking representative of the culinary art instruction that will not be forgotten. And ever after, that piece of cookery will be an exact copy of his first, and only needed lesson. On entering upon life in China I was told that I must not expect the servants to be in any degree nice and cleanly, according to our Western ideas. I was, however, so fortunate as not to be conscious of this; and although I regularly penetrated into nooks and corners,[1] — beyond what I should otherwise have done, — in order to mark the difference, the result was always favorable to the general neatness and tidy habits of our Coolies, as compared with most of the foreign servants we have in the United States.

With an Englishman his dinner is said to be the event of the day. It is, however, well known that an American is not altogether indifferent to that meal; but, be that as it may, inasmuch as English customs prevail in the little foreign circles at the ports of China, entertaining by dinner-parties is the dominant mode, and the arrival of a stranger is the signal for a round of "dinings out." If served by the better class of Chinese servants, even those people who live in the simplest manner have no care nor trouble about such matters of hospitality. All orders in relation to the entertainment are given to the head-servant, who, on being told the number of guests expected, makes all the arrangements *en regle*, and serves the dinner as handsomely as can be de-

---

[1] The housekeeper has the store-rooms, pantries, safes for food, etc., under her own supervision.

sired. The wealthy merchants live luxuriously, and they, as well as some of the representatives of foreign governments, keep butlers who are proficient in their calling. A well-trained Chinese waiting-man, however, never deviates from the prescribed forms, all of which are carefully attended to wherever he serves.

A gentleman on being invited out to dine takes his servant with him, the latter always coming under the direction of the butler of the host, although the place of each is near the chair of his master, and all are waited on with quietness and precision. Probably the English — who have better trained servants than we have in the United States — may not remark these little matters as readily as an American, who has seen her country-women, on account of inefficient domestics, well-nigh appalled at the prospect of inviting a few guests to dinner. To all such, a household served by good Chinese servants would seem, in some respects, an Elysium.

Foreigners usually breakfast at a late hour, and frequently, in the summer, the greater part of the business of the day is transacted before taking that meal. They are served, however, on first rising, with what in India is called the "little breakfast." This is brought to their rooms, and consists of a cup of tea, a bit of unbuttered toast, and some fruit. There are several varieties of the orange, and during the greatest part of the year that fruit is very abundant. The finest kinds are the mandarin, and the sweet Coolie orange. These, when in season, form a large portion of this early meal; and then the plantain, the lichi, a nice kind of plum, the peach, the mango, custard-apple, and persimmon, together with a few other fruits, reach into the early autumn, when the delicious oranges are again gladly welcomed.

The Chinese language knows but one gender, and when a lady speaks to a servant, he answers—"Sir," the same as he does to a gentleman. Indeed, among the Chinese, woman seems to be as completely absorbed in the other sex, as some of their devotee bonzes are in the essence of Buddha. For example: if, in telling a servant that guests are expected to breakfast or dinner, he wishes to ask for what number he is to prepare the entertainment, he says, — "How many piece man hab got come?" — or, how many persons are coming? a woman as well as a man being always designated as a "one piece man."

No reflecting woman, transferred from the pale of Christendom to a heathen land, can live there for any length of time without a profound feeling of gratitude that she was born and educated in a land of Bible religion. Foreigners rarely see the better class of women in China; but the condition of the lower class of females in any country is generally a pretty fair index to that of the higher classes, and judging by this standard, the condition of the highest in the " Central Flowery Land " is lamentable. The women of China carry their infants on their backs, and bind them to their persons with the same sort of contrivances that our Indians use in carrying their pappooses. It is common to see women, with their children thus snugly disposed of, sculling the sanpans, or engaged in other menial employments. This mode of carrying children is much approved by foreigners, whose Cantonese nurses often dispose of their infant charges in the same manner.

Most persons in the East are fond of boating; while those who are confined to " chop-life " are compelled, from the exigencies of their situation, to cultivate a taste for it. The well-appointed gigs and sanpans with which the Whampoa chops are supplied, afford a most agreeable manner of locomotion; the neatly-kept sanpan, in particular, with its nicely cushioned seats, and ample space for full dress, being a desirable substitute for a carriage, either for business or pleasure. Exercise in the open air is never more necessary than when living in a tropical climate; and if the weather did not admit either of boating, or walking on shore, we made use of our promenade. In fine weather, seeking the shores of French, or Dane's Island, and taking the paths that crossed the unfenced fields in every direction, (there are no roads in China,) we rambled among the graves, or along the hill-sides, where we obtained views that were more or less picturesque, and sometimes very beautiful.

Upon the summit of a lofty hill on Dane's Island, amid a fine growth of evergreens, is located the cemetery for the Parsee traders living at Canton. There are many charming landscapes to be seen from this eminence; and the country, with its well cultivated valleys, and populous villages, impresses one favorably as being a remarkably fertile region, and the inhabitants an industrious race of people. It not being deemed quite safe, we never ventured far from the river without having some one of our boat-people, in whom we had confidence, with us, as a sort of rear-guard.

The aspect of nature in China is not cheerful; nor does wandering amid its scenes always produce buoyancy of spirits, as it is wont to do in other lands. On the contrary, it is like wandering through a graveyard, for the country is one vast burial-ground, and the little tumuli, which one is constantly meeting at every step of out-door life, are but so many *memento mori* that lead one to the tenderly solemn thoughts with which one's own home-places of interment are invested. The place of burial for the foreigners of Canton is upon a pleasant hill-side on French Island. Our first Minister to China — the Hon. Alexander Everett — lies interred there. A granite obelisk marks the spot. At the base of the same hill, where it forms a steep river bank, are the graves of a number of foreign sailors, who were interred there in the early days of the East India Company, when the dislike and opposition of the Chinese to "outside barbarians" was such that they would not allow them to be buried anywhere else. These graves are so near the water, that, at the flow of the tide, many of them are partially submerged.

The Bethel "chop," which was occupied by the family of the chaplain, was provided with a large apartment built and fitted up expressly for a chapel, where services were held every Sunday. Where, however, as is the case in China, the boat-people, artisans, tradespeople, and pleasure-seekers are as intent in the pursuit of their several callings and amusements on Sunday, as on any other day, the soothing and grateful influences of a quiet Christian Sabbath cannot be enjoyed. The Bethel clergyman had also a place in Bambootown, where, during the week, he performed missionary work among the natives.

No people can exceed the Chinese in their love of noise ; hence, fire-crackers, gongs, tom-toms, and other musical instruments of harsh and strangely discordant notes are in request, not only at marriages, and other festivals, but also at funerals. Scarcely a day passed at Whampoa, without some one of these occasions producing a most heathenish racket. If asked what the uproar was about, the answer would sometimes be, " One piece man hab makee die," or, " One piece man hab makee marry;" or perhaps it was the festival of some heathen god, and then the reply would be, — " Some chin-chin joss," or, " Some joss pigeon." [1]

One day Mr. W—— having asked a worker in camphor-wood if he could have some articles which he was making for us completed at a certain time, he was answered with — " No can, my old muder hab makee die ; my must go bury he." Thinking that the woman had just died, and admiring the man's filial affection, our sympathies were at once excited. On making further inquiries, however, we learned that the man's mother had been dead two or three years, but that he did not wish to tell a foreigner that the season had come when he must visit the graves of his fathers, and perform the customary ancestral adorations. The first part of April

[1] That is, some god-worship.

is the season for performing this idolatrous service. It is called *pai shan*, or worshipping at the hills, and is the time when all the people — men, women, and children — visit their family graves; where, after renewing, or putting them in neat order, they present sacrifices of food, offer libations, and burn incense. After going through various idolatrous ceremonies and prayers, pieces of red and white paper are placed at the back part of the graves or tombs, where they are made secure by placing small fragments of turf upon them. These bits of paper remain a long time as evidence that the customary annual rites have been performed. In our daily walks upon the island, directly after this season, we observed that scarcely a grave had been neglected.

The worship of Manes is the chief idolatry of the nation; and besides their yearly adorations at the hills, nearly every house has an "ancestral hall," which is a room where wooden tablets, sacred to the dead, — called *shin chu*, i. e., "house of the spirit," — are set up and worshipped. These tablets are about twelve inches in length by three in width, and have the name, rank, date of birth, and death, carved in the wood. While at Fuhchau, the wife of a missionary of the American Board presented me with a tablet which had formerly belonged to, and been worshipped by, an old gentleman who is now a member of the Fuhchau Mission Church. It was, however, lost when I fell into the hands of the pirates, but fortunately the note accompanying it was among the few papers which I saved; and in order to illustrate more fully the nature of this kind of worship, I quote from it what my friend wrote in regard to the history of the tablet: —

"From the old gentleman to whom the tablet belonged, I have this morning gathered the following facts: It represented his father, and is fifty-six or seven years old. He says he used to think his father's spirit was in it, but now he regards it as wood, and does not think so. It was worshipped on the first and fifteenth of each month; also at New Year, and at feast times. By a little computation, then, we find that this senseless block of wood has been worshipped more than a thousand times; or rather, we should say, that the spirit which was supposed to inhabit it has thus been worshipped. Of course I cannot say definitely as to the number of times, as circumstances may sometimes have arisen to prevent the regular worship. This reminds one of Elijah's address to the prophets of Baal. The old man himself is sixty years of age. His name is Ka-Hang, and I believe he has been connected with our church more than a year."

The English Consul resided at Canton, and the

vice-consul, Dr. H——, who was stationed at Whampoa, occupied a three-decker man-of-war, which was the largest "chop" at the anchorage. This accomplished English official, — who is a naturalist, and well known to some of our men of science in New England, — with his cultivated family, added greatly to the attractions and agreeableness of the singularly novel kind of life which we led at Whampoa; while a few other pleasant neighbors, together with frequent intercourse with friends at Canton, afforded sufficient variety to prevent it from becoming wearisome.

Every kind of life has its disagreeable features; our own, during "chop-life," being made up of occasional fears lest we should be run into by Chinese vessels. Although these were not allowed to sail on our side of the reach, they were sometimes drifted by the current, driven by the wind, or perhaps badly steered, until they came unpleasantly near us. At night, notwithstanding both European and Chinese watchmen were constantly on the alert, if any unusual noise was heard without, the idea of a possible collision with a clumsy junk was fearful. One day, while at dinner, Mr. W——'s attention was arrested by an unusual noise, which evidently proceeded from Chinese sailors. He hastened out to inquire into the cause of the wild commotion, and in a few moments came rushing back, saying that an immense junk was coming upon the chop, and bade me follow him to our private entrance, where he had ordered our faithful boatman, As-sing, to bring round the sanpan and take us off. Our position was fearful; and even if it had not been, the frightful screams and vociferations of the Chinese would have well-nigh made it seem so, their dreadful clamor producing a scene of such terror and confusion, that, for a short time, we were nearly powerless. As we were about stepping into our boat, however, a message came that the vessel was clearing us, and we escaped with only a slight injury to the roof of our promenade. The poor sailors were the more terrified from the fact that they were aware the "chop" belonged to their Government; and knowing that they had no business on that side of the stream, they were appalled by the prospect of the severe punishment which would surely follow should they happen to sink us. Being panic-stricken, and unable to manage their craft, they must have drifted directly upon us, had not an European seaman been sent aboard the junk to get her out of the neighborhood of our vessel.

The mercury was at 80° in April, and averaged from 88° to 90° in May. Unless a thunder-storm was approaching, however, this degree of heat did not oppress us as it would have done at home.

Through the spring and early part of the summer, while the rainy season lasted, the dampness, which penetrated everywhere, covered many things with mould. Storms were then quite frequent, and the thunder and lightning very terrific. Sometimes there was one continuous roar and constant blaze during the whole night, while the rain fell in torrents; and on one occasion a fearfully crashing bolt struck the water within a few rods of our " chop."

CHAPTER VIII.

WHILE living at Whampoa we went often to Canton, passing, altogether, a month there in visiting friends, and places of interest. Steamers carrying passengers and freight were despatched every alternate day from Hong Kong and Macao, to Canton, — running up and down the estuary and river; but although these boats always stopped at Whampoa, my first sail up the river to the " City of Genii " — as an old legend terms it — was made in a sanpan, which was rowed by three Chinese boatmen, and sculled by a woman.

It was a clear and balmy morning in February, — the weather being more like one of our cool and perfect summer days at home, when one always feels the appositeness of Herbert's lines : —

> " Sweet day, so cool, so clear, so bright,
> The bridal of the earth and sky."

The New-Year festival had closed the day previous, but the Chinese vessels and boats were still bedecked with their holiday trappings. The newly painted junks with their butterfly sails, fancy streamers, and red flags, made quite a gay appearance, and together with the passenger-boats, cargo-boats, and sanpans, — from which were also fluttering bright flags, streamers, and red papers, — produced a scene at once unique and brilliant.

The land, on both sides of the river, which is low, is mostly used for the cultivation of rice; and husbandmen, with their rude ploughs drawn by buffalo oxen, were already preparing the soil to receive the seed. The plantain, with its long, heavy clusters of ripening fruit, was growing in great luxuriance upon the borders of the stream.

We had scarcely passed the pagoda in the neighborhood of Old Whampoa, and the towering one of nine stories on Lob Creek, when the Barrier pagoda came full in view. These tall structures, shooting up at different points in a landscape of low, flat country, not only relieve the monotonous sameness of the picture, but greatly embellish the scene. Here we also passed the ruins of the Barrier Forts that were destroyed by our lamented Commodore Foote. We observed while in China that the name of no American naval commander was as frequently mentioned as that of this officer; the most casual allusion to him always bringing forth an eulogium upon his gentlemanly and consistent Christian character, as well as upon his skill and fine judgment as an officer. Above these ruins we met a two-masted vessel of some petty Mandarin. Both wind and tide being against her, she was towed by Coolies, who ran along the river's bank, — like horses towing a canal-boat, — while pulling at the line of rope that was fastened to her. Near this scene an Imperial fleet of four men-of-war and eight gun-boats were lying at anchor. These were newly painted vessels, and although an occasional line of black and white relieved the garish brilliancy of the red, the latter was the prevailing color. This fleet was part of a naval force which was mustering at Canton, and were to be sent North to fight the rebels. For some months it made Canton its rendezvous, and finally numbered sixty vessels of war, besides a large flotilla of covered boats for soldiers. On the 27th of July following, however, when nearly ready to proceed North, it was dispersed and destroyed by one of the most terrible typhoons that ever visited Southern China. The men-of-war were huge junks, with monstrously fierce eyes — such as the Chinese always give their Imperial dragon — painted upon their prows. They were undoubtedly designed to strike the natives with awe; and their wildly grotesque and terrible appearance was admirably adapted for that purpose.

The appearance of Canton, as approached by the

12

river, is low, squalid, and uninviting. The most
conspicuous objects are the watch-towers upon the
city walls, and the pagodas, which tower above all
other buildings. The houses are mostly of one story,
and stretch along the river for more than four miles.
Those built nearest the water rest on piles which are
driven into the sand; and these, with the lower
parts of the city, are subject to inundations. Far
out into the river, and along the banks, the water
was nearly covered with boats of various colors and
sizes. The largest and most conspicuous were the
Flower and Mandarin boats, — these being, as a
general thing, highly ornamented with carvings and
gildings, and, being painted in brilliant colors, made
a very showy appearance. There was also a long
and narrow little craft called the Snake-boat, which
is much used in towing larger vessels when they
have to stem the tide. Near the city we passed
one of these having a Mandarin-boat in tow.

Some of the foreigners at Canton have a pleasure-boat called the *Matrimonial*, which, luxurious in
its appointments, is finely arranged to meet the necessities of a warm climate. Our countryman, Mr.
G——, the Commissioner of the Imperial Customs,
had one of these, which he kindly placed at our disposal whenever we were in the city; and all our
boating, when visiting the places of interest upon

the river, was done in it. The spacious cabin, which was furnished with divans and pillows, was also enclosed with Venetian blinds, which were so arranged as to be readily removed if the sun was obscured, or when at evening we visited the Macao Passage, in order to enjoy the cooling influence of the southwest monsoon.

In the middle of the river, nearly where the boat-life is the most animated, there is a little green island, called by the Chinese " Eastern Sea-fish Pearl," but by foreigners " Dutch Folly," — which, with its fine old trees, and few oddly fantastic Chinese buildings, adds greatly to the picture of busy life.

Before the bombardment of Canton by the Allies, the business hongs and homes of the foreign merchants, called the " Factories," were in the western suburb. These being situated on the river had an airy location, which afforded a cool and agreeable residence to Europeans. Since the destruction of these factories, however, the merchants have had their hongs at Honam. This is an island which lies directly opposite the city, and forms one of its extensive suburbs. Foreigners have now a more desirable place for building than that formerly occupied by them in the western suburbs. For this purpose a large portion of ground, also situated on the river, but farther up the stream than the factories, was ceded to the Allies in the last treaty of peace made between them and the Imperial Government. Along its border, facing the river, a high sea-wall has been built, and the whole area prepared for the erection of buildings. The place is called " *Shameen,*" or " new sand," " beach face ; " and being situated opposite the fork of the river that forms the Macao Passage, it is one of the most airy and desirable localities for foreigners in Canton. This passage is formed by the branching of the river at a point nearly opposite the Shameen. Here a large portion of the water from the rivers of the North (which flow in a southerly direction) passes around the island of Honam. A great part of this water, however, again joins the Pearl River near Whampoa ; while the remainder, continuing to flow south, enters the great Delta nearer the sea. During the summer months the southwest monsoon blows with refreshing coolness up this passage, which renders it the favorite resort of foreigners, who in their boats seek the middle of the stream, where, lying on their oars, they enjoy the delicious and gratefully invigorating air. When we were at Canton in the spring of 1862, very few dwellings had been erected on the Shameen. Large bungalows, however, with thatched roofs, and neatly covered verandas, had been put up by some of the merchants as temporary summer retreats from the stifling heat of their hongs at Honam.

" The earliest notices of the city of Canton date back two centuries before Christ; but traders were doubtless located here prior to that time. It grew in importance as the country became better settled, and in A. D. 700, a regular market was opened, and a collector of customs appointed. When the Manchus overran the country, this city resisted their utmost efforts to reduce it for the space of eleven months, and even then was only carried by treachery. Martini says that 100,000 men were killed during this siege, — the whole number who lost their lives while the city was invested being 700,000, if the native accounts are trustworthy. Since then it has been rebuilt, and has increased in prosperity, until it is regarded as the fourth city in the Empire in point of numbers." [1]

" The foundations of the city walls are of sandstone, and their upper part brick. They are about twenty feet thick, and from twenty-five to forty feet high, having an esplanade on the inside, and pathways leading to the ramparts on three sides. That part of the city within the walls is about six miles in circumference ; and its whole circuit, including the suburbs, is ten miles. The streets are narrow, and well paved with stone. Both the land and

[1] Dr. Williams's *Middle Kingdom*, Vol. i. p. 130.

water population, as computed by the most reliable data, is about 1,000,000."[1]

The chair-Coolies of Canton are said to be among the best in China. They are very strong, and from much practice acquire a carriage which gives a delightfully equal motion to the chair. They doubtless have learned this from being obliged to carry their own people with care; for if a disagreeable motion is given to the chair of a Chinese gentleman, or lady, the bearer will be sure to receive a reprimand. These men being remarkably fleet of foot, pass rapidly over the ground, and seem to prefer a brisk dog-trot pace to a fast walk. They usually wear a sandal made of strong grass, and with a gait peculiarly their own, touch the pavement with a nervously strong and firm tread.

Several of the American Missionaries live in the suburb called *Sun Sha*, which is nearly opposite the south gate of the city, and occupying houses that front on the river, they have the benefit of the refreshing summer breeze. The hospital connected with the Mission — which was formerly in the charge of Dr. Parker — is also located there, and is now under the management of Dr. Kerr. A Mission station, and a branch of this hospital, have also been established at Fatshan, — a town on the river, ten or fifteen miles west of Canton, — where the silk fab-

[1] Dr. Williams.

rics, matting, and most of the other articles exported from Canton are manufactured. This hospital is also under Dr. Kerr's care, who devotes a certain portion of his time in personal attention to the patients. We were indebted to the kind politeness of this gentleman — who speaks the language, and is familiar with the temples, as well as other places of interest — for most of the enjoyment of our first excursion in looking after the "lions" of Old Canton.

One morning early in March, taking sedan-chairs, with Dr. Kerr in advance, we left the Missionary quarters, and traversing several narrow streets, — among which was that occupied by the butchers and bakers, — finally entered a comparatively broad and quiet street in the New City, where the residences of the Chinese officials were situated. This brought us to the *Wan-shau-kung*, or Imperial Presence Hall, where, three days before, and three days after the Emperor's birthday, the high officials and people come to drink tea, and pay adoration to his Majesty.

The dragon, — that never-failing insignia of rank and grandeur in China, — together with the royal color, yellow, were conspicuous in all the embellishments of the establishment. This is the only building in Canton that is roofed with yellow tile. Here a large tablet is erected to the Emperor, upon which the expression, — " The Emperor of ten thousand years ; ten thousand times ten thousand years," are traced in Chinese characters. The characters for " ten thousand years " also appear upon some of the pillars sustaining the presence-chamber, and upon every panel of the low stone fence enclosing the temple. These expressions are doubtless designed to teach the people that their Emperor is an infinite superior, — a sort of deity, and an object worthy of adoration. Guarding the people's entrance to this temple were two rampant lions — frightful burlesques — sculptured in stone. Our bearers threaded the narrow and crowded streets with perfect ease. The confused bustle, however, together with the noise of our own chair-Coolies, calling out " *Lai ! Lai !* " or, clear the way, combined with that of the hundreds of other Chinamen, who in one unbroken stream were passing and repassing us, was in some degree fearful, and well-nigh deafening.

As we passed on in the midst of these surroundings, we finally entered one of the gates of the Old City, and threading a long street occupied by stone-cutters, reached a Confucian temple, sacred to the Goddess of Literature. The idols of this temple consist of simple tablets dedicated to Confucius, and other sages. Highly ornamented ones, also, of very large size, and brilliantly painted, — having been presented to the temple by different emperors, — were suspended above those of the sages. No tablets of the latter, — not even that of Confucius, — can receive equal honor and adoration with that of the Emperor. At each side of these, on tables or small altars, were arranged smaller tablets of the disciples of Confucius. The handsome roof of this temple — which had the appearance of being groined — was painted in a dark rich brown and deep red, reminding us of the fretted Gothic style.

The entrance to the Temple of Mars — which we next visited — was guarded by fierce-looking lions; and being in mourning for the Emperor, Heen Fung, then recently deceased, was draped with white. The floor was also covered with white calico. Here, when the Emperor dies, the high officials and military men repair; and for three days — bowing and prostrating themselves before an empty throne — mourn and bewail the dead. An appointed *groaner* leads in these wails and prostrations; and when the mourners have assumed the attitude of humble grief, a signal is given, and the yellow silk curtains in front of the throne being drawn around them, they are left to their sorrow.

Leaving the Temple of Mars, we were carried through several streets to the southwestern part of the town, where the principal college is located.

This institution is called the *Kung Yuen,* or Hall of
Literary Examination.   Students from the different
districts of the province come here for examination,
previous to taking their second literary degree.[1]   The
establishment is extensive, and has a large, open
space, in which are eight thousand cells, or low compartments, built of brick, where the candidates for literary honors are confined while writing their essays.
A student on entering his cell is only allowed to
take with him his writing materials and cooking
utensils, and is carefully examined to prevent his
secreting any book or manuscript about his person.
These cells are only about five feet in length, by
three or four in width; being built in parallel rows,
and so arranged as to form narrow passages between.   The entrance to each passage is guarded by
a small dragon gate, upon which the name is traced
in Chinese characters.   The examination hall, and
other apartments fitted up for the use of the examining committees and official visitors, are ornamented with blue, red, and yellow.   On the long
and spacious avenue leading from the street there
are three gates, each opening into a temple; the
further one, conducting directly to the cells, being
peculiar both in structure and ornament, as well as
lofty and imposing.   The place was much injured

[1] This institution is usually called by foreigners the "Provincial
College."

at the bombardment of the city by the Allies, the cells for the students being at that time destroyed. They have, however, been rebuilt, and the whole establishment thoroughly repaired, so that it was in very good condition at the time of our visit.

When going to the eastern gate of the city we traversed a portion of the fine military road that skirts a part of the north wall. It is macadamized, and was made by the English, on their first occupation of the place, for the more convenient carriage of supplies of food and ammunition to the troops stationed on the heights at the north part of the town. In order to have a ready communication between these heights and the city, there was also a line of telegraph wires put up along the course of this road. The houses in Canton are built close to the walls; therefore, in making such a road, many of the citizens were compelled to have their houses removed or torn down. The deep and lofty arch of the great eastern gate is built with outside bastions, and has a double gateway. A sort of citadel, in the pagoda style of architecture, is also built upon the massive walls directly over the arch. At the time of our visit this citadel was occupied by a small number of Chinese troops, who, under an officer called a " leader of sixty," were stationed there as a guard. From the upper story of this citadel there is an extensive view of the city, its suburbs, and the surrounding country.

The Chinese name of the street extending from the east to the west gate, and passing through the heart of the city, is, when rendered into English, the " Street of Benevolence and Love." By the foreigners, however, it is called East and West Street. As a striking instance of the " westward march " of the Chinese mind, we observed, in passing through this street, an advertisement of Dr. Jayne's medicines posted in a conspicuous place near a tablet of the sage Confucius. In this part of the town we visited a Confucian temple, which, *malgré* its Chinese architecture and ornament, was really beautiful. It belonged to the *literati* of the district or county, and was an educational establishment or college, where students take their first literary degree.[1] The buildings are of granite, having ornate roofs covered with highly glazed green tile.

Near one of the city prisons we met a deplorable-looking prisoner, who, chained and led by his keeper, presented a fitting introductory scene to the Temple of Horrors, which we were about to enter. The open space fronting this temple was mostly occupied by the stalls of fortune-tellers, gamblers, dealers in incense-paper, beggars, and crowds of Chinese. In

---

[1] Called the "District College."

fact, the appearance of the outer court was too much like Pandemonium to admit of a very close inspection, and I found myself oppressed with a sensation of fear as my chair was borne through it. I therefore merely took a hurried glance at the interior of the apartments where the different tortures of hell were represented. These were too cruelly shocking, and too painfully suggestive of Dante's " Inferno," to allow of any description. Apartments a little off from these were devoted to idols, before whom the poor, besotted people were bowing in worship.

Our transition from this temple of horrid spectacles to the *Yamun*, or residence of the Imperial Treasurer of the province, was delightfully refreshing. The avenue leading to this place was bordered with ancient banians, and in a large park deer were grazing. The grounds, besides having pretty flower-gardens, were ornamented with arches, rock-work, and little fancy buildings. Large sculptured lions, of fierce aspect, stood guard at the outer gate; but the roar of the Chinese lion has proved itself as deficient in power, as these representations were defective in truthfully delineating that animal, and we found the French flag floating above them. The place, although falling to decay, was like an extensive villa in the heart of a walled city. It was taken from the Chinese when the Allies entered Canton, and, as "might makes right," in accordance with the demands of the French Government, it fell into their hands. At the time of our visit it was occupied by Baron Trenqualye, a French official, who, in the very tranquil enjoyment of the poor treasurer's usurped abode, was taking his *siesta* when we sent in our cards.[1]

At a temple called the Pavilion of the Fire Genii, our attention was directed to the print of a man's foot in a rock, which, by the Buddhists, is called Buddha's Foot. The Chinese consider this temple one of the most remarkable "lions" of the city; but we had already seen so many gilded images that the fantastically arrayed genii of this pavilion made but little impression upon us.

In alighting from our chair at the Mohammedan mosque, — which is nothing more than a plain temple, — we were immediately surrounded and pressed upon by a motley crowd of men, women, and children. The greater part of them were miserable beggars, and as some were suffering from disease, as well as poverty, their near neighborhood was not only disagreeable, but fearful. Giving a hurried

---

[1] A street in this neighborhood, entirely occupied by the shops of booksellers, is called Book Street. Here are met the students and *literati*, who, like the cultivated and learned men of other lands, are fond of looking after, and gossiping about, whatever is new and wonderful in their world of letters.

glance, therefore, at the interior of the building, we returned to our chairs, and were borne to the Tartar portion of the city. There, happy and cheerful-looking women came to the doors, and smiling, bowed as we passed. The ears of these Tartar women were pierced in three places, and from every puncture little hoops of gold or silver wire were pendant.

There is no place in the world where a crowd collects in a shorter time than in the streets of Canton; and a woman from the West, when looking after the "lions" of the city, seems to be regarded with quite as much interest as a whole menagerie of wild animals. Whether at a shop or at a temple, we were immediately followed by a great crowd, so that it was not only difficult, but exceedingly disagreeable to move about. At one of the Confucian temples the students, or *literati*, occupying it were so eager and curious to see the European woman write her pencilled notes, that some of them drew near and looked over my shoulder. A woman educated to write was a *rara avis* to these civil and scholarly followers of the wise Confucius. Laughing, however, and chatting very agreeably with Dr. Kerr, they seemed to regard such an encroachment upon the sphere, which is almost entirely monopolized by their sex in China, very good-naturedly. Sometimes, when being carried along the street, I found it difficult to suppress a smile as the natives, with staring eyes and mouths agape, peered and gazed at me through the windows of my chair, or, stretching their necks, essayed to look in at the door.

I can never forget my first Sunday in Canton, nor with what painful sadness I passed through the busy streets of the suburbs of Honam, when on our way to attend service at the English Chapel. It was pitiful to see the poor shopkeepers, artisans, and laborers toiling and pursuing their avocations as usual. The streets were filled with the same restless, noisy, and jostling crowd. There were the open shops, and the money-changers sitting at the corners of the business thoroughfares, with piles of copper cash before them. It was a most melancholy reflection that the people had no Sunday, and knew nothing of its peaceful and soothing influence.

It is hardly possible to realize the sad condition of heathen people until one has lived among them. Perhaps this total ignorance and disregard of the Sabbath, and also of everything growing out of a Christian civilization, when witnessed among a people like the Chinese, who, besides being in a great measure civilized and educated, are much advanced in a knowledge of the arts, and also in the polite amenities of life, is more prolific of grievous thoughts than when met with among the untutored savage tribes. The people, however, were well aware that the day was sacred to the Christian; and a few — among whom I observed some of the better class of Chinese — were gathered in little groups at the corner of a street on which the chapel was situated, where they watched the gathering of the congregation with evident interest.

The marriage processions — which are common in the streets of Canton — are usually more curious than imposing. They consist of a display of highly ornamented and gilded sedan-chairs, which are occupied by the bride, her friends, and also by her *trousseau* and presents. These are preceded by a band of music, and followed in the rear by a number of men and boys wearing short red robes, and carrying red boxes that contain the marriage feast. If the parties are of high rank, there is a long procession of people carrying honorary tablets, flags, fancy lanterns, umbrellas, and various other articles. We, however, were not fortunate enough to meet any of this class.[1]

[1] The respectable Chinese, after having taken a wife according to the prescribed forms, do not go through the marriage formalities with another woman during the lifetime of the first. A man, however, may introduce concubines into his family without any other ceremony than a contract with their parents; but they and their children are not only subject to the will of the wife, but serve her.

Most of the business streets, both of the old and new city, have their specialties. Besides the streets of the butchers and bakers, we passed through several devoted to the dealers in fruits and vegetables, the street of the stone-cutters, a long street occupied by the workers in iron and brass, and also one made up entirely of cabinet-makers. The shops of the latter are large, and in many of them we observed that the mechanics were sawing and preparing their lumber with hand-saws. In Southern China, where there are neither horses nor machinery to aid the people in their labors, it is surprising to observe with what comparative ease and skill they perform their work. A street of old clothes and second-hand furniture shops, is called, by the foreigners, the Chatham Street of Canton. Itinerant tailors, cobblers, and barbers are found, in every part of the city, plying their trades by the wayside.

Groups of squalid beggars, intent upon the destruction of the animated nature that infests their miserable garments, are seen crouching at every vacant spot along the streets, and near the temples of both the city and its suburbs. Sadly diseased people, also, — some of whom were suffering from leprosy, — we frequently met near the temples. These, and kindred scenes, together with the vile odors often encountered, make many parts of the city the most disagreeably disgusting places in the world.

Chinese officials are regarded with great deference by the people; and foreigners also, who are in the service of the Imperial Government, are treated with much respect. In visiting the places of interest in the western suburbs, I was escorted by Mr. G—— and Mr. W——, both of whom belonged to the latter class, and consequently we did not suffer the usual annoyance from street crowds. Although Mr. G—— — who has, in another place, been spoken of as Imperial Commissioner of Customs at Canton — was in some measure acquainted with the language, a Chinese linguist also accompanied us, and going sometimes in advance to clear the way, caused a general stampede of all idlers, and prevented any disagreeable gathering of the people at the places where we stopped.

The gentry of Canton live in the western suburbs, and many of their residences are on Howqua Street, which is one of the widest and cleanest in the city. The private residences — which are built of a gray brick, with walls twenty-five or thirty feet in height — are situated directly on the street, their fronts presenting no opening except the door. Many of them cover a large surface, — stretching far along the street, — and are so constructed as to appear

like a series of small buildings, each of which terminates in an angle or recess. To form these angles,
the wall, which begins plumb to the street-line, gradually recedes until it reaches a point of perhaps not
more than one or two feet back of its commence-
ment, when it turns, and making a right angle, is
built straight back to the street line; another turn
is then made, and the wall is again carried in the
same receding line as at first; and in this manner
the work is continued until the front wall of the
mansion is completed. The Chinese — who are
always propitiating some evil power, or malign influence — believe that these angles will prevent the
escape of "good luck" from the street, and thus
shield themselves and their families from misfor-
tune.

Howqua and Pun-Tingqua — two well-known
Chinese gentlemen of influence and wealth — have
their private residences on Howqua Street. The
walls of their dwellings are built like those just described; and judging from the great extent of front
occupied by Pun-Tingqua, his establishment must
be very extensive.

On our way to the western suburbs we passed a
large stall at the corner of one of the streets, where
nothing but dog-meat was sold. That animal, which
we observed carefully skinned and dressed, was sus-

pended and exposed for sale like a lamb at one of our butcher's shops.

A few streets further on brought us to the cat-market, where the mewing creatures, well fatted and exhibited in cages, were being purchased for the table. We had always been rather sceptical in regard to the assertion that dogs and cats were used as food by the "celestials;" but having this ocular proof of the fact our incredulity vanished.

CHAPTER IX.

MANY of the Buddhist temples are very ancient and wealthy establishments. Although ancestral worship is the chief idolatry of the masses in China, the Buddhists, by incorporating this superstition into their own heathen rites have gained almost unlimited power over the people. What makes this fact the more remarkable is, that, aside from this worship of Manes, the Chinese are said to care but little for the Buddhist faith, or for their temples. Only the priests and nuns, however, are called Buddhists, — the first of which are very numerous, and have great influence among all classes. Dr. Williams remarks that "the demonology of the Buddhists allows the incorporation of the deities and spirits of other religions; and goes even further, in permitting the priests to worship the gods of other pantheons, so that they could adapt themselves to the popular superstitions of the countries they went to, and engraft all the foreign spirits into theirs." We had an exemplification of the truth of this at the Temple of the " Five Hundred Gods," which was one of the most remarkable places that we visited in the western suburbs.

The entrance to this temple was guarded by soldiers, but we were readily admitted, and passing on, were led to a veranda bordering the refectory, where the bonzes were at their mid-day meal. Leaving this apartment and entering the cloister, we made our way through several long passages, until we reached the great hall containing the gods.

The eye of the visitor, on entering this hall, is first greeted by two gigantic gilded wooden images elevated on high pedestals, and placed one on each side of the door. They are fat and jolly in appearance, and, sitting in a half reclining posture, are playing with little children. The merrily genial and gay physiognomy of one of them reminded us of Hackett's Falstaff, and his laughing face was quite as irresistible. Merry little children, in all kinds of baby attitudes, were sitting upon his knees, and also standing upon his feet and arms, or climbing upon his shoulders. Some of them were pointing, or pulling at his hair, eyes, and mouth; seemingly intent, in every conceivable manner, upon getting all the fun they could out of the old fellow, who appeared to be the happiest, — not of gods, — but mortals. To be childless is regarded by the Chinese as the greatest of all misfortunes; and these gods were doubtless intended to set forth the happiness of a parent. This large apartment was nearly filled with images, all of which were not only well kept, but as brilliant as gilt, paint, and bronze could make them. They were placed on shelves eight or ten feet in height, and arranged in a sitting posture, facing each other, with long passages between. They were represented in a variety of attitudes, — often with uplifted arms, — while some had six or eight arms, and one we observed with five eyes. Beyond these rows of idols, seated under a rich canopy, were large images of the Past, Present, and Future Buddha ; and a little in front, in a sitting posture, there was a statue of Kien-lung, the Emperor, whom Lord Amherst saw at Peking. He was here represented gorgeous in gilt and paint, and arrayed in his royal robes. This temple contains representations of nearly, if not all, the heathen deities of the East, and painfully impresses one with a sense of the moral darkness and gross superstition of the people. It deserves to be called the Pantheon of Canton.

The abbots of the Buddhist monasteries are not often seen, and rarely honor visitors with any particular civility. At the Temple of Longevity, however, the names of the gentlemen of our party being sent in, the abbot made his appearance in the reception-room, and treated us with distinguished attention. This room was furnished with chairs and sundry little tables, and opened upon a lovely garden, well supplied with trees, shrubs, and plants, and otherwise beautified with little artificial ponds, zigzag bridges, cascades, grottoes, and other rock-work. The space occupied by it was small; but we were assured that it was the handsomest garden in the city. A cup of tea of exquisite flavor, together with some delicious dried and confectioned fruits were served; while the abbot — who was a man of gentle address and quiet manners — condescended to join us in our repast, while, at the same time, he held some conversation with Mr. G——.

One of the idols of this temple was a gigantic reclining image of Noah, who, with dimpled cheeks and laughing eyes, may perhaps have been intended to represent a happy old age. Beyond this, in a dimly lighted place, were three large, dusky, and neglected looking images, representing the men, or superhuman beings, who, as the Chinese say, held up the ark at the time of the Deluge.

The largest Buddhist temple in Canton — as well as one of the oldest and most noted in China — is the *Hai-chwang-sz*, usually called by foreigners the Honam Joss House. It is situated near the river in the suburb of Honam; and the grounds, which contain several acres, are surrounded by a wall. The courts of the temple — as well as the avenue

leading from the outer gate — are shaded with
hoary banians, and the air is resonant with the caw-
ing of the numerous rooks which have their nests in
the wide-spreading branches. In order to be present
at Vespers, we visited this temple at five o'clock in
the evening, and, landing from our boat, entered the
enclosure at the outer gateway, which opens on the
street bordering the river. Traversing the gravelled
walk to the high portico, — which is guarded by
two frightful looking demons, — and passing through
a small enclosure to a porch containing four great
statues, we were conducted to the main temple,
which is a low building, about one hundred feet
square, — in the centre of which there are seated
images of the Past, Present, and Future Buddha.
These were more than twenty feet in height, and
were surrounded by altars and smaller idols.

The evening worship had just commenced as we
reached the door of this grand presence-chamber.
Here we found a large number of priests, — some in
full canonicals, — who were marching in single file
around the idols, and chanting in a drawling and
nasal tone of voice their idolatrous invocations, accompanied by a sort of drum, tom-toms, and the occasional ringing of a bell. The officiating priests
were arrayed in yellow, but most of the rest were in
flowing gray robes. We observed one who had not

performed the *tonsure* in a long time, and whose clothing was also old and much patched; but we afterwards learned that an old garb and an unshaven head were the perscribed mourning of the Buddhist monasteries. Towards the close of the worship, a few at a time, on passing before the idols, stepped out of the ranks and fell on their knees before them, until finally all were prostrate. The priest playing the tom-tom knelt upon a low stool, and bowed himself close at the base of the centre idol; but the increased vigor with which he used the instrument, together with the beating of the drum and the ringing of the bell, rendered it impossible to hear the chanting. Finally, in the midst of this noise, bowing themselves three times, and touching their foreheads each time to the floor, they all performed the *kotau*, and thus ended their adorations.

Although the bonzes, with clasped hands and downcast eyes, assumed the most devout attitudes, and chanted their vespers in most imploring accents, still many of them were more intent upon looking at their visitors, and appeared to be more interested in them than in their evening orisons. Nor could we observe any appearance of real solemnity in the officiating priests, who, on rising from their knees, and while taking off their yellow robes and other trappings, fell right merrily to chatting and laugh-

ing. Most of the invocation consisted of a repetition of the words, "*Omito fuh,*" (*Amida Buddha,*) or,
"Buddha, have mercy upon us;" which reminded
us of the words of our Saviour. (Matt. vi. 7.)

In another building beyond the grand presence-
chamber of Buddha, a marble monument is erected
to the Goddess of Mercy, in which there is said to
be a relic of Buddha.[1] A twisted pagoda-like shaft
surmounts a pedestal of extraordinary massiveness,
upon which the goddess is sculptured. We were
told by one of the priests that this monument —
which is more like the workmanship of India than
China — was brought from Siam. Tablets, commemorative of those who have given to the temple,
are set up at various points in the cloisters of all the
monasteries dedicated to the worship of Buddha.
Tablets, also, containing apothegms from Confucius,
are set into the walls bordering this cloister; and
here may be seen the "sacred hogs," which, having
been presented as offerings by some of the worshippers, have an apartment apropriated to them,
where they are kept and cared for as long as they
live.

After death the remains of the priests are disposed of by cremation. The bodies are burned in
a little stone-building, put up expressly for this

---

[1] Said to be one of his toe-nails.

purpose in the cemetery which adjoins the garden. In a line with the arched doorway of this building there is a grave-like excavation of about a foot in depth, where the fire is made; and an iron grate to receive the body is placed two or three feet above it. Small orifices in the back wall, together with the doorway, answer for the escape of the smoke; and the blackened wall and roof, directly over the arch, gave evidence that the building had been much used. The ashes of the dead having been deposited in earthen jars, are placed in another small building within the grounds; and if not taken by relatives, after a reasonable length of time, to be buried among their kindred, are finally interred in the cemetery.

In visiting the Buddhist temples, we observed that the ground and buildings, with all their belongings, were kept in remarkably neat order; which, together with their ample arrangements for tropical comfort, made them invitingly cool retreats. The idolatrous worship at this temple, together with the sickening accessories met with at the place of burial, were profoundly saddening; and we could not but wonder how any American or European reared within the pale of Protestant Christendom could, after witnessing such scenes, be at all at loss as to the Christian's duty in sustaining foreign missions in

China. Although the light of Divine truth has as yet illumined but comparatively few heathen hearts in that land, still its teachings are slowly but surely bringing forth fruit, and the way is gradually being prepared for the full reception of the Gospel. No Christian, even with the most limited knowledge of the heathen character, can be personally conversant with the American and European mission stations in Southern China, without being surprised at what has already been accomplished. Among the different denominations of Christians in heathen lands sectarianism is happily forgotten; and the delightful fraternization, which is a distinguishing feature of their little communities, savors of the true Gospel spirit.

The English Methodist missionaries at Canton have a large chapel and very comfortable dwellings, which were erected out of a fund bequeathed to the Church expressly for this purpose by some friends in England. From what we could learn, there is also a generous provision made for them by the society under whose patronage they are sent out. As to the American missions, we have frequently heard our countrymen in China remark that the salaries allowed them were not sufficient for their support, and that, consequently, they were obliged to economize more closely than was conducive either to health or comfort in such an exhausting climate. They are, however, too heartily engaged in their noble work ever to complain; and are always cheerfully contented, and happy to make any sacrifice in their Master's service.

While living at Whampoa my attention was attracted one morning by hearing the voices of children singing Sunday-school hymns. At first I doubted whether I might not be mistaken, for it seemed incredible that the sweet tones of so many childish voices could ever be heard, amid our heathenish surroundings, singing the same notes that are set to the little hymns found in the " Sabbath Bell," and other Sunday-school hymn-books. I was, however, soon relieved from my perplexity by the entrance of Mr. W——, from whom I learned that the singing proceeded from a Hong-boat, in which were Mr. and Mrs. Bonney,[1] together with the boys belonging to the school of the former. After they had visited the Bethel " chop," we had the pleasure of seeing them moored at our side, and entering the boat, heard the boys sing more of those agreeable home-strains, with which our ears had been so unexpectedly greeted. The hymns were the same that we had heard sung by the " little ones at home;" but when translated into the Chinese language, and

[1] Missionaries of the American Board at Canton.

sung in that far-off land by those boys of benighted parents, they were all the more sweet and touching. An American gentleman, — a resident of Canton, — having recently visited the school, proposed this holiday excursion, and paid the expenses of the trip. It was a remarkable affair for the little fellows, whose thorough enjoyment, together with the high degree of gratification which their happiness gave Mr. Bonney, must have more than repaid our countryman for his kind and thoughtful generosity.

Mrs. Bonney has also a school composed of twelve or fourteen Chinese girls, most of whom have touching little histories. One of them, who is now capable of assisting in caring for the younger girls, was originally sold for ten dollars, to be a servant-maid. She was redeemed, however, by an English lady, and given to Mrs. Bonney to educate. Another had been cast out from her home into the street on account of a lameness caused by cruel treatment, which had incapacitated her from doing much house-work. There was one, also, who had been sold by a wretchedly poor father for *five dollars*, but was redeemed by a Chinese woman, who had placed her with Mrs. Bonney for eight years. And still another, from Macao, whose mother — a poor widow — had wished to sell her for thirty dollars, but Mrs. Bonney would not permit it.

The names of these girls were very significant on being translated into English : — such as Miss *Wealth*, Miss *Summer*, Miss *Have*, Miss *Thoughtful*, &c. Mrs. Bonney keeps a Chinese female assistant, and the girls (who are taught in their own language) receive a useful and Christian education. In addition to their daily studies, they are also thoroughly instructed in the use of the needle and other womanly employments. Some of these children are supported by religious and benevolent women at home; and I could wish that many more of our countrywomen might be induced to become the patrons of this interesting and important branch of the missionary work. The other Mission schools, under the care of both American and English missionaries in Canton, are also assisting to advance the cause of Christian education, but I did not become as conversant with them as with the schools of Mr. and Mrs. Bonney.

To the Chinese nothing is more awe-inspiring, august, and powerful than their fabulous animal, the *lung*, or dragon. This is doubtless principally owing to the fact of its being adopted as the Imperial coat-of-arms; although, even aside from this, it is said to be more or less superstitiously regarded by all classes, and is peculiarly feared and worshipped by both boatmen and fishermen, who consider it the

.ruling spirit of the waters.   A festival to propitiate
this divinity — or demon of the ocean and rivers —
is observed for five days, in the month of May, and
is called the " Feast of the Dragon-boats."   The
chief feature in this festival is the racing of the
Dragon-boats belonging to the different villages.
These boats are about one hundred feet in length
by only thirty-two inches in width, terminating in
a point at either end.   They are brilliantly painted,
and have their bows ornamented with dragons.
Each boat is bedecked with flags and gay streamers, and contains sixty or eighty men, who, sitting
quietly, paddle their craft to the time produced by
the rude music of gongs, drums, and the jingling of
copper pans; the boats, when under full headway,
being in appearance not unlike huge centipedes in
motion.   While witnessing these races on the Pearl
River, both at Whampoa and Canton, I observed
that the time of the music and the speed of the
boats were always *pari passu.*   A man standing
near the helm was constantly waving a fancy flag;
while two men, who played a drum elevated in the
middle of the boat, led the band.   As the speed
of the boat and the din of the music culminated,
the excitement of the musicians exhibited itself in
various antics and gestures.   In consequence of the
very slight construction of these boats many lives
are sometimes lost by their breaking in two.

The private gardens of Howqua and Pun-Ting-qua — located a mile or two up the river from Canton — are much visited by foreigners. Both are enclosed by high walls; and although the garden of Howqua is not as well kept as formerly, it has spacious walks, pretty sheets of water, fine trees and plants, and altogether must have been a charming place when the avenues, ornamented buildings, and little bridges were in good order. We found the garden of Pun-Tingqua, on the contrary, not only well kept, but in a state of further improvement. One of the first things which strikes the eye on entering this garden is the handsomely covered walk bordering the walls. The grounds, however, are everywhere intersected with pleasant walks, — one of which, separating two artificial ponds, is bordered with fir-trees of a beautifully delicate foliage. A large house, standing within this garden, is the summer retreat of Pun-Tingqua's family, and the private theatre of that gentleman is also in the same building. These extensive grounds included every variety of ornament usually found in Chinese gardens. There were pretty kiosks, grottoes, and fancy bridges, besides a handsome pagoda of three stories, from the upper windows of which the *coup d'œil* of the whole was charmingly picturesque.

The *Fa-ti*, or Flower-gardens, — from which foreigners at Canton are supplied with the pots of rare plants that always adorn their verandas, — are also situated on the river above the city. In these gardens we observed some very lofty palms, and there was also a superabundance of other trees and shrubs, which seemed to be growing in all the wild exuberance of nature. Here, and also at the garden of Pun-Tingqua, a lovely orchid, called "the nun," was in blossom. In addition to the dwarfed trees and shrubs found in every Chinese garden, both at the Fa-ti and at the garden of Howqua, we noticed a small shrub, of a close, full, and delicate foliage, trimmed so as to form flower-baskets of elegant patterns. Animals, also, were delineated in the same manner, among which we observed many accurate representations of dogs and miniature giraffes.

Most of the shops in Canton are so constructed that their fronts can be removed during the day, thus giving the passer-by a good view of the interior. At one side of the entrance there is usually a little shrine containing some tablet or image, where incense is burned every day to supplicate a lucrative business. At some of the more wealthy and handsome shops, shrines, fancifully ornamented, are set up within the establishment, and these are not unfrequently embellished with vases of flowers. The Chinese — who have a superstitious notion that the blossoming of the peach-tree, at the time of their New-Year festival, betokens good luck and prosperity for the coming year — have a way of forcing that tree to bloom for the occasion. When making my first visit to Canton, I was shown, at the shop of Hoaching, — of whom I shall have more to say when speaking of shopkeepers, — a large branch of a peach-tree, which, having passed through the forcing process, was brilliant with flowers.

The shops at which foreigners make their purchases of china, lacquered ware, and articles carved in ivory and black-wood, are in the New City and its environs. A Chinaman is exceedingly clever at a bargain, and being quite as fond of money as an Anglo-Saxon, is no less quick to note and take advantage of every opportunity that may offer to increase his gains. During the occupation of Canton by the Allies, the artisans and dealers found their wares in such great demand by the foreign officers and others that there was a general rise in the old prices ; and as these still continued at their advanced rates, many of the most desirable articles were more expensive than formerly, — fine china-ware, at the time of our visit, being nearly as costly as the French article was in New York before the war. Besides this, many of the china-ware manufactories in the interior have been destroyed by the rebels, and it is more difficult for the dealers in Canton to obtain their usual supplies. Indeed, some articles formerly found at the shops are now not to be procured at all; and this has doubtless tended, more or less, to increase the price of all articles. A very curious, but handsome ware, called "open-work-china," was formerly made in the northern part of the Kwang-tung province, — of which Canton is the chief city. The rebels, however, have overrun and laid waste the country; and those who understood manufacturing this ware having passed away, the art is now said to be lost. This china is greatly in request, but is rarely found for sale. We saw only a few pieces of it, and these belonged to foreigners, who preserved them as curiosities.

Ushing's is a fine and extensive shop in the New City, where elegant china-ware, — comprising articles of every description, — and also furniture of curious, as well as beautiful patterns, elaborately carved in black-wood, are kept for sale. The prices of the most desirable articles range at very high figures; but they are so rare, and not unfrequently so superbly beautiful, that the shop is much patronized by wealthy foreigners. The patrons of this establishment are waited upon with much politeness; being usually met, on passing from the ante-room into the shop, by the portly Ushing himself, who, handsomely dressed in silk fabrics, approaches his customers, and, in spite of his obesity, greets them with sundry profound bows while leading them to the side and upper apartments, where there is a tempting display of his wares. Another shop much frequented by foreigners is kept by Pohing, who deals entirely in china, and has many beautiful things at less prices than Ushing. Pohing, however, is a noisy, curt, and blustering man, without the smooth polish and *savoir-vivre* that distinguishes Ushing, — his chief recommendation being, that those who possess purses of only a moderate depth can obtain many of the same kind of articles, and of as good quality, of him, as can be procured at Ushing's, and on far more reasonable terms.

The matchless skill displayed by Chinese artists in the workmanship of ivory is well known, and the exquisite minuteness of their carvings in that material is unrivalled. Hoaching — whose shop in the suburbs of Honam is filled with beautiful carved work in ivory, sandal-wood, and shell — is said to excel all others in the artistic finish of his articles. Foreign visitors to this shop always find something rare and curious to study. Once when there our attention was directed to some remarkable ornaments elegantly carved from the skull of a bird belonging to the egret species. It is a native of Cochin-China. We were shown the head of one from which pieces had been cut for carving. The bone, which is of a very fine and ivory-like texture, admits of being carved into the most minute representations of flowers and foliage, as well as of temples and people. It is of a delicate, but peculiarly rich, orange color, sometimes slightly veined with red; and the ornaments, when handsomely set in gold, are superbly unique.

The wealthy Chinese have a passion for fine carvings. We were shown, at Hoaching's, a superb piece in ivory, which had been ordered by a Chinese gentleman at the cost of five hundred dollars. It was a mass of elaborate and exquisite carvings, representing men, animals, birds, and scenery. The article itself was of a peculiar design, and, from what we could learn, was intended to ornament the shrine of a household god, or, perhaps, the ancestral hall. Temples — and their never-failing adjuncts, the sacred banians — embellish most of these carvings, and the latter are remarkably well given.

The cultivated Chinese greatly admire antiques, and highly value an old piece of curious china, an antique bronze, or a rare carving. It is said that no city in the empire has more of the antique, the rare, the curious, and the grotesque, to interest a foreigner, than Canton,—the shops of Curio Street, in the New City, being mostly occupied by dealers in such articles. Some of these shops are large, and well filled with articles of rare and handsome workmanship. At any of them one can soon invest a thousand dollars in elegant pieces of furniture, rich carvings, and other valuable works of *vertu* and art. Many of the articles in bronze, however, are too ugly or too disagreeably grotesque to tempt a foreigner. The studio of the noted painter, Lamqua, and the shop of " Old Siqua," — whose lacquered ware is considered the finest in Canton, — are also in the Honam suburbs. Lamqua is an artist of much talent; and having profited by the instruction of Chinery, — the Anglo-Eastern artist already mentioned, — his pictures are free from the gross inaccuracies in perspective, and many other points that usually mar the sketches and paintings of his countrymen. He is noted for his fine fruit-pieces, and I also observed in his studio some very good pictures of foreigners. His finely painted miniatures, copied from photographs, and done on ivory, are also excellent.

The Chinese women are very fond of ornaments made of the "jade-stone." [1] Vases, also, and other

---

[1] An imitation of jade, or serpentine, of a vitreous composition between glass and porcelain, and of a cloudy-green color, is manufactured into ornaments that are much worn by the lower classes.

fancy articles manufactured from it, are highly prized, and sold to the wealthy at fabulous prices. A daily market expressly for the sale of this article, which is located in the western suburbs, is regulated by certain laws, one of which requires it to be closed at twelve in the morning.

Judging from the extent of the street occupied by the artificers in fans, and the infinite variety of that article exposed everywhere for sale, China is very properly called the "land of fans." No people, however, need them more; and nearly every city manufactures its own style of the article; hence there are Peking fans, Canton and Swatow fans, besides many others. Those, however, that are made at Suchau, — a city situated on the Yellow River, in the province of Kiangsu, — being either very tastefully and delicately painted, or elegantly finished in black and gold, are much in request. In fact, at one time these fans were so much the mode among the higher classes of the Chinese, that, for one to say that his fan was from Suchau, made the same impression as for us to speak of an article imported from Paris. Suchau is also noted for its dark, bronze-colored, lacquered ware, prettily ornamented with etchings of birds, trees, and flowers, the outlines of which are touched or finished in gilt. The rebels, however, have nearly destroyed the city, and both the Suchau fans and lacquered ware having become scarce, — except at some of the shops on Curio Street, where they command a very high price, — they are now rarely met with.

Canton is said to rank next to Peking in wealth, and no one can visit either the New, or the Old City without being impressed with the opulent appearance of a great portion of the people; for although beggars of the poorest and most wretched class are met everywhere, many of the streets are thronged with Chinese gentlemen, who, walking or in chairs, are arrayed in garbs of the most expensive silks. A large number of streets are also lined with spacious and handsome shops, which are filled with the richest fabrics of the East. In passing through some of these streets the extensive view afforded in either direction, with the moving crowds, brilliant signs, and other gorgeous adornments, is very picturesque, and to a traveller from the Occident has an air of enchantment about it, which is almost a realization of the tales of the Genii of old.

CHAPTER X.

ALL classes of women in China pay much attention to the cultivation and arrangement of the hair,
and often display much taste in their picturesque
styles of wearing and ornamenting it. In some of
the Northern provinces the women of every class
are at all times seen with beautiful flowers in their
hair; but at Canton, and at the South generally,
we observed that this tasteful fashion was confined
to the ladies. Among the flowers used to ornament
the hair of the few Chinese ladies we met at Canton, the rose was conspicuous, and we learned that
it was as great a favorite among the Chinese as it
is with us. There are twenty native species of the
rose in China, besides a good many varieties, and
it is very extensively cultivated.

The women very seriously injure their skin by the
free use of cosmetics. A Chinese lady, when making her toilette for any grand occasion, blackens her
eyebrows so as to form an arch; and after making
a free use of white paint upon her face, finishes by
deeply rouging her cheeks and lips. To avoid tot-
tering, the women of small feet step quickly, and

swing their arms in order to keep their equilibrium. At the same time they have a mincing gait, peculiarly their own, which is doubtless considered very elegant; as I frequently observed that the large-footed, but smartly dressed, women of the common classes endeavored to imitate it.

A descendant, and the representative of the noted hong merchant, Mingqua, of Canton, was, with one exception, the only Chinese gentleman we met who could speak English with fluency, and some degree of correctness. He is a man of very *suave* and courtly address, which, combined with elaborate manners, make up a gentleman well suited to his Oriental style, and in fine keeping with his character and conversation.

For several years before the Allies obliged the Chinese to open the gates of the Old City of Canton to foreigners, the wife of Mingqua occasionally received and returned the visits of some of the foreign ladies then residing at the old factories. The wife of Howqua also occasionally received such visits; but at that time the opportunities of coming in contact with the Chinese ladies were not common, nor have they become so since. On the contrary, the inner apartments, (as the rooms occupied by the women of a Chinese family of rank are called) are guarded as carefully as ever; and up to this time a woman from the West, when invited to enter their tabooed precincts, receives a distinguished favor. Mingqua, however, on account of his knowledge of our language, and from his having had a great deal of intercourse with foreigners, has in some respects become an exception to this rule. Seeming not to dislike our modes, but to rather approve of ladies having more liberty than they are allowed in China, he not only invites foreign ladies to visit his family, but, as will be seen, occasionally permits the gentlemen accompanying them to see the women of the household. He had frequently expressed a wish that I should visit the ladies of his family; therefore at our last visit to Canton, — notes and cards having been exchanged, and all the forms, according to Chinese etiquette, being complied with, — at the appointed time we took chairs and proceeded to his residence.

In making this visit, (besides being attended by Mr. G—— and Mr. W——,) we were accompanied by an English gentleman, — who was also in the employ of the Imperial Customs. To this gentleman — who was a Chinese scholar — I was indebted for the translation of a note from Mingqua, in which the latter, after the fashion of Orientals, affects great humility, and in language of the most extravagant hyperbole, speaks of my visiting at his

" humble abode." This note was written upon paper of an India-pink tint, and the elegant card accompanying it was also of the same color, being over nine inches in length by four in width. Mingqua's humility, however, was not of a character to induce him to live anywhere but in the western suburbs; therefore we not only found his residence in Howqua Street, but in the aristocratic and wealthy neighborhood of Pun-Tingqua, and Howqua. A few people were gathered in the street, near the great doorway, when we arrived; but as our coming had been expected, the portal was directly opened, when we passed quickly through the porch to a little court, where we were welcomed by Mingqua with elegant politeness, and then led with Oriental ease and grace to a reception-room in the rear of the court. This room communicated with the inner apartments by two doors, near which the women and children of the household were congregated to receive us. Their dresses were of some dark material, and very simple and unpretending in style; although the faces of the ladies showed the free use of white paint, while their cheeks and lips were deeply rouged. Their hair was also elegantly arranged, and tastefully ornamented with flowers.

The gentlemen of our party — who had expected that I alone would be admitted into the presence of the ladies — were both surprised and gratified with the arrangement which Mingqua had made, in order to allow them to see the whole of the family; and although his disposing of them in this manner prevented my visiting the inner apartments, the fact of a Chinese admitting foreign gentlemen to the presence of his women was so unlooked-for and agreeable to my escort that I was soon oblivious of disappointment. A slight entertainment, consisting of candied fruits, sweetmeats, and cakes, was already waiting on a little table in the reception-room when we entered; and soon after we had been presented to the family, tea was brought in and served with these refreshments.

Fearing to appear too inquisitive, we did not ask any questions in reference to the daughters of the family; and no allusion being made to them, we presumed that Mingqua, like all his countrymen, regarded them of but little consequence. On the contrary, presenting his sons in due form, he first introduced the eldest, who, being a young gentleman, spoke English very well, and was not unlike his father in the elegance and polish of his manners. We were the most interested, however, in the youngest, — a fine, bright lad of only six years, — whom Mingqua said he desired to send to England, or America, to be educated. The higher classes of

Chinese who are not exposed to the sun are whiter than those in the common walks of life; and this boy having a remarkably fair complexion, one of our party remarked to his father,—"Why, Mingqua, this is a fine little fellow, and has a remarkably fair complexion." The father evidently pleased with the compliment, giving one of his courtly bows, replied,—"Yes, high-born always whiter." The house was exceedingly plain and simple in all its appointments; but we were informed that, in consequence of some business difficulties, Mingqua affected a parsimonious style of living, and it was therefore difficult to pronounce upon his true condition.

Chinese etiquette does not permit them to shake each other's hands; on the contrary, politely bowing when they meet, they shake their own while clasping them before them. Mingqua, however, in his intercourse with foreigners, adopts our mode of greeting; and on our taking leave the ladies, holding out their little hands in a very polite manner to me, made their adieus, Western fashion.

When about taking our leave, Mingqua informed us that his cousin, living only a few doors from him, wished us to make a call at his house. Being aware that the well-bred Chinese regard any breach of etiquette as an unpardonable offence, and fearing that by making so unceremonious a visit we might compromise ourselves in their estimation, we hesitated. The gentlemen, however, learning from Mingqua that his cousin, — who was a wealthy member of the Pun family, and belonged to the class of Mandarins, — having been aware that we were about to leave Canton, had already arranged the matter of etiquette in such a way that it would be *comme il faut* for us to go there at once, we gladly assented. This Chinese gentleman had at one time filled the office of Taou-tai, at the North, whence, after amassing a handsome fortune, he returned to Canton, and built a splendid mansion on Howqua Street, which is said to be the finest residence in the western suburbs.

A servant having been despatched to apprise the Taou-tai of our coming, accompanied by Mingqua we were again in our chairs, and following our *avant courier*. The spacious portal of the Taou-tai's residence opening on our approach, we were conveyed through a fine large porch, into an inner court. Beautiful lanterns were hanging in the porch, and the guardians of the household, in the shape of two brilliantly ornamented images, stood one on each side of the door leading into the court. Leaving our chairs, we were met at a door entrance, connecting with one of the apartments of the house, by the Taou-tai himself, who, without raising his eyes [1] towards me,

[1] According to Chinese etiquette it is very impolite, if not highly

bowed, and waving his hand, without a word, and almost without volition, I moved on in the direction indicated, to a door that opened apparently without aid from any one, and which, as I passed through it, closed in the same unaccountable manner. The spacious porch, the inner court, and the apartment where the Taou-tai first received us, being in construction, arrangement, and ornament very much superior to anything I had seen, my surprise and admiration increased at every step until I reached the rooms occupied by the ladies. But these Inner Apartments — as they are termed — as far exceeded the rest of the house, in the superb brilliancy and beauty of their adornments, as the finest china in Ushing's shop, in the elegance of its design and painting, surpasses the common and cheap article which is sold at the little stands by the way-side.

Recovering a little from the maze into which the peculiarity of my position and the fairy-like appearance of its surroundings had thrown me, I perceived a middle-aged lady, handsomely dressed in dark material, standing on a dais at the further end of the room; who, as I looked towards her, directly bowed, and with a quiet dignity, shaking her hands before her, greeted me with the Chinese salutation — "Tsing!

indecorous for a gentleman to look at a lady. The Taou-tai, therefore, treated me with marked respect.

Tsing!" — i. e. Hail! Hail! Drawing near, I also
bowed while saluting her in the same manner; but
with the exception of these words of salutation, and a
few simple phrases, I knew nothing of the language,
and our intercourse was consequently continued in
pantomime. This lady led me through a door
opening back of the dais into another apartment, at
the further end of which there was again another
dais, with a broad passage leading from it to the
rooms beyond. On each side of this passage
tasteful boudoirs led to richly furnished bedrooms,
near which we observed two very pretty and elegantly dressed young women standing one on each
side of the entrance. They were leaning in graceful attitudes against the corners of the boudoirs,
and as both continued to bow and repeat their
salutations during our approach, in order to return
them properly I was obliged to advance bowing
and shaking my hands, first to one and then to the
other, until we reached and ascended the dais.
They then led me into one of the boudoirs, where,
standing a little back of a table, on which was lying
their embroidery, chairs were placed, and I was
motioned to be seated. The middle-aged lady, —
who evidently occupied a position of honor in the
household, — took the chair next to mine, while
the two younger ladies stood, one on our right and

the other on our left, during the whole interview.
With their small feet this must have been fatigu-
ing to them, but if etiquette demanded it they were
obliged to endure the discomfort without complain-
ing.   They were in costumes of rich silk fabrics
ornamented in gay colors, and their hair was elaborately arranged and dressed with flowers.   They also
wore elegant ornaments of gold and precious stones,
and had their cheeks and lips rouged; their gentle
and lady-like manners, as well as their entire demeanor, being of that cast which belongs only to
the most delicate refinement.   We were scarcely
seated when not only the room was filled, but there
was also a group about the door of the apartment,
and I soon found myself not only a curiosity to the
ladies and children, but also to the servants, which
last stood in the outer circle, and were very respec-
table-looking women and girls.

Tea having been brought in by a sprightly and
laughing serving-woman, one of the young ladies
receiving the cup designed for me, and observing
that the tea was very hot, lifted the delicate china
cover, and fanning the steaming liquid until it was
cooled, proceeded, with inimitable ease and grace,
to hold the cup to my lips while I drank the bever-
age.   This ceremony being over, my dress was next
closely inspected and commented upon by the whole

group; while, amid smiles and an occasional merry laugh, we carried on a pantomimic conversation, which afforded infinite amusement to all. My bonnet, with its trimmings, attracted particular attention, but a delicate *mouchoir* was their especial delight. The ladies then displayed their beautiful embroidery, which was done in silk floss, and fastened in the same sort of frames as those used by us.

The furniture of the boudoir, and bedroom leading out of it, was of black wood, ornamented with carvings. The bedroom was small, but the bedstead was a massive piece of furniture, elaborately carved, with a highly ornamental tester, from which hung mosquito-curtains of green silk gauze. In addition to the rooms through which I was first conducted, I was shown several brilliant apartments, and an open court finished in the same style, which contained a variety of beautiful plants in bloom. The partitions of the rooms were of fanciful lattice-work, and were painted in delicate shades of stone-color, and brilliantly ornamented in gilt, with red, blue, and different shades of green. Every room was supplied with little stands of curious design, upon which were beautiful porcelain vases and jars, while screens and other ornamental articles completed the furniture. There were also a variety of beautiful Chinese lanterns suspended from the ceilings, and some of the rooms were provided with handsome European chandeliers.

The latticed partitions with their embellishments, the ornamental furniture, and the general arrangement of the whole, as seen in the soft radiance admitted through the skylight, had an air of superb elegance. Each room, however, was a gem of itself, and of so unique a character that the place was invested with an Arabian Night-like charm. Finally, on taking leave, my middle-aged friend politely accompanied me to the door at which I entered, and I once more joined the gentlemen of our party, who, not having been as highly entertained, were becoming a little impatient for my return. Having made our formal adieus to the Taou-tai and the courteous Mingqua, we then took our departure, greatly pleased and gratified with this our first peep at high life in China.

These visits were made on Saturday, and while at Mingqua's house he politely invited me to dine with the ladies of his family on the Monday following. Having, however, not forgotten our visit to the dog and cat market, and also not having any assurance that the better classes of the people were not fond of cat meat, but rather the reverse, I felicitated myself on being able to say that we intended to leave for the North on that day, and could not ac-

cept the invitation. The excellent tea, together with
the delicious sweetmeats and candied fruits which
are served when on visits of ceremony among this
people, are always acceptable and agreeable entertainments; but when it comes to the question of a
formal dinner, it is not quite so pleasant to fancy
the possibility of being served to a cat ragout or a
dish of kitten cutlet! A ceremonious dinner would
have greatly gratified our curiosity, and doubtless
given us some further insight into the secluded
mode of life led by the Chinese ladies; but in view
of these considerations we felt little regret in being
obliged to decline Mingqua's polite invitation.

CHAPTER XI.

Mr. W—— having been ordered by the Chinese Government to remove to Swatow, a seaport one hundred and eighty miles north of Hong Kong, our "chop"-life drew rapidly to a close, and one morning early in the month of June, 1862, we found ourselves *en route* for our new home, and once more on board the American steamer *Spark*, bound for Macao.

A few weeks previous to this time some Chinese pirates had taken passage at Hong Kong on board a small English steamer bound for Macao, and while on their way thither, in attempting to take the vessel, had killed one of the officers, besides injuring some of the passengers. In consequence of this, we found the large crowd of Chinese passengers on board the steamer properly secured below. There was also a small force of well-armed Malays, who not only guarded that part of the boat, but were also stationed at other exposed points, giving to the little vessel quite a warlike appearance. Each officer had one of Colt's revolvers in his belt, and the foreign passengers were also armed; so that, although sailing under our own flag, we felt that we were not altogether among friends. The number of European passengers was, however, larger than usual, and in case of any difficulty, they would of themselves have constituted a very efficient force. In view of all this, and being at the same time aware that the Chinese pirates seldom attack foreigners unless they are greatly off their guard, we went on board with no real solicitude in reference to our safety.

We had sailed on quietly for several hours, and had made the Kumsing-moon Passage, — which, together with the neighboring islands, was formerly fearfully infested with pirates, — when, in consequence of an accident happening to our machinery, we were compelled to lie to and anchor for several hours. Soon after the vessel had stopped, Mr. Perry, — our Consul at Canton, and Mr. G——, both of whom were passengers, — discovered that the boat was on fire. At about the same time, and before the extent of the fire could be ascertained, a number of Chinese boats were seen to be bearing down upon us. We then began to fear that our engineers and firemen, — who were Chinamen, — might be in collusion with these boatmen, and that they possibly intended to take and plunder the vessel, in which case they would also capture the foreign passengers, and (as is their custom) keep us in durance until they received an exorbitant ransom. After the fire was subdued, it was two or three hours before we could get up steam sufficient to proceed on our voyage ; but as soon as there was any likelihood of our doing so the native boats disappeared. This accident occurred just as it was announced to the passengers that *tiffin* was ready; and to Mr. Perry — who refused to go below to partake of it, until he could learn the nature and extent of the difficulty — we were providentially indebted for our safety. If there was any compact between the Chinese employées and the boatmen, it was thought that some signal must have been given the latter, indicating that there were too many armed foreigners and Malays on board to admit of their meeting with any success. In fine, whatever may have been the true state of the case, we learned, after reaching Macao, that we had strangely escaped the danger of steam as well as fire ; it being then discovered that the boilers of our vessel had been so much burned as to be ruined, and that we had been mercifully preserved not only from apparent but from real perils.

Macao is exceedingly attractive in winter ; but in June and the early part of July, when its gardens and lovely environs are brilliant with flowering trees, shrubs, and plants, it is one of the most charming places in the world. Few settlements in the East have as great a variety of shrubs and trees, for many of which the colony is indebted to the East India Company, who adorned their gardens and grounds with the finest that could be procured in India, and the various islands of the East. The beautiful nym — called the Pride of India — is here seen growing in the Government Park; and the gardens of the foreign residents are beautified with a variety of flowering trees, among which are the *Bauhinia, Poinciania* and *Lagerstræmias.* The delicate, crape-like flowers of the latter are almost unequalled, and, as an ornamental tree, it has few compeers. Among the flowering plants, several species of hibiscus, the magnolia, plumoria, oleander, and jasmine flourish in great profusion; while of creeping plants, the *Quisqualis Regina* — which was in bloom — exceeded in elegance all the flowering vines we had seen in the East. The lotus, also, with its delicately tinted flowers, and the regal blossoms of the night-blooming cereus, — *Cereus grandiflora,* — both flowering in July, delighted us with their resplendent beauty.

The deliciously soft atmosphere of the bright evenings in early summer, at Macao, is unrivalled; and every one goes forth to enjoy " the quiet and the

beauty of the scene." The native Portuguese ladies
— who rarely venture out in winter — then saunter
in little groups along the beautiful Praya Grande, or,
seated on the green (the Alameda) which adjoins it,
may be observed quietly listening to the music of
the military band. The whole circuit of the settlement is only eight miles, and yet there is a great
variety of interesting points in the scenery, — the
suburbs affording many charming walks besides that
of the Praya. Among these, the finest and most desirable for enjoying the refreshing summer breezes,
is the winding road which passes over the high ridge
of cliffs that face the sea. This road — which skirts,
in a part of its course, the finely curved shore of
Cacilha Bay — is called the *Estrada de Cacilhas.*
The pandanus, or screw-pine, grows in wild luxuriance at various points along its border, and the
gullies that seam the steep hills around which it
winds afford a variety of beautiful ferns. There
are, also, at the more elevated points of this road
fine sea views, where the air is always delightfully invigorating. The *Estrada* is therefore the
favorite promenade of invalids, and foreigners generally, who, if they manage to exist through the
exhausting heat of the tropical summer, may here
be seen at evening in large numbers walking, or
being borne around the cliffs in their sedan-chairs.

The precipitous and rocky formation near the shore of this part of the peninsula, together with the old fortifications crowning the elevations which rise abruptly beyond, give the settlement, when approached from the sea, a formidable and ancient appearance.

In Macao — as in all communities under Roman Catholic rule — the festivals of that Church are celebrated with much display, and, being under the patronage of the Government, are very generally observed by the people. One of these festivals is known as Corpus Christi Day, on which occasion we witnessed the elevation of the host, — the procession being composed of the bishop, the high officials of the colony, with several orders of priests in their different habits, proved a most imposing pageant. The consecrated wafer was carried by the bishop, — assisted by some of the high dignitaries of the Church, — over whom a satin canopy was upheld by the first civilians of the colony. The procession, with its chanting priests, having issued from the Cathedral, marched through the streets amid the firing of salutes from the guns of the Guia fortress ; the military, who were drawn up near where it was to pass, falling on their knees while their canopied bishop moved by, and the band, also, — although continuing to play, — assuming the same posture of adoration.

Hundreds of poor Chinamen were gathered to witness this august spectacle, most of whom were doubtless unable to perceive any difference between prostrating one's-self before the host, or before their ancestral tablets and the gods of Buddha. It was a sad sight, and the more so, as these Romish priests and their people are looked upon by the Chinese as representatives of Christianity. Such displays, however, are well calculated not only to attract and gain the hearts of the Portuguese and the mixed races of the colony, but also those of many of the Chinese.

A small company, composed of the soldiers garrisoning the forts, constitute a military dancing troupe, who, at the festival of St. John, hold a sort of carnival which lasts through several evenings, and is thought by the Portuguese to add greatly to the festivities of the occasion. As this festival occurs in the month of June, we had an opportunity of witnessing some of these evening entertainments.

The whole troupe maintain, under all circumstances, a strict silence, and are called the "Mummers." Accompanied by a ludicrously dressed harlequin, who directs the dancers and their changes by blowing a whistle, it is customary for them first to visit the governor and other high officials of the colony, where, upon the verandas, or in front of their residences, they perform beautiful fancy dances, which frequently terminate in fine tableaux. At every place a sum of money is given them, which is appropriated to a charity established expressly for the benefit of their regiment. The dancers are arrayed in fancy costumes, and preceded by musicians, who are also accompanied by men clad in antique armor. When marching through the streets by torch-light, they present quite an imposing as well as picturesque appearance, and their dances seem to have a fascinating influence which attracts all classes. To make a dancing troupe, however, an accessory to a Church festival, is, to one unused to any but a purely Protestant atmosphere, strangely out of place.

A handsome *fête,* or *soirée musicale,* commemorative of our national anniversary, was given at our consulate in Macao, on the evening of July Fourth, 1862. This proved to be the event of the season, and being detained until after it took place, we were happily among the invited guests. Mr. Nye's spacious mansion is situated in the heart of the city, two or three rods back from the street, — its grounds forming a little park in the rear, and the whole enclosed by a wall which in front is twelve or fifteen feet in height. With the exception of the gateway, the entire face of this part of the wall and the columns ornamenting it were covered with the foliage and flowers of the *quisqualis*. On approaching the grounds, the evening of the *fête*, the first thing that attracted our attention was the display of hundreds of brilliant lights forming eight stars, which were arranged with charming effect against the dark green foliage on the walls, and illuminated the street, where a large crowd of Chinese, as well as Portuguese, had already been attracted to admire the scene. The Portuguese military band were playing our national airs as our sedan-chairs passed into the compound. From this a stately entrance led into a hall, and ascending a handsome staircase which conducted to the family apartments, we found ourselves in a small ante-room, furnished with a well-filled black-wood bookcase, an arrangement for hats and coats, and a few classical engravings. Here the band was stationed, and from this we entered another saloon situated in the middle of the mansion, which was furnished in fine taste, and contained some European and Chinese articles of *vertu* and art. Passing through this saloon, — upon the left side of which was the ladies dressing-room, and on the right the supper-room, — we entered the chief drawing-room, on either side of which, and leading out of it, a handsome room was also thrown open, making a suite of three, extending the entire length of the house. The concert was to be given

16

in the centre room, where a grand action-piano had
been placed for the occasion; but the arrangement
of this apartment being purely classical, it only
contained a few pieces of rare furniture, and some
ornamental works of art.   Its walls, however, were
decorated with fine old paintings and engravings;
and the rooms leading out of it — although simple
and tasteful in arrangement — were furnished with
large centre-tables of elegant workmanship, upon
which were placed immense bouquets composed of
superb tropical flowers.   These were arranged by
the Baroness Circal, — the wife of the Brazilian
Consul, — who presented them to Mr. Nye, as an
offering to his national festival.   They were in porcelain vases of beautiful design, and were standing
on mats made of Berlin wools done in our national
colors.

Arched doorways and windows led from this suite
of apartments into a spacious veranda about eighty
feet in length by fifteen in width, and built the
whole extent of the mansion.   It was covered with
a high arched roof, and enclosed with glass windows
which were shaded with Venetian blinds.   In the
evening, however, both the windows and the blinds
were removed, leaving only the high arches and pillars between.   From this veranda a door led to an
open terrace, which looked down upon a lawn beau-

tified with flowering trees and shrubs, and leading
to a little park containing a few deer.   To the right
was a flower garden, and to the left a large tank,
in which were luxuriant lotus plants in full bloom.
The terrace, which was simply covered with mats,
was enclosed with a brick parapet three feet in
height, the top of which was gay with pots of flowering plants.   The arched windows and doorways
leading from the veranda into the drawing-rooms
were ornamented with wreaths of dark myrtle tastefully interspersed with delicate flowers, among which
the *quisqualis* was prominent, — its lovely pendant
fascicles contrasting with the rich shining green of
the myrtle with distinguished effect.   The dark and
richly polished timbers running across the veranda,
just under the curve of the roof, as well as the arched
windows opening upon the terrace, were also decorated with garlands, and an elegant basket of exquisite flowers was suspended from the centre of
each arch.   At one end of the veranda the American
flag was so draped as to form a background of stars
for a large portrait of General Washington, which
adorned the centre of the arch, and was the most
conspicuous object at the *fête*.   At the other end the
" Stars and Stripes " together with the flags of Portugal, England and Brazil, were tastefully draped
together, while the national colors of Portugal and

Spain were prettily arranged just above the centre arches which led out upon the terrace. These, as well as various other national flags used in adorning the veranda, were embellished with chaplets of myrtle and flowers. Nothing could exceed the elegance of these decorations, nor the fine taste displayed in all the arrangements of the brilliantly lighted apartments. Twenty-six stars, which were also disposed among the trees about the grounds so as to have their dark foliage for a background, made, with those that illuminated the front wall, thirty-four, and showed conclusively the loyal sentiments of our Consul.

The Governor of the colony was absent at Peking, but all the other officials, and the Portuguese army officers, together with the foreign Consuls, were present, in full court-dress. The Baron Circal — who takes his title from the little town of Circal, in Portugal — was also present in full regalia, with a diamond star of the first magnitude making a brilliant display upon his left shoulder.

The Portuguese ladies, although elaborately arrayed and showing a decided taste for gay and striking colors as well as for ornaments, were in what a Portuguese writer, in describing the festival, called " simple toilettes." The stateliness of both the men and women bordered frequently upon stiffness,

and although some of the former were able to con-
verse a little in English, the ladies knew nothing of
the language. In fact, one rarely meets in Macao
with a Portuguese lady who speaks English. Among
the gentlemen there was a superabundance of gold-
lace and bright buttons, and, as at all entertainments
given by foreigners in the East, they greatly outnum-
bered the ladies. The concert, which lasted until
twelve o'clock, was performed by French and Italian
artists from Hong Kong, and the music, consisting
chiefly of selections from popular operas, was delightful. At the close of this musical entertainment,
being requested to step out upon the terrace, we
found the twenty-six stars — which were arranged
among the trees, and during the evening had only
been partially illuminated — beaming in full reful-
gence. Before we had more than cast a glance at
this resplendent scene we were surprised at hearing
distant martial music, and soon the military dancing troupe, accompanied by torch-bearers, was seen
marching under the shadow of the trees that bordered the walk on the other side of the grounds.
On reaching the lawn near the terrace, the musicians
struck up a contra-dance, which being performed by
that picturesque company amid the brilliant light
of so many burning stars, and in a spot so charming, was quite enchanting. This agreeable surprise

added more to the entertainment because it was so unexpected, and was a source of great enjoyment. As the troupe left the grounds, and while the band in the small saloon were playing our national airs, we were handed to the supper-room. The table was brilliant with flowers, whose superb arrangement, in connection with the display of fruits seen peeping out from beneath buds and blossoms, evinced much delicacy of taste and gratified one's relish for the beautiful, while the elegant supper, refreshing the inner man, prepared the gayer portion of the company for the amusement that was to follow.

Directly after supper the veranda was cleared for dancing, and the spacious apartment being occupied throughout its entire extent, the *coup d'œil* of the long vista was very beautiful. Indeed the tasteful decorations of the room, together with the showy toilettes of the ladies, and the bright buttons and epaulettes of the gentlemen, produced a scene of rare splendor, and the few Americans present entered into the spirit of the festival with grateful alacrity. The fact that our country was in affliction only made us the more anxious to be known as loyal citizens of the Federal Government; therefore the toilettes of our countrywomen were slightly embellished with our national colors, while the gentlemen wore badges combining the same hues. After supper, some small photographs, taken from the portrait of Washington, which hung in the veranda, were distributed among the ladies, and gave much satisfaction. A French naval officer among the guests having also received one of these little pictures, remarked to me, with evident satisfaction, — " I, too, have one picture of Mr. Washington!"

In a description of this entertainment, which was written in Portuguese by the Secretary of the Colonial Government and appeared in the Government paper, there occurs the following passage in regard to this happy idea of our Consul: —

" Not willing to omit the smallest point of etiquette, — notwithstanding the picture of the great Washington was seen resting on the ensign of the United States, to preside over the feast, which was proceeding with great spirit, — still Mr. Nye offered a photograph of the hero to each of the ladies."

Being gathered to celebrate the natal day of our nation at a time when a melancholy war was raging at home, the conversation naturally turned upon its condition and prospects, and the probable result of the rebellion. We have a pleasant and grateful remembrance of our intercourse with the English friends whose acquaintance we made in the East, and no one can more admire the social life of a well-bred and cultivated English family than we do. No people are more delightful, and no hospitality can be more charming; yet, with few exceptions, the English people met with abroad know so little of the true spirit, character and condition of the United States, and consequently have such vague, and not unfrequently monstrous ideas of our institutions and government, that when one discovers the reason for their erroneous opinions, it is vastly more amusing than annoying to hear them express their views in regard to our final destiny. It is therefore the better way, when brought into contact with this class of our cousins, to be quietly reticent; leaving them to learn, as they finally must, that being of their own stock, and not having any taint of the convict element which we fear flows in the veins of some of the Southern rebels, (whose States were originally penal colonies,) we not only can contend stoutly for a principle, but will also fight for it as patiently, persistently, and bravely, as they do.

CHAPTER XII.

AFTER several weeks of genial quiet and enjoyment in the somewhat dilapidated, although still stately old settlement of Macao, — whose soft and balmy summer atmosphere first taught us to understand and take pleasure in the fascinating *dolce far niente* of the South, — we proceeded to Hong Kong, and while there, as the guests of our friend, Mr. P——, of the house of Olyphant & Co., were the recipients of that lordly and charming hospitality which one meets with among most of the polished and cultivated foreign residents in China.

The colony of Hong Kong is not favorably situated to receive the full influences of the cool southwest monsoon of the summer months, and the extremely warm weather which prevailed at this time produced the most intense tropical languor. After a brief stay, however, the 23d of July found us on board the English coasting steamer *Undine, in transitu* to our new home in Swatow, at which place we arrived the next day.

Swatow — which is one of the five ports that a few years ago were thrown open by treaties to foreign trade — is situated on the river Han,[1] which is navigable for vessels of a light draft for some distance. There is also a spacious harbor at its mouth, with sufficient water to float ships of large tonnage. The river has several branches, which intersect a populous and fertile region of country, throughout which are scattered villages and large cities, as well as walled towns. In fact, it is said that no district in China presents greater natural advantages for agriculture and commerce than that in the neighborhood of this port.

Double Island — which is the residence of foreigners — is situated a little off the mouth of the river, being about a mile distant from the main land, and five miles from the native town of Swatow. The area of land upon this island is small, a brisk walker being able to accomplish its entire circuit in half an hour without inconvenience. Standing high out of the water, it has two conspicuous and verdant hills, situated, the one at the northern and the other at its southern extremity. These hills overlook the two entrances to the harbor, and upon one of them are still to be seen the ruins of a native fort which once guarded the chief passage. The settlement, which faces the harbor, is built in the valley between; and most of it is so situated under the lee

---

[1] Called, also, by foreigners, the Swatow River.

of the high ground as to be sheltered from the worst effects of the terrible typhoons which occasionally visit this region. The climate is very salubrious, and the island is considered one of the most healthy places for Europeans on the coast. Situated quite out into the sea, the inhabitants enjoy the cooling influence of the southwest monsoon through the summer, at which time invalids visiting the place receive much benefit from the pure and bracing sea-air. In fact, we were informed that at one time there had been some talk of establishing upon the island a *sanatarium* for invalids, and that the scheme was favored by one of the best medical men in Hong Kong.

Notwithstanding the fine sea-air at this place, the heat of the summer, which is of long continuance, is very exhausting to all foreigners; and here — as everywhere else in Southern China — the more temperate October days are welcomed with pleasure. The very warm weather, however, does not commence quite as early in the season as it does at Canton and Whampoa; but as we were at the South until midsummer, we did not have the mercury below eighty degrees from April until the 8th of October, and for by far the greater portion of that time it was some degrees higher.

There being no low lands nor rice-fields upon

Double Island, mosquitoes — which are the greatest of all plagues in the south of China — are not numerous. It is only necessary, however, to live in Canton or Macao for a short time, in order fully to appreciate the blessing of being freed from the venomous assaults of this insect. While living upon the water at Whampoa we were seldom troubled with them, but when at Canton, if we chanced to have our beds shielded by defective mosquito-curtains, the night was fearfully woful, and the noise of their shrill trumpets, together with their stinging attacks, not only dispelled sleep, but destroyed all comfort and repose. The species of this insect met there is *sui generis*, and being striped on the back something like a tiger, has been by some very appropriately called the " tiger mosquito." The drapery of my sleeping-room at Macao was so infested with these hatefully irritating creatures that the moment I disturbed any part of it they swarmed forth in great numbers. Indeed, even during the day, we frequently suffered such depredations from these bloodthirsty tormentors, that, with the mercury ranging as high as eighty or ninety degrees, it was exceedingly difficult to sit quietly or patiently at any employment. We therefore, on reaching Double Island, felicitated ourselves upon being freed from this, the most intolerably keen annoyance that we met with while living in the East. Even the frightful centipede is not so much to be dreaded, for he always seeks the darkness, and instinctively shuns the presence of man.

The name of this island — which was conferred upon it by Europeans — is derived from its shape, which appears double when seen from the east or west. It has also three very significant Chinese names: viz., *Fung-shan*, *Fang-ke-shan*, and *Ma-seu*, or *Ma-soo*. We are indebted to a member of the English Consulate at Swatow — who understands the Chinese language — for the following interesting explanation of these names. "*Fung-shan*," he writes, "may be translated Phœnix Island, — it being understood that the imaginary supernatural bird of the Chinese, which we call the 'Phœnix,' does not correspond with the Phœnix of western legends. The island gets this name from its shape; — the light-house promontory on the east representing the head of the bird, and the main part of the island stretching north and south, the outspread wings. The Chinese, with their geomantic notions, attaching a real importance to this, believe that the light-house erected on the head of the Phœnix has brought bad fortune to the port, in the shape of typhoons[1]

[1] Some of the most fearful typhoons ever experienced in China have visited Swatow since this light-house was built. When I

and divers other calamities. The word *shan*, in *Fung-shan*, may be translated island. Its proper meaning, however, is hill, or mountain, although it often occurs in the names of hilly islands.

" *Ma-seu*, or *Ma-soo*, is the most common name among the Chinese, and is not unknown among foreigners. It means the island of Ma-tsoo, the name of a Buddhist goddess, or saint, who has a temple here, which at times is much resorted to. She is a sort of sailors' goddess, much worshipped by them and others, especially in the provinces of Fuh-kien and Kwang-tung. She was a native, it is said, of Chin-chew, or that neighborhood, in Fuh-kien, — and is sometimes called the ' Holy Mother,' ' Queen of Heaven,' but is not to be confounded with the Goddess of Mercy, *Kwan-yin*, whose worship is much more widely diffused all over China, and beyond it, and whose rank is considered higher.

"*Fang-ke-shan* may be translated — ' the island where fowls are let go.' I am told that some time ago, when there were no residents here but the people of the temple, live fowls used to be presented at the temple of Ma-tsoo, and then let go on the island, and that rice was given by the junk-people for the

was at Swatow, it had, however, fallen into disuse ; and, from recent letters received, I learn that it has finally been pulled down by the natives.

food of the fowls. It is also said that people did not dare to steal and eat them, and that any one who did so would get the stomach-ache."

The Buddhist temples in China are — as we have already seen — placed in the most picturesque situations, and frequently command views of the most charming scenery. This is also the case with the small but elaborately ornamented temple of Ma-tsoo, which is shaded with huge old banians, and located in one of the pleasantest spots on the island. A festival in honor of this goddess — which lasts five days — is held in September of each year, and is attended by crowds of people, who at that time flock to the island from the villages and cities on the main-land, in order to make offerings to their favorite deity. It is the custom of these people to blend various kinds of amusements with their devotions, which, to one so unfortunate as to be within hearing distance, are chiefly characterized by a most heathenish racket. At all of these festivals itinerant theatricals constitute a favorite source of amusement; and at Double Island the temporary theatre — which is always constructed of bamboo-poles and covered with matting — was frequently erected disagreeably near to some of the foreign residences. In September, 1862, one was set up so near our house, that, with the intense heat of the season and the noise of the performers,

together with the clangor of their musical (?) instruments, we nearly went mad.   The performances —
which were continued every evening until an hour
or two after twelve o'clock — "made night hideous."
The actors were arrayed in rich satin robes, elaborately embroidered, and, judging from the sea of
upturned faces[1] that surrounded the place, the plays
must have deeply interested the spectators.

Previous to 1860 there were but very few foreigners living at Swatow.   During that year, however, a
Mission station, under the auspices of the American
Baptist Board, was established at Double Island by
the Rev. Mr. Johnson.   At that time there were no
religious services held on the island, and the natives
knew nothing of the Christian religion, or of any of
its observances.   Under these discouraging circumstances, — which might well-nigh have appalled the
most hopeful, — Mr. Johnson purchased a billiard-
room, — which was the only place that could then
be procured for a chapel, — and at once commenced
holding Divine service on Sunday evenings for the
benefit of the foreign community.   Since that time
the building has been converted into a neat little
chapel, which is appropriately fitted up, and gener-

[1] The front of the theatre is entirely open, and is built high, so
that the performance is in the second story, while the spectators
stand in crowds outside.

ally well attended by persons who are grateful for its privileges. Such missionaries as Mr. and Mrs. Johnson are a blessing to all classes of people among whom they may be placed; and one on the spot can readily see in how many different ways the influence and teachings of this mission have tended to improve the natives, as well as to make the place more home-like to Europeans. While I remained at the island Mr. Johnson's house was the favorite gathering place of all the foreigners in the settlement; and the ladies looked to Mrs. Johnson for advice and aid in every emergency.

The house in which we were to live not being ready for occupation until a fortnight after our arrival at Double Island, and during that time being members of Mr. Johnson's family, I saw something of the workings of the mission, and became much interested in Mrs. Johnson's school of Chinese girls. Mr. Johnson was missionary at Hong Kong for several years previous to establishing himself at Swatow, and some of the girls composing Mrs. Johnson's school while there, being originally from the neighborhood of Double Island, accompanied them on their removal to that place. Some of those who early became Christians have now attained to womanhood, and, still retaining the integrity of their religious profession, are not only leading exemplary

17

lives, but are also making themselves useful to their people.   One of them is now the chief native assistant in Mrs. Johnson's school.   When we left Swatow this school numbered eleven boarding pupils, besides five or six day scholars; and a letter received from Mrs. Johnson, since my return to the United States, informs me that six of these pupils have recently become Christians.   From what we learned of the influence of this school, not only upon the girls, but also upon the families with which they were connected, we were more than ever convinced that a practical Christian education given to the young, and particularly to the daughters, who, among the Chinese, are rarely taught to read, must in time contribute much towards Christianizing the people.   This school — with which I became more familiar than with any other in China — is said to be managed in a wise and very judicious manner.   Like that of Mrs. Bonny's at Canton, the girls are frequently *proteges* of benevolent and religious women in the United States.   We doubt much whether any more wisely appropriated foreign charity, than that extended to these schools, can be found; and in speaking of Mrs. Johnson's, we would wish to do so in such a manner as to induce our countrywomen of the Baptist churches at home — as well as of other denominations of Protestant

Christians, whose enlarged benevolence inclines them to do good whenever an opportunity offers — to become its patrons.

Some of the Chinese youth who have become Christians after coming under the instruction of Mr. Johnson, have, on their refusing to join in the idolatrous ancestral worship of the country, been very cruelly treated by their friends. One of these — a young shopkeeper — was sadly persecuted by his parents, as well as by his brothers and sisters; who not only beat him, but would give him no food, nor suffer him to enter the house. This young man became a Christian after attending, from motives of curiosity, the services at the Mission Chapel which Mr. Johnson established at *Tat-hau-po*, — a place on the main-land about five miles from Double Island. Finally his business was entirely broken up, and in order to support himself he peddled rice, eggs, and fruit. We often procured our supplies of these articles of him, and long before being made acquainted with his history had observed his meek and chastened appearance, as well as his quiet and gentle demeanor. Older persons, also, on forsaking their idolatry, have suffered very bitter persecution. One of this class, — who is a member of the Mission Church at *Tat-hau-po*, — previous to his conversion, kept a shop for selling small idols, incense-sticks and incense-paper. This man, after coming under the illuminating and sanctifying influence of the Gospel, decided to abandon a business that was so entirely supported by idol-worship, and therefore immediately closed his shop. This course did not meet with the approbation of his wife or children, none of whom would associate with him, and he was thrust from his home as an outcast.

Just before war broke out between China and the Allies, As-sune, an old native teacher in the employ of Mr. Johnson, being a Christian, suffered imprisonment in the city of *Chau-chau-fu*, which is situated forty miles up the river from Swatow. When taken before the Mandarins, this man refused to kneel, saying that " he kneeled to none but Jesus." Then, when attempting to preach the Gospel to them by relating the history of our Saviour, and telling them of his death upon the cross, an effort was made to silence him, which being unsuccessful, he was severely beaten on the cheek with the heavy shoe of a Chinaman, until his face was badly cut and two of his teeth were knocked out.

The native Christians under the watch and care of the mission, always attend the communion services held at Double Island, and have the advantage of profiting by the valuable teachings of Mr. Johnson several times during the year. These services commence on Friday, and continue until Sunday evening; and the communicants, coming from the main-land, frequently travel a distance of forty or fifty miles to be present. In summer the boats of these people arrive at the island in the morning, and our house being situated near the landing-place, we watched with interest for the arrival of three aged Christians, who, fifteen or twenty years ago, while living in Siam for business purposes, had, through the faithfulness of some Baptist missionaries, been converted to Christianity. The countenances of these men — who were over sixty years of age — were spiritual to a degree that reminded us of the old man given in the last picture of Cole's paintings of the "Voyage of Life." One rarely meets with such faces, nor with more happy and devoted Christians. We learned from Mr. Johnson that these men, with a few other native converts in humble life, were doing much good among the people where they lived; and that it was not an uncommon thing for persons who had become Christians through the influence of their teachings and example, to come to him for the purpose of further instruction, and to be admitted into his church by baptism. One of the old men mentioned cultivated a small piece of ground, and selling whatever it yielded, appropriated the avails of it to printing parts of the Bible, and religious tracts, which he distributed among his countrymen. This little plot of ground he called "Christ's Garden."

The London Missionary Society also had two missionary clergymen stationed in towns forty or fifty miles from Swatow. These men — who were devoted to their work, — occasionally visited the island; and although living where there were no foreign residents, their isolation from the world made them none the less cheerful, nor earnest in doing good.

The different dialects prevailing in every new district one visits in China, are no less noticeable than the difference which is observed in the appearence of the people. This first attracted our attention on reaching Swatow, where we thought the people more hardy looking, as well as rougher, than the same class of natives seen farther south. In fact, the natives of this district have had the reputation of being a savage and quarrelsome people; and a few years ago it was thought to be as much as a foreigner's life was worth to venture living in their vicinity. The difficulty, however, was greatly owing to their inefficient rulers, together with the dreadful feuds which existed between the inhabitants of different villages. This state of things increased until the people of some of the villages could not pursue any honest employment, however much they might desire to do so. They were often attacked when at work in their fields; and if the crops were left unmolested until ripe, they were sure to be harvested by bands of plunderers. A number of large fishing villages were prominent in creating the anarchy and suffering that finally prevailed, and, being located near the coast, were able to make successful depredations upon the commerce between the sea and the interior, until they nearly destroyed it. By reason of this, foreign vessels, being able to resist the marauders, found lucrative employment at Swatow long before the port was opened by treaty to foreign trade. In consequence of this deplorable state of things, the people were finally reduced to the most abject poverty; and starvation being the only alternative to emigration, Swatow speedily became the centre of the Coolie traffic. At first, the trade being confined to Singapore and Siam, was not marked by those horrors which characterized it after it fell into the hands of the Europeans.

This wicked traffic, like the African slave-trade, resulted in the natives kidnapping one another; and it was the custom of the people of different villages to make raids, — the stronger upon the weaker, — simply for the purpose of procuring men to sell as Coolies to the Europeans. These unfortunate creatures were put into receiving-ships lying in the harbor, and being poorly cared for, as well as placed in very crowded and close quarters, they died in great numbers before the vessels were ready to leave port.

Near a portion of the sea-beach which formed a part of our favorite walk on Double Island, there were two large mounds where many of these Coolies were buried. The sand with which they were originally covered had in some places been washed away by the rains, and occasionally we noticed the bones of an arm or a leg protruding from some part of the elevation. It required only one sad look at these huge graves to convince us that the Asiatic, when once within the grasp of the money-loving and rapacious European, meets with the same fate as the poor African. We observed the *Ipomea maritima* — a beautiful creeper, which is found trailing in great luxuriance over the sandy beaches of the China sea — growing near these tumuli, and partly covering the surface of one of them with its rich foliage and flowers.

It is stated that during the worst stage of the Coolie traffic the people of the district were demoralized to such a degree that they so far violated all Chinese ideas of propriety as to sell their women, who were sent in large numbers to Singapore and

Siam, and that some were also exported to Cuba. The prices received for them ranged from fifteen to thirty dollars, and at that time they constituted a regular article of merchandise to Singapore and Bankok. With the legalization of foreign trade at the port of Swatow, this shocking condition of things underwent a change, and the cruelty attending the Coolie traffic ceased. This being followed by a great increase in trade, and a corresponding increase in revenue, induced both the Government and the people to interpose with a strong hand and put a stop to the enormity. Nothing is now heard of the Coolie trade, nor of the suffering that first caused it; in fact, so few can now be induced even to emigrate that the establishment of the British Emigration Company — which is situated on the Otow shore upon the main-land, and opposite Double Island — was abandoned during the summer I was there, and the agents either left the port, or engaged in a different business.

If, in Southern China, there were accessible mountain regions, where, as in India, sanatariums could be established for the invalided, doubtless by resorting to such places for a few months, — while undergoing the process of acclimation, — foreigners would be enabled to remain in the country with some degree of comfort and safety, for a much longer time than they now do. As the interior of China becomes more and more occupied by Europeans, such places will probably be found; but until then, foreigners, when seriously affected by the climate, must seek a change in visiting the more salubrious coasts of Japan, or by returning home. During the summer months I was gradually prostrated by ill-health; and in September, — notwithstanding my agreeable life in China, and the lively interest which I had taken in regard to the country and its singular people, — I was obliged to prepare for returning home.

CHAPTER XIII.

Mr. Johnson had been for some time anxious to send his only son, Master Charlie, — a lad in his fifteenth year, — home to be educated; and it was accordingly arranged that he should be my *compagnon du voyage.* Our passage to New York was taken in the clipper ship *Jacob Bell,* which was then loading at Fuh-chau, — a port situated about three hundred miles north of Swatow. The *Jacob Bell* was expected to be ready to put to sea by the 15th or 20th of October; and Mr. W——, having received leave of absence to go on to Fuh-chau, and to remain there until we sailed, our preparations were soon made, and on the 10th of that month, bidding adieu, with many regrets, to the kind friends we had met at the island, and once more embarking on board the English steamer *Undine,* we were soon sailing up the coast, *en route* to Fuh-chau.

Although steaming against a northeast monsoon, we arrived at Amoy [1] the next day; and the vessel remaining there three days, not only enjoyed a quiet and church-going Sunday, but, as far as

[1] This is the ancient port of Zoi-tun mentioned by Marco Polo.

health would permit, were able to see something of the place. Some of the small islands, which form the boundary of the bay seaward, are surmounted with pagodas and temples; which, together with the high hills and verdant country in the background of the city of Amoy, renders an approach to the place from the sea charmingly picturesque.

The town is built on a large island, called *Hia-mun*, or island of Amoy, which according to Dr. Williams, is forty miles in circumference. The same author also states the circumference of the city and its suburbs to be about eight miles, containing a population of 300,000, while that of the island is estimated at 100,000 more. Most of the foreign residents live on the lovely island of *Ku-lang-su*, or the " drum wave island,"[1] which lies in the harbor, directly opposite the city. The house of Mr. Bradford — our consul — is on this island, — the little avenue leading to it being bordered with beautiful palms.

On Sunday we attended the Mission Chapel, where the Rev. W. C. Burns — a missionary of the English Presbyterian Mission — performed the religious services. Mr. Burns — who always wears the Chinese costume — frequently travels into the

---

[1] So called because the noise made by heavy waves beating against one part of the shore, where there is a cave-like formation, is very similar to the beating of a drum.

interior of the country, and visiting the cities and villages, prepares the way for the permanent settlement of other missionaries. He has been several years engaged in his heaven-directed work, — having assumed the native dress at the outset, in order as much as possible to go unobserved among the people. In this garb he is able to enter new places quite unmolested, and easily gains the attention of the multitudes which throng the streets of all Chinese towns. He labored at one time in the district of Swatow, and was imprisoned for Christ's sake at the city of Chau-chau-fu, at the time that As-sune, — Mr. Johnson's old teacher — suffered for his Divine Master. From recent information I learn that, in the region about Amoy, the labors of Mr. Burns, in connection with the efforts of other missionaries, have been greatly blessed, and that many of the people have embraced Christianity. These native converts, however, have suffered severe persecution; and their enemies, in order to entirely root out Christianity, at one time threatened to drive them from their homes and property. The missionaries, however, appealed to Mr. Pedder — the English Consul at Amoy — for their protection; which being obtained, according to the treaties made at Tientsin, the persecutors entered into a bond not to interfere with the native converts; and in a few days the Mandarins issued a proclamation stating that the matter was settled, and forbidding the people to molest any persons "who may enter the holy religion of Jesus." There is a very prosperous mission of the American Dutch Reformed Board established at Amoy; and to the Rev. Mr. Doty — who has for more than twenty years been one of its most efficient and devoted missionaries — we were indebted for various kind civilities. Mr. Doty had just recovered from a slight attack of fever; and it was evident that his long residence within the tropics was telling disastrously upon his health. We observed, however, that his deep interest in the Mission cause made the thought of leaving his post exceedingly painful.

Every city in China is noted for some article of manufacture peculiarly its own; and the Amoy bracelet — formed of olive-stones exquisitely carved, is a unique ornament of rare elegance. Beautiful brooches, also, carved in pseudo sandal-wood, — which is of the color of the olive-stone, — are made to match the bracelets. These ornaments are much in request among the foreigners visiting Amoy, and are particularly sought after by the English, who send them home, where they are said to be highly prized. The Amoy pumelo,[1] — which is noted for

---

[1] The fruit of the *Citrus decumana.*

being superior to any grown elsewhere, — was in perfection at the time of our visit. This delicious fruit gained but little in its change of name, when introduced by Captain Shaddock into the West Indies.

Leaving Amoy on Monday afternoon, we met a very heavy monsoon sea outside the harbor, and before nine o'clock had a stiff breeze, which finally increased to a gale, and made our passage to Fuh-chau very tempestous. The next evening, however, we reached the three islands called the White Dogs, which lie off the mouth of the river Min, and anchored under the lee of one of them, where we remained until the next morning, when at flood tide, crossing the bar at the mouth of the river, we sailed up the latter to the Pagoda anchorage. Fuh-chau is situated about forty miles from the mouth of the river; and the passage being difficult, large vessels proceed no farther than this anchorage, which is off an island of the same name.

Thirteen or fourteen miles from the mouth of the Min, the stream, for the distance of nearly three miles, is less than half a mile wide, with the water from twelve to twenty-five fathoms deep. The hills rise on each side of this pass to the height of from fifteen hundred to two thousand feet, and are defended by forts. Dr. Williams has well said that

" the scenery on this river, though of a different character, will bear comparison with that of the Hudson for sublimity and beauty. The hills are, however, much higher on the Min." On sailing up the river the scenery varies, although the bold and romantic hills give a certain uniformity to the stream. These elevations are for the most part covered with verdure, while those of a less rocky and rough surface are terraced, and cultivated to their summits. At two points near which we sailed we observed establishments for firing or curing tea, and some of the furnaces were so situated as to be in full view. In the valleys, and upon the low lands bordering the river above the narrow pass, we observed small hamlets and extensive farms, furnished with buildings, and orchards of fruit-trees, which, from our point of view, seemed more like country life at the West than anything we saw in China.

On reaching the Pagoda anchorage, — which is at the termination of ship navigation on the Min, — we learned that the *Jacob Bell* would not be ready to sail for two or three weeks, during which time, through the kind hospitality of the house of Messrs. Olyphant & Co., we were entertained at their residence in Fuh-chau.[1] With the exception of Hong

[1] I cannot refrain from expressing here our gratitude to Mr. O——, an Englishman, —who, at that time represented the firm of Oly-

Kong and Macao, there are no hotels for the accommodation of foreigners in any of the ports of Southern China. At every place, however, strangers meet with the most agreeable hospitality from the foreign residents, who throw open their houses and welcome them with a delicate heartiness and kind sincerity which no grateful words can overpraise. Their houses are spacious; and as every one travels with a servant who takes charge of his apartment, the guest is quite as much at home as he would be in his own house.

We made the sail from the anchorage to the city of Fuh-chau — which is about twelve miles further up the river — in a pleasure-boat belonging to the Imperial Customs. The boat, which was large, and furnished with sails, — although differently constructed from the Canton "matrimonials," — had a cabin which was fitted up in a similar manner. When leaving the anchorage we not only had the tide with us, but the wind was also favorable, and until we had taken one or two turns in the river, — which brought us under the lee of a considerable mountain, — we sailed with very good speed. We then, however, came to a dead calm; but after our eight stalwart Fuh-chauan boatmen had been for

plant & Co. at Fuh-chau, — for his many acts of thoughtful kindness, and his gentlemanly attentions while we were his guests.

a long time sitting quietly and waiting for a propitious wind, we heard a low, wind-like whistle,
and as it became louder discovered that, sailor-like,
they were whistling to call to their aid a friendly
breeze.   How long this would have lasted I cannot say, as here Mr. W—— interposed, ordering
the chief man to bid them take to their oars, which
they readily did; and while plying them sang in a
nasal, and at times in a harsh, guttural tone a monotonous refrain, to which they not only kept time
with their oars, but also with their feet.   Landing
at the hong of Messrs. Olyphant & Co., we were
soon comfortably domiciled in their new and spacious mansion, which occupies a beautiful location,
upon a fine eminence, on the south bank of the
river, where most of the foreigners have their residences.

Fuh-chau-fu — or the Happy City — is built in
a plain, through which flows the river Min.   This
plain is entirely surrounded by mountains, forming
a vast amphitheatre of about twenty miles in diameter, in the northern part of which the city is
situated, while the river enters it from the northwest, through a narrow pass said to be similar to the
one we have described as occurring fourteen miles
from its mouth.   The land is of great fertility, and
that part of it unoccupied by the city is intersected

by little canals, and covered with cultivated fields, which are interspersed with hamlets, cottages, orchards, gardens, and beautifully wooded knolls. The Rev. R. S. Maclay, in his "Life among the Chinese," says that "the city proper is surrounded by a substantial wall built compactly of brick, and resting on a foundation of granite. The wall is about twenty feet high and ten feet thick, surmounted by a parapet five feet high, with bastions at regular intervals. The gateways are of great size and strength, and so constructed that a small force in charge of them could hold at bay almost any number of attacking troops."

The extensive southern suburb — called the suburb of *Nantai* — reaches three miles from the south wall to the river, and stretches along both sides of the stream. Along the southern shore, and particularly upon the handsomely swelling hill beyond, this suburb is not as densely built. It is, however, the centre of both the native and foreign trade; and the business hongs of the foreigners are situated near the river, while their residences occupy the eminence that overlooks them. From this hill the south gate of the city — which is six miles distant — is reached by a single street. The two bridges spanning the river are substantially built of granite, and are connected by a little islet in the river, which is called by the natives *chang-chau*.[1] The bridge crossing the northern branch of the river — which is called " The Bridge of Ten Thousand Ages " — is composed of twenty-six spans, each measuring twenty feet, and is furnished with a stone balustrade. The piers and spans are constructed of granite; and the floor of the bridge is also formed of the same material. The bridge crossing that portion of the stream, between the island and the southern bank of the river, is built in the same manner, but comprises only nine arches. These remarkable structures — over which crowds of people are continually passing and repassing — are said to be at least a thousand years old.

Ill-health prevented my thoroughly "doing" the city; but being guests for two days in the family of the Rev. Mr. Hartwell, — one of the missionaries of the American Board, who was living within the walls, — we visited a few places of interest, and learned more in regard to the city proper than I could otherwise have done.

The street of six miles, which we traversed in going through the suburb of Nantai, on our way to the south gate of the city, is lined on both sides with shops and residences, and always crowded from morn till night with a busy, jostling, and noisy moving mass of shopmen, mechanics, hucksters, and the

[1] In the local dialect it is *Tongchin*.

bearers of heavy burdens. We had up to this time considered ourselves thoroughly acquainted with the power and depth of the lungs of a Chinaman, and supposed that the deafening vociferations and noisy cries, that we had heard in the streets of Canton, could not be emulated; but after our brawny sedan-bearers had threaded their way through the suburb of Nantai, and, entering the city gate, were trotting briskly through North and South Street, we cheerfully awarded the palm to the sturdy, rough, and noisy Fuh-chauan. The increase of vile odors also, as compared with Canton, was in the same ratio; while the people, as a whole, looked much stouter, — or rather more brawny, — as well as rougher and poorer. At different places along the street we observed establishments, furnished with chairs and little tables, where people were drinking tea, and refreshing themselves with food. These places — which reminded us of the restaurants of the West — are called tea-pavilions. Very soon after passing one of these places — which was not far from the south gate — we were surprised at having our eyes greeted with the sight of a church, which has been built at that central point by the American Methodist Episcopal Mission. The edifice — which reminded us, in its exterior, of some of the village churches at home — is built with a cupola, and furnished with a bell.

It is well located to attract the crowds of people who, during the day, always throng that great thoroughfare, and, at any hour it is only necessary to throw open the doors in order to gather a congregation.

The principal street within the walled city — which is called *Nanka,* that is, South Street — runs from the south gate nearly to the north, and is therefore usually called by the Europeans North and South Street. For a Chinese town, it is a wide and well-paved street, and in it are located the finest shops in the city. This place had been open to foreigners for so short a time that we were more of a curiosity, while in Nanka Street, than in any spot that we visited while in China. In fact, when entering some extensive china shops, we were so pressed upon and closely pursued by the crowd on stepping out of our chairs that we were obliged to rush through the front apartments of the shops into the large warerooms beyond, in order to escape them. The gentlemen and Master Charlie were in open chairs, and the latter was an object of special interest. A foreign boy of fourteen years is rarely seen in the streets of a Chinese city, and of course our young friend was a great lion to the curious Fuh-chauans, who turned their heads and gazed after him as long as he could be seen.

In Fuh-chau, — as in Canton, — the residences of
the Mandarins, and other persons of position and
wealth, are in the western portion of the town, and
it is said that some of their establishments are arranged and furnished in a style indicating refinement and good taste. The city and its suburbs
contain half a million of inhabitants, who are a very
energetic, persevering, and independent people, and
are also represented as being more or less refractory,
and consequently not over polite.   Indeed they are
much less courteous than the Cantonese; and a foreigner from the south of China will quickly observe
their harsh, guttural dialect, as well as their independent bearing.   The boat-people are numerous,
and the river — like all rivers near Chinese cities —
presents an animated picture.   The boat-women
have also a fashion of wearing flowers in their hair;
which, together with the flower-pots that ornament
nearly all the boats, give the scene a peculiarly
attractive aspect. The women, in fact, of all classes
are in the habit of dressing their heads with flowers;
and however gray the hair, or bald the head, or
soiled and tattered the garments, these beautiful
ornaments, tastefully arranged in little bouquets, are
seen fastened with metal pins to the side, or near
the top of the head.   The pins used are ornamental,
and we observed some made of silver wire that

matched well with the hoop-rings of extraordinary circumference which they wore in their ears. Many of these floral ornaments were composed of china-asters of exquisite tints, which, in regard to the contrast of colors, showed much fine taste in their arrangement. Not unfrequently bouquets are worn on both sides of the head; and the charming effect of these decorations, as viewed in the constantly changing crowds which one encounters in the streets, must be seen in order to be fully appreciated. No description — at least none that I can give — is adequate to the subject. Natural flowers are much in favor with these women, although many of them wear artificial ones; and for the purpose of answering the constant demand which this fashion has created, artificial flowers are extensively manufactured. Upon many of these I observed butterflies of brilliant hues, which were represented as having alighted to taste their sweets. Of course the flowers made for the use of the ladies are much more elegant and expensive than those used by the lower classes. The field-flowers, however, — which are particularly designed for the latter, — are very beautiful.

There are two Confucian temples within the walls of the city; one of which having been burned a few years ago, has since been rebuilt, on a grand scale, by the Mandarins, and is said to be the finest build-

ing in the town. The main temple has a lofty
portico, and a fretted roof which is supported by
huge columns of granite. From this temple we
went to a picturesque elevation overlooking the city,
and the whole amphitheatre of hills in the midst of
which it is built, and which is called *Wu-shih-
shan*, or Black-stone Hill. At one place, more than
half way up the steep and rugged ascent of this hill,
there is a Buddhist temple, with ornamental buildings scattered here and there; and upon the highest
point there is also an altar, constructed of stone,
which supports a sort of iron vase, in which the
superstitious Fuh-chauans — who resort thither thrice
a year for the purpose of worshipping the heavens
and the earth — burn their incense-paper.

Strong sedan-bearers carried me with much apparent ease for some distance above the monastery,
from which point I clambered up the remainder of
the rock-ribbed summit, where the widely extended
and beautiful view, not only of the city but of the
mountains, the hills, and the rice-fields on the low
land, — with the river and little canals intersect-
ing the latter, — more than repaid for the fatigue
which I encountered. The view of the city from
this point is one of great interest; the two nine-
storied pagodas,[1] together with the watch-towers on

---

[1] One of these is called the White, and the other the Black

the walls, greatly relieving the monotony of the low, tiled roofs; while the scene is still further diversified by the great numbers of noble old banian-trees for which Fuh-chau is noted.[1]

Passing down the other side of the *Wu-shih-shan,* we reached the city wall, and continued our walk upon it until we came to the south gate. The top and sides of these walls were everywhere covered with vines, grass, and lovely ferns.

Some of the mountains, five or six miles below the city, are two or three thousand feet high. One of these, called Kushan Peak, has already become something of a sanatarium for foreigners; and the place is also noted as being the location of one of the most extensive and celebrated Buddhist monasteries in China, which is situated far up the side of the mountain, occupying a charming spot, only a few hundred feet from the top of the peak. Strangers visiting Fuh-chau usually make a pilgrimage to this spot; but the ascent of two or three miles — although it could have been accomplished in a mountain-chair — was too formidable an undertaking

Pagoda. They are very old, and are connected with Buddhist temples. The White Pagoda, however, is in such a state of decay that no one is allowed to ascend it.

[1] Fuh-chau is sometimes called by the natives, the " City of Banians."

for an invalid, and I was obliged to be contented
with a view of the broad and well-made path leading up to it. This path, which is shaded most of
the way by lofty pines, has "rest-houses" erected
along its winding course; and in the vicinity of the
monastery — which commands a prospect stretching
far away among the distant mountains and fertile
valleys — huge camphor-trees are growing.

The hills and mountain-sides on the south bank
of the river are covered with graves and tombs, interspersed among which are beautiful little groves
of lofty pines, and occasional patches of land where
a plant is cultivated, whose flowers are used for the
purpose of scenting tea; or, perhaps, the spot is used
for vegetables. The graves of the Mandarins are
always expensive. On our excursions, however, to
enjoy the cool evening air, we frequently passed a
new tomb of the Greek-letter form, which was built
with a tasteful, altar-like arrangement, where the
offerings were placed at the time of ancestral worship. This was one of the most costly and showy
tombs I ever saw, and was simply the sepulchre
of a private gentleman of great wealth. Many of
the foreign residences look out upon this vast cemetery, and the delightful house at which we were
guests was built in the midst of these tombs and
tumuli. The spot on which it stands, and the

compound surrounding it, were originally used for the same purpose. When it was purchased, however, the friends of the dead removed their remains. There are some very ancient tombs, situated near the wall enclosing the grounds of this residence, which have been occupied several hundred years.

Low buildings, constructed of wood, and of sufficient height to admit of three or four rows of shelves for the support of coffins, are also scattered here and there in this vast resting-place of the dead. Within them, closely sealed, coffined relics are placed, and remain until what the surviving friends consider a "lucky day" arrives, and then, the "lucky spot" in which to inter them being procured, they are buried. I was assured that not unfrequently years elapsed before everything was regarded as propitious for the interment of these remains. And also learned that some were placed there because of the poverty of their friends, and were left until the latter could afford the expense of a fitting burial. We observed that many of these, temporary little wooden sepulchres were so old and dilapidated that the coffins were plainly visible to the gaze of the passer-by.

The foreigners have so far widened and improved some of the many winding paths — which lead in every direction among the graves, and stretch far out into the country — that there is ample room for equestrians. A few European horses are kept, but we observed that the little Tartar pony of the North was also used. This animal reminded us of the Canadian pony, although he looked a trifle smaller, while his mane was much heavier.

Many of my countrywomen would doubtless be appalled at the idea of having no promenade but that bordered by graves and tombs. I have already intimated, in speaking of this subject in connection with our life at Whampoa, that they do not tend to make the aspect of nature cheerful; and if we found this the case before having seen the unbroken miles of beautiful hills and the steep mountain-sides, which at Fuh-chau are covered with these reminders of our mortality, this change in our location did not render us the less inclined to solemnity. It is not difficult, however, to become cheerfully habituated even to this funereal landscape; and the country about Fuh-chau is so incomparably beautiful that in spite of the graveyard use to which most of the uncultivated ground is put, one cannot but admire and enjoy the scenes around him. In fact, the suburbs and surroundings of this city were more attractive in situation and scenery than any other place we visited in China. The hill-sides offer finer locations for residences; where, excepting in the hottest weather, Europeans can be as comfortable as at home. For although it is very warm from May until the first of October, the mountain-breezes continue to be bracing until late in the spring; and returning early in the autumn, the climate is not as exhausting as at the ports further south. In China, however, the humidity of the atmosphere is such that the same degrees of heat and cold are more seriously felt than in the United States.

Kite-flying is a gentlemanly pastime among the Fuh-chauans; and groups of men are frequently seen moving about among the graves, upon the hills, engaged in this amusement. Sometimes the kite is made to represent a flock of birds; and on one occasion we observed that they were so natural and bird-like in form and motion, that, had we not been assured to the contrary, we should have taken them for what they only appeared to be. The Chinese, in fact, are said to succeed so admirably in making and flying these bird-kites that an Englishman, on first arriving in the country, being out on a hunting excursion, fired into a flock of them before perceiving his mistake. We also saw a centipede-kite, — said to be a hundred feet in length, — which was flying, and in its motions was not unlike the frightfully disagreeable reptile it represented.

I was more and more impressed at every place we visited in China with the skill exhibited by the people in their own peculiar works of art, but found none more worthy of notice than that of the Fuh-chauans, whose exquisite carvings in marble are not only excellent representations of themselves, but also of the local scenes in and about the city; many of which are beautifully done. The people of a district about sixty miles from Fuh-chau are famous for the manufacture of flowers, which are made of silver. We shall not attempt a description of these beautiful creations of artistic taste and skill, which represent delicate foliage and flowers, and are formed into wreaths for the head, as well as made into little ornamental clusters or bouquets. We saw one wreath of exquisite workmanship, which was admirably adapted to adorn the head of a bride. The people of this same district manufacture also a very curious but handsome fire-screen, woven of paper, on which are represented not only flowers, birds, and animals, but also figures of men and women, together with various scenes common to the country. The most remarkable thing about them is that the figures are made in the weaving. The threads of paper are colored before the material is woven, and the scenes and figures are given in the most brilliant hues.

For the benefit of the foreign community the services of the English Church are held every Sunday in the English Chapel,—which is a small Gothic edifice, occupying a fine situation in the neighborhood of the English consulate, and upon an eminence which is quite the centre of the foreign community. The premises of the American Methodist Episcopal Mission are also in the same neighborhood with the foreign residences ; and a small church — which is erected within the wall enclosing them — is arranged into two chapels, one being appropriated to services for the benefit of Europeans, and the other for such natives as may choose to attend upon the ministrations of the missionaries. The American Board have a mission station within the walls of the city, which is occupied by two mission families. They have also another station in the suburbs, where, at the time of our visit, two other families were living. The ladies at these stations were doing all they could for the religious and domestic education and other improvement of the native women and their daughters.

At the station within the walls, Mrs. Hartwell was teaching a number of native women, but was in great need of a convenient room apart from her own house, where at stated hours she could receive and instruct them. On account of the state of the finances at home, the mission was unwilling to appeal to the Society for aid to build a house for this purpose, but an effort which was being made, when we left Fuh-chau, to raise the necessary funds among the foreigners, was successful ; and from letters subsequently received from there, we have been informed that the building is completed and occupied, much to the satisfaction of the mission. The school under the care of the wife of the Rev. Mr. Baldwin, — one of the missionaries of the station in the suburbs, — and also that of the Misses Woolston, — of the Methodist Mission, — were spoken of as flourishing, and as quietly assisting to do the same good work among the Chinese girls of Fuh-chau which is being accomplished by the same kind of schools at Canton and Swatow.

19

CHAPTER XV.

BEING advised, on the 3d of November, that the *Jacob Bell* had received her full cargo, and would sail in a few days, we hastened the few remaining preparations for our long voyage, and embarked on board of her. On Friday, the 7th of the month, our regretful adieus were made to the friends we were leaving, and the ship was towed from the anchorage down the river by the English steamer *Fieloong*, when she anchored for the night at Sharp Peak Island. The next morning, being again taken in tow, we were soon beyond all rocks and bars, when the steamer left us in charge of a pilot, who was also to leave us at the White Dogs. On reaching the neighborhood of these islands, however, we encountered a very short and heavy sea; and not being able to pass sufficiently near under the lee of the island to make it safe for the pilot-boat to come off for him, he was compelled to go down the sea with us. In such rough sailing it was impossible not to come somewhat under the influence of old Neptune, and poor Charlie suffered severely. We were, however, too good sailors to be long affected,

and the next day all such disagreeables were forgotten.

Our accommodations were excellent; and although
we were the only passengers, the fact that Captain
Frisbie — the master of the vessel — had his wife on
board was encouraging, and enabled me to look forward the more hopefully to the safe termination of
the long voyage before us.

A strong northeast monsoon drove us down the
channel of Formosa and the China Sea at the rate
of eleven knots an hour, so that on Sunday we were
passing Namoa Island, which lies not far from the
entrance to the harbor of Swatow; and on Monday
morning were sailing within forty miles of Hong
Kong. After sighting Victoria Peak we fell in with
a native pilot-boat, which enabling the captain to
send his Fuh-chauan pilot to Hong Kong, we did
not suffer the detention we had feared, in being
obliged to go into port in order to land him.

On the 18th day of the month — when below the
fourth degree of north latitude, and in the neighborhood of the Natura Islands — our fine breeze left us;
but, under the influence of light winds, we sailed
on slowly, — the mercury indicating a heat of from
eighty to ninety degrees. The weather soon became so oppressive that, on the 21st of the month,
one of the sailors had a *coup de soleil*, and fell while

at the wheel. Happily it did not prove a fatal case, and after a few days of care the man was again performing his duties. While near the Natura Islands we had several ships in sight, and speaking two of them, learned that they were bound to London. During the night of the 21st we had severe squalls of wind and rain, and in a few hours "boxed the compass" seven times. Calms succeeded these squalls, but when off the island of Borneo strong southerly currents floated us gently onward, and at noon on the 23d of November we crossed the equator.

When about two miles south of the equinoctial line we were suddenly greeted with the cry of "A sea-serpent, a sea-serpent!" and at the same time Master Charlie came rushing into the cabin, and begged me to go up on deck and see the monster. With the Nahant sea-serpent, however, in mind, and stout incredulity in my heart, I followed my young friend. The serpent — or whatever it might have been — was on our larboard side, and floating with the current at a distance of what seemed to be not more than two or three times the length of the ship from us. On ascending to the deck I found the captain and his crew watching the movements of the creature, which was then quietly floating opposite the vessel. There was not a ripple to be seen upon the mirror-like surface of the ocean. In a few moments, however, the object moved in a very slow manner, and raising what was pronounced to be his head, made some disagreeably sinuous motions with his body, after which he again relapsed into a state of quietude. This continued but for a short time, when there was another general movement, which was more decidedly animated and serpent-like than at the first; and this time the so-called head appeared to be raised nearly above the water. This demonstration was too terribly frightful; and, having a great horror of anything so suggestive of a reptile, I fled directly to the cabin. Nor did I regret our having passed this nondescript creature, which appeared to us very like a huge snake floating along while basking in the fiercest heat of the torrid zone. Many parts of the China Sea are infested with snakes, which are often seen swimming near the surface of the water; and the captain of the *Jacob Bell* declared that he had seen them ten feet long. This creature, however, — which he and all his crew persisted in calling a sea-serpent, — was pronounced by him to be forty feet in length, and one old sailor went so far as to say that it was as long as the mainyard. It was of a dark snuff-color, and was said to be covered with barnacles.

I do not relate this exciting incident with any intention of proclaiming that we saw a veritable sea-serpent; nor do I say that it was a living monster of any kind, but merely state the case in accordance with appearances. Furthermore, I do not acknowledge to any belief about it; but leave the decision that it was a sea-serpent — which was made by the captain and crew of the *Bell* — to be sustained or reversed by the citizens of Nahant, whose superior wisdom and vast experience in such matters is universally acknowledged and always deferred to.

Reaching Gasper Strait, and sailing through the Staltz Channel, we passed the islands and dangerous shoals in that vicinity with safety, and entered the Java Sea on the 26th of November. Ship supplies can always be procured at Anjer, which is a small port on the coast of Java, and just within the Strait of Sunda as it is entered from the Java Sea. When the wind is fair, vessels frequently stop there and take in their supplies while at anchor; when, however, the weather is unfavorable, boats loaded with the necessary articles go out and meet them.

Having calms and light winds we sailed very slowly; but finally, after passing the North Watchers and the Thousand Islands, on the afternoon of the 29th — when about fifty miles from the Strait of Sunda — two native boats, or *prahus*, were seen making vigorously for us. The little craft — which were manned by Malays — were from Anjer; and besides being loaded with fowls, fruits, and vegetables, had also on board some monkeys, and a pair of little moose deer of Java,[1] besides a few cages of Java sparrows. With the approach of the Malay boats we were visited with a breeze; and after purchasing the necessary supplies, our captain took the little vessels in tow, when we sailed on at the rate of eight knots an hour. During the night one of the boats parted her cable, and we left her, while the other continued with us until morning, when, coming alongside, our letters were given to the chief man on board, with instructions to deliver them into the hands of the Dutch governor at Anjer, when we

---

[1] The deer — which were purchased by Captain Frisbie — throve well, and were doing finely when we were taken by the pirate steamer *Florida*. Then, however, they passed into the hands of the chief buccaneer, Captain Maffit, who, soon after we were transferred from his vessel to the Danish bark *Morning Star*, visited the island of Barbadoes, and being dined and fêted by the Governor of that English colony, he presented these beautiful creatures to the daughter of his kind and hospitable entertainer. It was also reliably stated in the public prints that Captain Maffit and his officers made presents to the English ladies of beautiful articles from China and Japan. These ladies were also highly delighted with some small canisters of choice tea which Captain Maffit gave them; and as these were all from our packages, I cannot say less than to express the fear that if our English cousins *enjoy* the possession of the Oriental articles which we lost, they may also have disposed of their self-respect when drinking our tea.

parted. This was on Sunday morning, as we were nearing the islands of Java and Sumatra, with the dark peaks of the Radjah Bassa mountains and the entrance-way to the strait in full view. We, however, had a head-wind; and although our captain made every exertion, by constantly tacking ship, to enter the passage, he was finally obliged to come to, and anchor for the night near the coast of Sumatra, and under the lee of the Radjah Bassa range.

Besides taking a long sea-voyage, one must be a wakeful invalid, and also pass through a day of the disagreeable sailing and noise incident to the frequent tacking of ship, in order to appreciate the quiet and delicious sleep which I enjoyed that night. The next morning, being more successful in our efforts, we entered the narrow pass on the western side of Renjang, or Thwart-the-way Island, and, getting safely through, were soon sailing past the little settlement of Anjer.

Renjang, or Thwart-the-way Island — which, as its name indicates, lies athwart the mouth of the Strait — is jagged-looking, and of singular shape, having sundry acute angles, whose rocky points shoot directly out into the water. It is, however, covered with trees, shrubs, and vines, and with its tropical luxuriance, displayed, as we sailed near, some very exquisite bits of scenery. At one place, near the beach, the ground and rocks formed high arches, over which trailed vines of the richest foliage. We also observed a remarkable ravine, and an elevation which rose perpendicularly from the water's edge to the height of five hundred feet.

On the 2d day of December we passed Cocketoo Island, and sailing on reached Princess Island, which lies near the entrance to the Indian Ocean, having a passage leading into it both upon its east and west side. Taking the western passage, we were in a short time out on the broad ocean ; and as Java Head faded in the distance, not only felicitated ourselves in having escaped the dangers of the China Sea, but already began to look forward with much hopeful courage for the future.

Our fine breeze had again died away, but having gentle zephyrs we still moved slowly onward, and lost sight of Java Head before evening. During the night, however, we met with a heavy swell from the south, and our wind entirely failing us, we drifted so far back that in the morning Java Head was again plainly visible. In the afternoon, being again favored with a fair wind, we sailed on our course, when Java Head faded permanently from our view. Up to this time calms and adverse winds had prevailed to such a degree that for seventeen successive days we had only made, on an average, two and a half miles an hour.

While in the East I observed that meteors were of much more common occurrence than in our Western hemisphere. Indeed, when at Swatow, our evenings were usually passed, until a very late hour, in an open veranda; and I fail to remember a night in which we did not note one or two, which, passing athwart the heavens, made the blue vault, which sparkled with brilliant stars, if possible more splendidly glorious. From the deck of the *Jacob Bell*, however, on the evening of the 5th of December, I observed one which far exceeded in brilliancy, and in the length of time that it remained luminous, any I had ever seen. This appeared at first in the eastern portion of the heavens, and taking an oblique direction to the south passed over a great space, and then, for a few seconds, displayed a flame-colored tail, — while the nucleus assumed a rich golden hue, — when it exploded and vanished. The spotlessly white and ethereal-looking fleecy clouds — which are always seen when sailing on the Indian Ocean — seemed to be more numerous and beautiful than when on our voyage out; and when lighted up by the departing rays of the setting sun the scene was enchanting. I may, in time, forget our perils by sea, and the more painful perils that we were afterwards placed in by our treacherous countrymen, but I can never forget the sunset glories of the Indian Ocean. The Magellan clouds and lovely Southern Cross, attended by its brilliantly sparkling pointers, were also our nightly visitors; and, as on our outward voyage, the stars in the Cross, as well as those composing Orion, Taurus, and other southern constellations, appeared more brilliant than when seen in the Atlantic tropics.

Although we had a favorable trade-wind within a week after entering the Indian Ocean, it lasted only for a few days, and before the 21st of the month, as we neared the latitude of Mauritius, the heat greatly increased, and we were again visited with light winds and calms. For a week after leaving Fuh-chau it was pleasantly cool, but from that time the mercury had not fallen below eighty degrees, and sometimes it was as high as ninety and ninety-six degrees, which made an atmosphere that, without the sea-breeze, would have been almost unendurable. On Christmas Day we were passing the Isle of Bourbon; and at night, having severe squalls of wind, were made painfully aware that we were again in the hurricane latitudes at an inopportune season. These squalls, however, lasted but for a short time, and, leaving us with a fair breeze, we had passed the longitude of Madagascar and were sailing prosperously onward, when we were suddenly visited with a terrific squall from the northwest. This came on during the afternoon of January 1st, 1863, when we were about off Port Natal. As I had never before taken a voyage in a sailing vessel, and this being the most fearful wind we had encountered, the loud screaming tones of the captain, giving his orders, and the noise of the sailors as they hastened to furl the sails, together with the howling of the wind through the rigging, was appalling. It blew a gale during the night, nor did it abate so that we could make sail until the following afternoon ; and yet this squall, and the few tempestuous hours that followed it, bore no comparison to the sharp southeaster we encountered three days afterwards.

We were then nearly off Great Fish River, with the prospect of soon rounding the Cape. The gale, which commenced on Saturday, reached its culminating point on Sunday, and we were obliged to lie to until Monday morning. For several hours, fastenings arranged with pulleys were attached to each side of the wheel, in order to keep the rudder steady; and for still greater safety, a man crouched upon deck was stationed to hold at each of the fastenings, while two men stood at the wheel, and carefully guided the ship. The gale had continued many hours before I could call sufficient courage into requisition to take a view of the scene of awful gran-

deur about us. Being assured, however, that our
vessel was in no danger from the storm, I finally
ascended to the quarter-deck, from whence the huge
and extensive waves of the broad ocean presented
a sublime though fearful spectacle. The ship, although tossed about by the waves like a frail canoe,
at the same time rode them so easily that I soon
learned to view the scene with less terror and more
satisfaction than I ever expected to regard so fierce
a tempest. We frequently shipped seas upon the
main-deck; and occasionally a wave dashing over
the cabin, swept also the quarter-deck. One of these
waves, in fact, finally drove me below, where I was
glad to remain.

This dreadful gale — which began to lull about
twelve o'clock Sunday night — also left us with a
fair breeze, which wafted us around the Cape of
Storms; and on the 9th of January we were in
the South Atlantic, with our prow pointing homeward, and beginning to indulge in the fancy that our
long voyage was fast drawing near to an auspicious
close. As we neared Cape Lagullas the air became
bracing; and before we had reached the Atlantic
Ocean the atmosphere was delightful.

While rounding the Cape we fell in company
with several kinds of sea-birds; most of which, being new to us, were objects of much interest. The

albatross, in particular, — whether on the wing, or floating with majestic grace upon the waves, — was always greeted with admiration.

The fair breeze with which we entered the Atlantic continued until we reached a favorable trade-wind ; and — the latter accompanying us until the 15th of January — we were at that date but seven miles from the southern tropics. Here the weather becoming again very warm, the little vigor which I had gained while sailing within the bracing region of the Cape, was soon dissipated; and it seemed as though the long days and nights of prostration and suffering, experienced before our ship had reached and passed the equator, would never end. On the 2d of February, however, we were nearly one degree north of the equinoctial line, and beginning to feel, in a slight degree, the influence of the bracing wind from the north. On the 10th, — being nearly out of the tropics, and hoping to reach New York in ten or fifteen days, — with the assistance of my young friend and only protector, Master Charlie, I began to pack and make a few preparations in anticipation of that event.

CHAPTER XIV.

FROM the 2d of February to the 12th we had favorable winds, and for three or four days our speed had averaged ten or eleven knots an hour. At noon of that day, when in latitude 24° 1′ north and longitude 65° 58′ west, our captain and officers observed a sail in our wake, which gradually gained upon us, until it could be plainly seen that she was a steamer. At this time the wind had lulled, and we were only making eight knots an hour; so that about three o'clock in the afternoon the strange sail was distant from us perhaps six miles, and following directly astern, with the " stars and stripes " run up on her foremast. We had not thought of being molested by southern pirates,[1] but hoped she might

[1] Lawful and honorable privateering never admits of plundering and appropriating the luggage and private property of the passengers found on the captured prize and seamen, of whatever nation, committing such outrages, are pronounced by all honorable men of the Christianized world, as pirates. In view of this long-established truth I am obliged, however I may regret the necessity of doing so, to give, at the outset of this narrative, the *chivalric* Southern officers, into whose gentlemanly (?) hands I was so unfortunate as to fall, their only appropriate name of *pirates.*

prove to be a gunboat of our Government; and being nearly famished, after a five months' fast, for news
from home, were happy in the prospect of hearing
how it fared with our country. A little before four
o'clock I went to the quarter-deck, and seated myself on the starboard side, not far back of the stern.
She was then directly in our track, and evidently
making for us with much speed, having every stitch
of canvas out, even to her studding-sails, and her
steam power in full operation. Soon after this an
order was given to unfurl our flag at the peak, and
I observed that our captain, who was constantly
using his glass, and watching the approaching vessel,
seemed a little nervous and ill at ease. Indeed,
doubt had already begun to settle upon us all, for
the steamer was gaining upon us at the rate of three
miles an hour, and her appearance, to say the least,
did not bode us any good. We were making all
the sail we could, and had the wind which had
favored us the day previous continued, we could
have kept out of the range of her guns until evening,
and then probably have been able to elude her. But
it was otherwise decreed, and down she came upon
us, firing a shot when about three miles distant,
which struck the water a ship's length and a half
astern of the *Bell*, on the port side. That shot was
potential, carrying conviction to all that our vessel

was doomed, and that we were about to fall into the hands of an enemy. It required but little reflection to make us painfully conscious of the fact, the whole truth of which flashed upon us as suddenly and unexpectedly as the booming of the distant gun which seemed to announce our doom; in an instant, as it were, paralyzing all thought and feeling. Directly on the firing of the gun Captain Frisbie rose up, and turning his face towards the bow, looked first at his ship and then at the sail, saying, — " Well, I guess you 'll heave to, now!" and ordering his men to "clew up the crotchet sail," and back the yards, we quietly waited for the decision of our fate.

We had just sailed through the heat of the tropics, and having been ill for more than three weeks, and of course weak and easily perturbed, the firing of the gun sent me directly into the cabin; but, through Master Charlie, I learned that in about ten minutes after I had left the deck, the steamer, which proved to be the *Florida*, — a pirate, officered and manned by the rebels of the Southern States, — came round our stern to the port side, and when within two ship's lengths of us ran up the rebel Confederate flag, — taking down the " stars and stripes," — and hailed us. On being answered, and told whither we were bound, we were ordered to strike our colors; and no answer being returned, nor any movement made

20

to carry the order into execution, there came a second and more peremptory summons, with which Captain Frisbie complied, and our colors were struck! The steamer, meanwhile, made a circuit once or twice around us for purposes of observation, very much in the same way that a cat toys with a mouse, after having made sure of her victim. Having no efficient armament, we were powerless; yet she did not raise the rebel flag until she had us broadside under her guns, — a circumstance which indicated, as clearly as anything could, the conscious guilt of these pirates, and their extreme care lest they should be caught in some trap, thus getting their retribution somewhat in advance of their calculations. The pirate captain then sent a boat alongside, with a prize-master; who, accosting Captain Frisbie, exclaimed — "You are my prize." The captain replied — "But this is English property." " I can't help that," rejoined the prize-master; "I must obey my orders." Captain Frisbie then said — "Is this the way you take English property on the high seas?" "Yes, sir!" was the reply; "Lord John Russell has recently said that if English subjects put their property in United States vessels, they must look for pay to the Confederate Government." The prize-master than told Captain Frisbie that he must prepare to go on board the steamer, while he took possession of the ship; and on being asked what was to be done with the passengers and crew, the officer said they were also to be taken on board, but that all private property should be saved, and after taking what they wished from the *Jacob Bell*, they should burn her.

There being no appeal from this *ex cathedra* decision, or rather doom, our captain went below and directly made preparations to leave. In a few minutes after this another boat coming from the *Florida*, in charge of one of their doctors, our crew were immediately taken on board, and we were only allowed the time taken for their transshipment, — which could not have exceeded half an hour, — to gather up a few things and get ready to follow.

Complying with the suggestions of our faithful and kind colored steward, I gathered together the few things that were in the drawers of my stateroom, and throwing them hastily on my bed, tied them securely in the counterpane. 'I also put the few books which were in my state-room into a small calico bag; and notwithstanding my confused and nervous state, had sufficient self-possession and forecast to take a small hand-trunk, in which I put a change or two of linen, and a few night-clothes; being careful to add flannel articles, warm stockings, boots, and gloves for the cold weather on our coast, together with our toilet articles. To these I also added some pocket-handkerchiefs, one or two books valuable from association, a few pieces of jewelry, and some other articles, which, together with the little money we had with us, would be absolutely necessary in case we should never get any more of our luggage. We were bidden to make all haste, and the little trunk, together with two Chinese baskets,— the only articles that we could take with us,— were soon ready; our trunks of clothing for sea use having been also got out and placed in the cabin, along with our two emigrant-looking bundles. There was no time to give any attention to one's personal appearance, and it certainly would not be entertaining to know what kind of plight I was in when taken on board the pirate. I have already alluded, however, to the fact of having been more ill than usual during our passage through the Atlantic tropics; and my lady-readers can readily imagine how they would look *en déshabillé*, with a loose gown of cotton print, an old shawl thrown about their shoulders, and a straw hat in place of a bonnet.

The boat came for the third time, when, with the captain, his wife, and child, we were transferred to the pirate. Happily for us the wind had continued to lull, and although there was something of a swell, there was no heavy sea running. For this we were thankful;—but to be fastened into a chair, and hoisted over the ship's side by means of a rope-tackling, into a boat, and then to be re-hoisted in the same manner, and lowered upon the deck of an armed vessel prepared for piratical warfare, amid the gaze of brutalized and vicious men, whose vulgar, jeering expression of countenance was enough to make any one shrink back involuntarily with loathing and indignation, was a severe test for a woman, who, both in body and mind, was greatly weakened by a long voyage and months of disease in the tropics of the East; and yet all this was but a slight foretaste of what was to follow.

The flag of the *Jacob Bell* — claimed as a prize by the pirates — was to be taken with us on board their vessel; and Captain Frisbie laying it over the chair in which his wife and I were to be placed, in order to be hoisted into the boat, we gathered the loose folds into our laps, so as to partly cover us. The gleam of comfort and sunshine that flashed through my confused brain when my eye first rested on one particular star in those folds can never be forgotten. It was still a star of hope and trust, making even the heart of a feeble and unprotected woman glow with an emotion of joyful pride in that she was permitted to suffer in a cause like that of constitutional liberty; which, next to our holy religion, is more sacred and precious than anything else for which man can be called upon to lay down his life.

When we were alongside the *Florida*, the officer who had us in charge, while re-arranging the chair in which we were to be re-hoisted on deck, proposed substituting the rebel flag in place of our own; but our captain, with prudent tact, in an apparently indifferent manner, said, — "This will do just as well," — whereupon, no objection being made, we were again wrapped in our own colors, which was doubtless the last honorable service of the flag of the ill-fated *Jacob Bell.* On being lowered to the deck of the steamer, and freed from our chair-tackling, I heard a rather cultivated voice on my right, saying, — "Please take my arm, madam." I saw nothing, for my first glance at the deck and the rough men with upturned faces rudely gazing as I hung in the air, had caused both head and eyes to droop. But woman's natural instinct, when in a position of fearful suffering and rude exposure, to readily and gratefully receive civility and protection, — no matter from what source it may come, — led me to accept the proffered arm, and suffer myself to be conducted by Captain Maffit, — the leader of this band of buccaneers, (as he proved to be,) — to his cabin. This was done with a cool *sang-froid*, and also with the patronizing, host-like air of one about offering the most agreeable hospitality. Soon the whole of our party were in the cabin, which we were told was at our disposal; and also that the captain's private state-room, leading out of it, could be occupied by one of the ladies. It was, however, only appropriated by us for one night, it being dark and close; and we therefore abandoned it for sleeping-purposes, greatly preferring the cabin lockers, where mattrasses — some of them taken from the *Jacob Bell* — were placed, and the remainder of our party slept.

The knives of our crew were taken from them, and they made to sign a paper that they would offer no resistance while on board. There had been great haste made in transferring us, in order to follow up another United States vessel then in sight; and it being late in the afternoon, it was not possible for them to pillage the *Jacob Bell* and destroy her that night. A prize-crew was therefore put on board of her, and told to steer in a certain direction, while we were to steam after the " Yankee," as they sneeringly called her; but during the evening she managed to get out of their range; and as ours was a case of misery not admitting of a wish for company, we silently rejoiced, giving thanks that the prowling marauders were foiled of their prey. Our speed was then lessened, and in the morning we were again in the neighborhood of the *Jacob Bell.*

That was a fearful and strangely eventful day to us; and although we had been told that our private effects would be saved, I had many doubts in regard to the fulfilment of the promise. During the first part of the night previous I plainly heard, from the place where I was lying, portions of a conversation held by the ward-room officers, who had been on board the *Jacob Bell* for the purpose of seeing what plunder could be taken from her. They were making out an inventory of what things were to be brought on board the *Florida* for their own use; and it being evident that they were arranging for a long day's work, I feared that the captain would perhaps demur to the trouble of saving and bringing on board the packages belonging to us; it, however, never once occurred to me that they might open and plunder them there.

Before leaving the *Jacob Bell* our captain obtained permission of the prize-master to leave his steward and a waiting-man on board, who were to look after his effects and our trunks of sea-clothing; which, with our bundles and a small basket of stores that they were to put up for us, we hoped to receive on board the *Florida*. In the morning, on learning that Captain Frisbie had already gone on board the *Jacob Bell*, I handed Captain Maffit, as requested, a list of the packages we had in the ship, which having read, he returned to me, saying, — " Mrs. W—— I cannot take all your things on board ; for we have not room, and we cannot have much on deck, as it will prevent the free working of the guns." I then said, " It will be very hard, Captain Maffit, to lose all our packages; for those in the hold contain the greatest and best part of our wardrobes, besides some household supplies, and many other articles of rare value ; and we were assured by your officer when taken that all our private effects should be saved." " Yes," was the reply, " but it is quite impossible in this case; and you must take what you most need. I shall then allow you more than is usual in such cases." After this conversation I mentioned to Captain Maffit the fact of my having a small insurance on my property, but remarked that I was not sure of its being good for anything in this case. At his request I then handed him the policy, which he read and returned to me, saying, — " Yes, that is a war risk." In a few moments after, he asked to look at the policy again; and once more having conned it apparently with great care, remarked, " Yes, your policy is good in this case, and I am surprised that any one will attempt to travel with valuables in these times without being properly insured. I advise you to leave the insured packages. They are not numbered, and you can take whichever parcels you please, only be sure to leave twenty packages, for if you do not, your policy will be contested."[1] In this seemingly disinterested manner he advised me what to do; telling me he could not save our property, but at the same time appeared to deplore the necessity of the case, and expressed his regret at what I must suffer in seeing the destruction of so much of the nice, curious, useful, and valuable. He thus so completely deceived me that I never once suspected his object; nor that his officers would be allowed to break open and plunder our property. He then told us that he was going on board the *Jacob Bell*, and would send the few packages that we were to have on board his vessel. I directly handed him the meagre list, saying,— "Then all the rest, Captain Maffit, must burn and go down with the ship.". I also interceded in every possible way that I could, in order to save Master Charlie's large box-like trunk, which was not

---

[1] Mr. W—— gave me a copy of my insurance policy a few days before we left Fouchau, remarking at the time that, in case anything disastrous happened, I must not trouble about my luggage. Not being accustomed to business, and ignorant of the rights or duties of the insured, when Captain Maffit said that he could not save my property, I unfortunately repeated to him Mr. W——'s remark, saying, also, that I had the impression it would injure the policy if I took any one of the insured packages. The captain at once assured me that it was so, and that unless I left the whole number named in the document, I would get nothing. My loss was between two and three thousand dollars.

insured, but was of great value to him, and was in the hold with my packages. I was the more anxious on this point for the reason that Charlie's father, who was a missionary in China, was sending him home to be educated; and the package contained books and articles of value, the loss of which the lad would feel during his whole course of study. Charlie was much perturbed when we were first taken; and from agitation failed to secure the effects which he had in his state-room. It therefore became necessary that he should go on board and look after them, and another boat putting off for the *Jacob Bell* soon after Captain Maffit had gone, I obtained permission of the officer in charge for him to go on board also.

While I was still remaining on deck the crew commenced bringing boat-loads of property from the ship, although I am not positive that any luggage had as yet been sent. In a short time, however, to my amazement I observed some of the officers and crew of the pirate coming over the side of the vessel, each with an armful of things from my packages. There was bed and table linen, towels made up and in the piece, articles of my wardrobe, silver plate, a box of rare china, two chairs from Canton, Oriental table-mats, a box of India sweetmeats, our stores, and two cases of claret; which, with the sweetmeats, were marked with my name in full. There were also boxes of spools of sewing-silk and sewing-cotton, boxes of pins and of dress-trimmings, and various other articles required for personal or housekeeping use. There was therefore no mistaking the fact that our boxes, trunks, camphor-chests, and camphor-chest of drawers had all been rudely broken open, and plundered by these outlaws. The *officers* of the *Florida*—the so-called boasted *chivalry* of the South — were now shamelessly enacting the burglar and shop-lifter, directly before my eyes; and carrying my property in tumbled, confused masses, — some of it dragging and trailing on the deck, — into their ward-room. I saw Lieutenant Reed with a huge armful of cotton-sheeting and unmade table-linen, — grasping at the same time in one hand my cake-basket, (the wrappers of which being torn off it was exposed to my gaze,) — rush from the side of the ship to the ward-room entrance; when seeing that I was watching him in mute astonishment, he dropped his eyes and hurried below like a detected thief. This scene of pillage continued for several hours. Finally, Charlie returned, and related to me the scenes he had witnessed on board the *Jacob Bell*. He saw my packages brought up from the hold of the vessel, and also saw the *officers* of the *Florida* split and break them open, rummaging their contents, and tearing off wrappers of small parcels in the greatest eagerness, which if not desirable, or such as they could not make use of, were thrown on deck and trodden under foot in a manner which would have almost made an ordinary pirate blush. Laces, and other delicate fabrics, were thus used; and a valuable bonnet was soiled and destroyed in the same manner. Private papers also, and photographs of friends, met a like fate; nothing, in fact, escaped their shamelessly sacrilegious hands. There was a large number of curious, rare, and elegant Oriental articles, — presents from friends and acquaintances in the East, — beside many that were not only handsome, but useful, which I was bringing home as presents for friends; all of which met the same fate. One officer was seen examining and helping himself from a box of fans, — taking them out one by one, and fanning himself, to see which he liked the best. Another laid hold of a hoop-skirt, and putting it on, tripped over the main-deck with a grace and delicacy doubtless unattainable except by a representative of Southern *chivalry !*

While this scene of rioting and plunder was going on, Charlie begged of them three times to save his large trunk, but was told that nothing from the hold could be taken on board the pirate; nor was his package brought from the hold until he left the *Jacob Bell* to return to the *Florida.* Then some of our crew, who were still remaining on board the ship, saw it brought up, broken open, and plundered in the same way they had served mine.[1]   But to cap the climax of this scene, a fat pig, — one of the animals remaining of the *Jacob Bell's* supplies, — was killed on her main-deck in a most barbarous manner, and pieces of the creature being savagely cut from its sides, the marauders took such portions as they desired, while the entrails were thrown about the deck, where the blood had been permitted to flow in every direction, and in which articles of my wardrobe, expensive fabrics, family relics, and souvenirs of friends left in the East, were also thrown, and mingled with the clotted mixture in the most offensive and disgusting manner. After witnessing this, Charlie returned on board the steamer, and approaching me with teeth firmly set, while indignation flashed from his eyes, exclaimed in an undertone, " I never was so mad in all my life!   O! it was a fearful scene; I shall never forget it;" and afterwards added — " I hope yet to meet them with a gun in my hand!" I was frightened as well as surprised to see the gentle,

---

[1] Most of Charlie's money, which was in Mexican dollars, was in this package, and his father has since written him that the value of the contents of the trunk was two hundred dollars. It also contained the only mementos the boy possessed of his deceased mother.

quiet boy wrought up to such a pitch of indignation; but that scene, together with the compulsory
piratical cruise of five days and nights which followed, seemed to arouse and mature in the boy all
the noble and brave qualities of the man. He only
wished that we could meet one of our cruisers, and
have an engagement with her; declaring that he
would gladly serve his country by going to the bottom, if the steamer could be sunk, carrying down
with her the piratical officers and her crew; nor
would the boy ever acknowledge to an emotion of
gratitude to Captain Maffit for the common personal
civilities we received; but if it was referred to, always said that he saw too much of the plundering
scene to desire anything but the destruction of the
captain and his officers.

There was now much confusion on the deck of
the pirate. It was nearly four o'clock, P. M., and
trunks, stray articles from our packages, boxes of
the ship's stores, and some of our own, together
with a few of the sailors' chests, bags of sailcloth
filled with clothing, and boxes of tea, were lying
about in every direction. The pirates had become
so completely engrossed in their work of plunder as
to be oblivious of all else; and before they were
aware, the *Jacob Bell*, with all her sails set, was fast
drifting against the *Florida*. That was a terrible

scene.   She seemed a sentient being, — "a thing
of life."   There was a little swell, but thanks to a
kind Providence, no sea ; and as she came down on
the *Florida* her prow seemed absolutely to stretch
eagerly forward as if in haste to avenge her wrongs.
The fires of the steamer had been banked, and as
there was no steam to enable us to back off, for a
time there was general confusion ; until finally I
heard Captain Maffit giving orders to put oil and tar
on the fires.   By this time the jib-boom of the *Jacob
Bell* had become entangled in the fore-rigging of the
Florida, and broken the ratlines ; when there was an
attempt made to cut it away, — all on board of her
being congregated at her bow for this purpose.   The
crew of the *Jacob Bell*, as well as those of the *Florida*,
assisted by means of spars in keeping the former out
of the way ; but she finally came up with greater
force, getting the jib-boom under the main-top-mast
stay, but doing no serious damage.   We very soon,
however, got up sufficient steam to move a little out
of the way.   To say that this was a scene of immi-
nent peril can impart but a faint idea of the over-
whelming consternation and dismay which we suffered during these moments of intense anxiety and
terror.   I was already in a pitiable condition from
the alarm and agitation which a consciousness of
extreme exposure produces ; and not having yet

recovered from the shock received on finding myself in the power of lawless men, this new and crushing terror seemed to subdue and benumb every faculty.

As soon as the pirate had become disentangled from our vessel, our captors having placed combustibles in three places on board of the *Jacob Bell*, she was fired about four o'clock, when she was abandoned, and we steamed away from her neighborhood. The distressing circumstances under which we were placed rendered it impossible for us to feel the sublimity of the spectacle she presented while the flames crept steadily up her sails, spars, and rigging, until she became a pyramid of fire. Not that our thoughts dwelt so much upon the wicked destruction of property, as upon the fact that we were being completely cut off from home and country; and knew not how, when, nor where we could look for release. To us the last sight of our noble ship a little before her masts fell, when with her sails and rigging all a-blaze, she was quietly floating on, impressed us with a scene of awful and melancholy grandeur. The sublimity of such a spectacle depends altogether upon the circumstances under which we behold it. Our ideas of things are merely relative, and depend for their moral effect upon the power of association. Hence, the contemplation of any wide-spread ruin may be the height of the sublime

21

to a disinterested spectator; but to another, whose
worldly interests, or, as was feared in this instance,
whose life is depending upon the character and extent of the calamity, it can be nothing else than a
scene of horror and dismay.

The next day (Saturday, the 14th) we had a fair
wind, and the steamer, having only enough coals for
two days' use, was put under sail, and her screw
raised upon deck. The armament of the pirate was
very heavy: there being six sixty-eight pounders,
three on each side of the ship; and two immense
guns, called chasers, one at the bow and the other
at the stern, which were said to be one hundred
and twenty pounders. There were about[1] one hundred and sixty men on board beside the officers, the
latter consisting of the captain, a sailing-master, four
lieutenants, four midshipmen, and two physicians,
besides three or four minor officers. The small
arms of the *Jacob Bell* which were taken enabled
some of the crew to supply themselves with fine
cutlasses, and thus complete their accoutrements.
The lieutenants and physicians were very young
men, none being over twenty-five years old; and
the midshipmen were quite young striplings, — mere.
boys in fact,—but some of them hard-looking young-
sters. Both the lieutenants and midshipmen were

[1] According to Captain Maffit's statement.

evidently regarded as belonging to the class called " Southern gentlemen!" There was a Reed from Charleston, and a Floyd from Georgia, — (of the former I shall say more by and by,) — both of the best blood of the South, and the rest of the officers were also reputed to be of highly respectable lineage. One officer — a young man from Mobile, whose name I have forgotten — became so intoxicated, on some brandy we had among our stores, that he was put under arrest, which was the only case of discipline that occurred while we were on board. The steamer was shockingly dirty, and in an almost filthy condition,—the deck affording no place where a woman could remain with unsoiled skirts. Indeed, excepting in the most miserable hovels of the foreign poor in the outskirts of the city of New York, I never met with such disgusting untidiness and want of cleanliness. With these surroundings personal neatness was out of the question, and my garments became shockingly soiled and unsightly. But *malgré* this pitiable plight, with all its attendant exposure to the vulgar gaze and criticisms of the low and degraded men composing the officers and crew of the *Florida*, it was, with the exception of an occasional emotion of contempt and righteous indignation, entirely lost sight of in the absorbing thought and prayer for a speedy deliverance from such an unhallowed atmosphere.

Saturday wore slowly away, and after another fearful night the Sabbath found us again chasing one of our vessels. On such a ship as the *Florida* any appearance of properly regarding the day would have presented an anomaly, — the habits of both officers and men, and the iniquitious business in which they were engaged, being so thoroughly in keeping with their surroundings. The crew were at work as usual during the whole day, some scraping the masts, and all on the *qui vive*, and animated with the idea of bagging and burning another "Yankee." Captain Maffit did not know that it was Sunday until the fact was alluded to by one of our number in his presence, which caused him to exclaim, — "Sunday! Is it Sunday? I did not think of its being Sunday!" The burden of our prayers during the day was for the final escape of their anticipated victim, which proved to be a schooner, and got rid of her pursuers by skilful management, obliging them to tack ship repeatedly. The crew of the pirate, not being experienced sailors, were awkward and slow in performing their duties. They were mostly composed of the lowest class of Irish, with some few English and Scotch, — most of whom had formerly been in the rebel army, and were mere tyros in nautical matters. Captain Maffit told us, however, that he had drilled them at the guns until they could manage them with great celerity and effect.

Early in the afternoon Captain Frisbie, on coming below, remarked that we were gaining on the schooner, and he feared she would be taken; and at a later hour Captain Maffit descended into the cabin with a countenance beaming from delighted exultation, and, throwing something of the theatrical into his air and manner, seated himself, remarking, — " Well, I fear there is 'one more unfortunate'!" He did not proceed with the quotation, but it was continued in some of our hearts by the supplication, — God forbid that she should come " to her death" by you and your lawless crew! It is almost needless to add that we secretly rejoiced and gave thanks, when, as the shadows of evening gathered around us, the expected prey escaped.

When the *Jacob Bell* was captured we had nearly used up all our fresh animal food, and there was but little poultry and one pig remaining. To the killing and disposing of the latter I have already alluded. The few fowls left were also killed and taken on board the *Florida*, and we were once served with a dish of them, and once with the fresh pork. With these exceptions, we lived almost entirely upon salt-beef and pork, together with a little rice and hard biscuit. Captain Maffit said he gave us the best he had, and professed to regret not having better for the ladies. Our food, however, was of little moment, no one having the heart to expend any thought upon our common sea-fare, and some of us being too ill to care for such matters. We suffered most from want of good water, — that on board the *Florida* being condensed steam, and evidently produced in a defective apparatus, which imparted to it so strong a taste of kreosote that one could scarcely swallow it. Indeed we feared that it was injurious, and dared not drink it; nor was the tea and coffee made of it at all palatable.

All but one of the packages promised me from the *Jacob Bell* were sent on board; that contained a valuable article, — a present from a French baron, formerly one of the French legation at the court of Peking, but now Commissioner of the Imperial Customs at Fuh-chau. Captain Maffit, on being told of its elegance and rare value, and that it was in a part of the ship near my state-room where it could be readily found, and transferred with our trunks of sea-clothing. and Captain Frisbie's luggage to the steamer, said, in an earnest manner, " Mrs. W——, you shall have the box, and I will see that it is sent on board "; but on returning to his own vessel very coolly said that he had looked for it, but it could not be found. I was not sensible

of any feeling of indignation in relation to the pillaging and wanton destruction of our property. A kind
Providence had ordered that the stunning effect of our
unexpected capture should render me unfit to care for
or realize the loss of my property ; nor, with the exception of some occasional agitation, — when a view
of our terribly fearful position, and the perils with
which we were environed flashed across my mind, —
was I conscious of any emotion, but was much like
Dr. Livingstone when the lion's paw was on him, —
" without feeling."

Captain Maffit had said, when we were first
taken, that we would be only two or three days on
board his ship, as he would probably, by that time,
meet some friendly vessel, and be able to transfer
us, but if not, he would take us into a neutral port ;
yet day after day we continued sailing in every
direction, and unfurling the flag of whatever nation
best suited his purpose, in order the more successfully to play the corsair. In the course of three days
the debilitating effects of the increasing heat warned
me that we were again seeking the heat of the tropics ; and nearly at the same time the fact that the
captain feared to attempt entering· a neutral port,
and that in essaying to do so we must run the
risk of an encounter with some of our Government
cruisers, began to dawn upon my excited imagi-

nation, making the possibility of an early release
from our unhappy condition seem more remote than
ever. This unnatural excitement was followed by
great depression, — a sort of despair, — under which
nature gave way, and, like a child, I could not
allude to our painful situation without weeping.
Despair is said to give courage to the weak, but it
failed in my case ; and when the day closed, and
the gloom of night settled around us, the fear and
anxiety which seemed to make up the sum of those
dismal hours may be perhaps imagined, but no
description of their terrors can be given which will
not fall short of the reality. A soul suspended in
Dante's " Limbo " could scarcely be more hopeless.
We could not disrobe, but laid ourselves down to
rest in the clothes worn during the day. Sleep
was far from being the " sweet restorer," and
every movement of the armament above, or noise
about the ship, roused me, until everything seemed
one confused and horrid nightmare. One night,
after slumbering a short time, I was awakened by
an unusual noise on deck, and as the wind had increased, and we were sailing more rapidly, I feared
that a heavy gale was approaching. The most courageous rarely desire a repetition of a storm at sea,
and the timid are always agonized in the prospect
of one. Belonging to the latter class, an undefina-

ble sensation of fear and dread seized me. There was no light in the cabin, but quickly rising and groping in the dark as best I could, I reached the companion-way, and on climbing the stairs, a man stationed at the top, armed *cap-à-pie*, forcibly reminded me of our captivity. Fearful of giving offence, I asked the sentinel to excuse me, and added that I was very timid at sea, and observing that the wind seemed to be increasing, feared that we were about to have a gale. The man,—who was one of the rough crew,—after civilly assuring me that all was right, and that we had only a fine breeze, added, "I knows you's not fit for the likes of this." There was real kindness of heart in the tones of Erin, and I was sorry that the "likes of him" should be engaged in so desperate a business. I afterwards learned that several of the crew from Mobile and New Orleans, in private conversation with the crew of the *Jacob Bell*, deplored being on the *Florida;* but said that they had been compelled to ship so as to get food, as they were without employment and without means. Moreover they expressed regret that they also were not to be transferred to a neutral vessel, or to be landed at some port from whence they could go to the North.

I knew nothing of Captain Maffit's antecedents, nor of his standing when an officer in our navy. I

learned, however, from Captain Frisbie, that he had
at one time been attached to the coast-survey, and
that his charts were much used by mariners. The
captain himself valued them highly, and spoke of
the author as having been one of the first officers in
our service in point of ability. When we were first
taken on board the *Florida* he simulated the air and
tone of an honorable man, and stoutly disclaimed all
wish or intention to war on women and children, telling us that all our private effects should be respected
and saved for us, and was altogether so civil that
although we could only look upon him as a sort of
buccaneer, we were led to hope that he might still
retain enough of the elements belonging to the character of a *civilized* man of the nineteenth century,
as to really mean what he said ; in other words, we
did not suppose that it was a part of his code of
chivalry to impose upon a defenceless woman and
child. In this, however, we were mistaken ; for with
the exception of a box of Captain Frisbie's china
which was stolen by the ward-room officers, and the
general pilfering practised by the pirates upon the
powerless crew of the *Jacob Bell*, Master Charlie
and I *were the only persons plundered ;* and Captain Maffit, notwithstanding his fine words, seemed
to make us the special objects of his treachery. He
affected to regret the necessity which he was under

of destroying our captain's favorite ship, and pretended to be sorry that the charts and most of the nautical instruments belonged to the latter, as the orders of his Government were imperative, and obliged him to take them as his prize. He was very sorry such misfortunes should fall upon men like Captain Frisbie, but assured him that all his private property should be saved; and all of it, consisting of several trunks and chests, beside a number of well-filled sail-cloth bags, and four boxes of china, were taken on board the *Florida*. All of this property but one box of china (to which reference has already been made) was safely transferred to the Danish bark. The officers probably kept the one box of china by order of their captain, so as to give the impression that they had not expended all their purloining energies upon us.

While on the deck of the *Florida*, the day after the burning of the *Jacob Bell*, one of the officers did the agreeable by offering to lend me books to read; but looking at him with surprise, I directly exclaimed, — "Books! it would be impossible for me to read just now, — neither in body or mind am I equal to the task!" It certainly betokened a great degree of impudence and hardihood, for one to assist in the plundering of our private effects, and then unblushingly attempt to recommend himself in this way to my regard. I also had, during the same day, a few words of conversation with another officer in regard to the rebellion ; in the course of which he made some malicious remark that led me to say, — " We do not hate you as you seem to hate us. Why is it that you at the South hate the North so much ? " With the coolest effrontery he answered, — " We have more reason to hate you." The tone and manner in which this was said was too much even for the benumbed senses of a powerless and defenceless woman, and I quickly answered, — " No, you have not, sir. I feel that I am suffering in a good cause, nor should you hear a murmur from me were I strong and in good health." Thus to beard the lion in his den was unquestionably imprudent and unsafe ; but the unmitigated arrogance and impertinence of one who, from what we had experienced, could be classed only among shoplifters, was rather too much for our sense of honor to let pass unrebuked, and the words leaped from my lips like the " stir of an unbidden thought." Although outwardly civil, it required no extraordinary power to see plainly that, could it have served their purpose and benefited their cause, it would have cost them no pang to act the pirate to the *death*, as they were acting it to the life ; but to carry their feelings of hatred to such an extent, they well knew, would array the whole civilized world against them.

Captain Maffit boasted of his daughter, and related the circumstance of the capture of the rebel vessel — in which she was going from Nassau to Charleston — when attempting to run the blockade. He commented with great *goût* upon her bravery, in telling the Government officials — before whom she had to appear in New York — that she acknowledged no Government but that of the Southern Confederacy, and no President but Jeff. Davis. He also told us of a letter written by his youngest son, in which the hopeful youth requested his father to " send him a Yankee's head with the teeth all in!!!" The boy, we understood him to say, was only *five years old!* [1] None of us dared to give utterance to the thoughts suggested on hearing of so savage a request from such a child, — if, indeed, the child ever made it; — and it is difficult to think that Christendom, in this age of the world, is capable of producing a father willing thus to advertise the disgustingly

[1] Since the above was written, a person who has some knowledge of Captain Maffit's children, has suggested to me that he may have said *nine* years, instead of *five*, — his youngest son being then about the age of nine years ; and, as we may have misunderstood him, I cheerfully give him the benefit of the doubt, which, however, does not very materially ameliorate the cruel character of the child.

precocious ferocity of his little son. The bloody request indicated the Nero-like training to which the
child had been subjected, and the malicious hatred
he was already capable of bearing towards his kind.
If this is the child, what will be the horrid proportions of the man ?

From a late New York paper — for the perusal
of which we were indebted to Captain Maffit — we
learned of the noble generosity of the merchants of
that city, in sending a ship loaded with food to the
starving Lancashire operatives ; and on observing
the name of A. A. Low, Esq., — the owner of the
Jacob Bell, — as one of the most active in that work
of mercy, we involuntarily looked around the cabin,
the finishing of which, with all its furniture and fixtures, told us what was too true, that to England —
or rather to a class of her grasping and unprincipled
merchants and cotton-brokers — Mr. Low owed the
loss of his ship, and we our fearful perils and captivity. Whatever else may be forgotten, it certainly
is to be hoped that when the history of this war is
written, the noble and truly Christian manner in
which the New York merchants returned good for
evil will not be lost sight of.

Captain Maffit was much in the cabin during the
day, making himself very facetious, and was always
full of anecdote. He often mentioned incidents in

regard to the rebellion, — giving us what he termed the truth as to the condition and suffering of the North, — which, not then knowing his true character, and having been months without news from the United States, gave us painful uneasiness.

On the afternoon of Monday, February 16th, we were in hot pursuit of a bark that bore the French flag, and early in the evening, getting within hailing distance, brought her to without firing a gun. She was boarded by some of the piratical officers, and proved to be what her colors indicated; and being direct from the island of Martinique, bound to Havre, the pirates neither gained a prize nor were able to dispose of us by transferring us, as passengers, on board of her. This was a sad disappointment, for we had hoped she might prove a neutral vessel bound to some of the West India islands, and be willing to take us to her port of destination. But another long night, with its doubts and fears and weary hours, came and passed away, when, with heavier and more hopeless hearts, we greeted the morning of the 17th, the evening of which day was to bring the wished-for release.

As usual, the beardless midshipmen, armed to the teeth, were constantly ascending aloft and prowling at the mast-head, or on some of the higher parts of the rigging, watching for more prey ; when, early in the afternoon, some one of them on the lookout described a sail far off upon the horizon, which, from the whiteness of her canvas, as well as from its arrangement, was pronounced a " Yankee." The *Florida* was put speedily on her track, but not until late in the afternoon were we sufficiently near the stranger to enable Captain Maffit to play the decoy; which he essayed to do this time by unfurling the English flag at the mast-head. The bark then ran up the colors of Denmark, and, courting our vicinage, seemed for a time to be bearing towards us. At the sight of the strange flag, (for strange it was, indeed, not one of the officers or crew of the pirate being sufficiently versed in nautical matters to tell to what nation it belonged,) there was an extraordinary fluttering among these highly cultivated and well-read (?) men, which finally ended in their referring to the officers of the *Jacob Bell* for the desired information. This point being settled by our not overlettered " Yankee" captain, and the bark not appearing to be in any hurry about courting our acquaintance, but, if anything, gradually shying off from us, Captain Maffit sailed more directly for her, and in the evening, after eight o'clock, fired one of his guns at her, which brought her to, and an officer boarded her.

Captain Maffit had told us in the afternoon that,

should the bark prove to be a Danish vessel, bound for any of the islands, he should transfer us to her in case they would take us as passengers. We were, therefore, in no ordinary state of solicitude, — not daring to hope for our release, for fear of meeting with another painful disappointment.

The boat returned from the bark, and, after a little consultation among the pirates, was despatched a second time. It was already quite dark, and we, to all outward appearances quiet and composed, were sitting in the cabin, — the prey to thoughts and emotions which cannot be expressed, — silently awaiting our fate. When the boat returned for the second time, Captain Maffit held a consultation with several of his officers on a retired portion of the deck ; after which, descending into the cabin, he told us that the vessel was a Dane, bound for the island of St. Thomas, and that her captain had consented to take us as passengers. Then, turning to Captain Frisbie, he said : " What do you say to taking her ? " " I say take her ; any port in a storm," quickly replied the captain. It was then after nine o'clock. The sky was clear, and a few stars were shining, but there was no moon. There was, also, a sharp breeze, and considerable swell in the ocean ; enough, certainly, to impress us with a sense of the formidable character of the adventure which we were about to make, the fearfulness of which now flashed upon our minds in all its appalling reality. It was like being on the roof of a house with all on fire beneath and around. Liberty, and life, for aught we knew, both depended upon facing the danger, and it did not take us long to understand and weigh the dreadful contingencies of the case; but, trusting ourselves to the guiding hand of that same kind Providence who had hitherto protected us, and hoping to reach the deck of the friendly bark in safety, we gathered up the remnant of our luggage, and prepared to take our departure.

We have already mentioned the fact that the officers of the *Florida*, although *high-minded Southern gentlemen*, were possessed of decidedly large organs of acquisitiveness. True to their natural or cultivated instincts, they could not let us depart without practising a little more of their honorable handicraft. When our luggage was brought out and piled on deck, just before our departure, we were assured that all of it should be safely sent on board. We had an undefined fear that some of it would be retained, but dared not intimate to Captain Maffit that we should like our things taken on board *first*, for fear of giving offence, and involving ourselves in some new trouble. We therefore concluded to patiently await the issue of events; but, as will be seen in the sequel, our fears proved well founded.

The reader must not lose sight, in what follows, of the fact that Captain Maffit had all along led me to believe that from kindly motives he had done all he could to protect us and our effects; and that, could he have controlled the pillagers, our packages would have remained untouched to burn with the ship. He also asserted that he had allowed us to have all the luggage he could, and that he greatly regretted we should have been so unfortunate. With these things in mind, the conversation held with him as he accompanied us from the companion-way of his cabin nearly to the bow of the vessel, where we were again to be lowered into the boat that was to receive us, will be readily understood; but we had little idea of the extent of the deception which he was again to practise upon us.

After remarking, as we passed the pile of luggage, that we had placed ours there, hoping it would all reach us safely, Captain Maffit said, — "It shall all be sent on board, Mrs. W——." I then expressed my thanks for his civilities, adding, that we were grateful for his protection, and that our friends would also be thankful that, in our misfortunes, we personally had fared so well; whereupon he remarked something about it being very disagreeable for ladies to be situated as we had been, and expressed himself as extremely sorry for not having been able to make us more comfortable; after which I remarked, — "Captain Maffit, if you are taken, we hope you may be treated as well as you have treated us." Responding quickly, he said, — "I hope I shall not be taken at all." I dared not, in the midst of such surroundings, say, as I must, if a reply were given, that I wished him to be taken, and therefore was silent. Meanwhile we walked several steps, when the captain, divining my thoughts, continued, — "But I suspect, Mrs. W——, that you wish I may be taken?" This said interrogatively, enabled me to escape from my dilemma by the ready rejoinder, — "I shall not pray for it, Captain Maffit." He then assisted me to disembark, and shaking hands, said, with great show of fervor and sincerity, — "Goodbye, God bless you"; which piece of acting being concluded, I was soon over the side of his disgusting vessel and being let down into the boat. This undertaking was no less perilous than our transfer to the bark, nor did we face either with undaunted nerves.

It was now half past nine o'clock. The steamer was rolling and pitching a good deal, and the wind had increased until the white caps, notwithstanding it was quite dark, were plainly visible. I shall not soon forget the terror experienced while suspended over the boat. Her appearance was as frail as a cockle-shell, and being tossed about like a feather, she was continually rising and falling with the sea, which rendered it difficult to keep her properly off from the steamer. While thus suspended, Captain Frisbie, sailor-like, clambered over and down the side of the vessel, and getting into the boat, called out, — " Now let her down easy." Down went the chair for a moment, and then came the cry, — " Hold on ! be careful ! get her more from the side of the ship." For a few moments a state of rest, with both mind and body *in suspension*, followed ; then, again, was heard, — " Now, easy " ; then up came the boat, reaching nearly to the top of the ship's bulwarks ; but directly I was lowered, and, being freed from the chair, grasped nervously the gunwale of the boat, and sitting down, awaited in dread and dismay the hoisting and lowering, in the same way, of the captain's wife. The sailors then assisted Master Charlie and the captain's little son down the ship's side ; and all being ready, we left, and were rowed half a mile in the darkness, through the breaking sea, while our boat leaked so much, that, although there was constant bailing, the water gained on us so fast that it was soon over the tops of my slippers, and I could feel and calculate its increase of depth. I observed that the sailors used great care, aiming to keep the boat in such a position that she would ride the waves as safely as possible; but Charlie, who sat near the bow, said that we twice came near shipping a sea and being submerged. On approaching the bark we found her also rolling and pitching fearfully, and the idea of getting sufficiently near her side to be taken on board seemed truly formidable; but, by God's blessing, we also passed safely through this peril, and finding ourselves on her deck, were relieved of an herculean weight of anxiety and hopeless fear, such as no one can feel or understand unless made to pass through the same terrible ordeal.

The name of the bark was the *Morning Star*, then eight days from New York, and bound to the island of St. Thomas. She was in reality what the pirates first suspected, a " Yankee "; but having been recently sold, and placed under Danish colors, was saved from sharing the fate of the *Jacob Bell.* Like most of the small trading-vessels plying between New York and the West Indies, she was prepared to carry a few passengers, and had a nice cabin, with comfortable accommodations. We were received and welcomed on board in the most humane and kindly manner, — the captain directly giving up his private cabin, and having it arranged with two berths, for the use of Mrs. Frisbie and myself. Indeed, this little *Morning Star*, (Sterling, master,) proved herself a whole constellation of light, hope, and joy to us; her captain also proved a *sterling* commander; nor shall we cease being grateful to her officers for their warm-hearted civility and kindness.

It was after eleven o'clock when all the luggage was said to have been brought on board. The breeze had still further increased, and we were put under sail as speedily as possible; the captain and officers of the bark meanwhile congratulating one another on having escaped unscathed, and evidently glad to widen the distance between themselves and the pirate as fast as possible. I reached the deck of the bark not only with wet feet, but with the lower part of the skirts of my garments in the same uncomfortable condition. In my hand-trunk, it will be remembered, had been put what would make me comfortable in such an emergency; but the steward, after looking for it among the luggage as thoroughly as the confused state of things and the imperfect light of a lantern would permit, reported that it could not be found. We therefore conjectured that it was hidden under the pile of luggage, and would probably come to light in the morning. Happily Charlie was enabled, soon after we reached the cabin of the bark, to get at his trunk of clothing designed for the homeward voyage, and brought me a pair of his woollen hose, which were a comfortable substitute for my wet ones. The little trunk, however, not being found, I was compelled to seek another night's rest in the same condition of personal discomfort in which we all slept on board the *Florida.*

In the morning my hand-trunk was still missing. It was secured by two locks; and, as already mentioned, was full to repletion with what was then to me more valuable than gold, and without which I must not only suffer, perhaps disastrously, from the cold weather on our coast, but be deprived of the means of making a respectable toilette. Through all the destruction of our property I had not thus far shed a tear for any of the many sacredly associated treasures destroyed so ruthlessly by men worse than Goth or Vandal; but the fact of the complete destitution to which I was reduced, in being deprived of all means of personal tidiness and womanly comfort, was too much, and the tears could not be repressed. My two trunks used for sea-clothing on the voyage were sent on board, but nearly all the supplies they contained when we left China having been worn and soiled, had been put into a large clothes-hamper, which was one of the lost packages. I was not certain, even, that I had clothes enough remaining to give myself a respectable garb; nor was it convenient, while on the bark, to get at the trunks in order to make a proper examination. Fortunately, on retiring I had placed my wet stockings where they dried during the night, and, as a dernier resort, was glad to be able to put them on again in the morning. Finding, also, in the counterpane bundle a forlorn old delaine frock, only intended to be worn in times of wretched sea-sickness, (when one, in order to recover, must be on deck in all kinds of weather,) it was soon appropriated, enabling my personal appearance to be only that of bare decency; while Miss Flora McFlimsey's complaint of "nothing to wear," (minus only the poetry,) came home to me in all the eloquence of *unadorned* truth. Perhaps some of the ungrateful Floras among my countrywomen might have learned a valuable lesson by being put to such straits; but I could not be wicked enough to wish any of them a taste of my experience unless they make themselves morally monstrous by claiming to sympathize with the Southern rebels, and boast of their disloyalty to our Government. For the thorough-bred Southern woman, with her rebelliously educated heart, I have much pitiful regard; but none for the shameless Northern defamer of her Government and the land of her birth.

On further search it was discovered, that besides the small trunk, the outlaws had kept a small package, well tied up with a rope, which contained a

folding-chair, designed for sea-travel; a large fur rug
from the Amoor River, which had been purchased at
Fuh-chau, for comfort and protection from the cold
as we neared the coast; an East India pillow, covered with fine matting, and a most desirable article
in the tropics; and a silk sun-umbrella, having an
outer covering of white calico, after the fashion of
the East, together with several other articles of value
from association.   On leaving the pirate we had little thought of losing the trunk, but did have some
fears that the roped package might be retained.
When obtaining permission for the folding-chair
to be brought on board the *Florida* with the rest of
our luggage, I was careful not to tell Captain Maffit
that it was made of a piece of oak taken from the
old English man-of-war *Minden*, on board of which
Mr. Key, during his imprisonment, wrote the " Star-
Spangled Banner"; but Charlie, on returning from
the *Jacob Bell* to the steamer on the day of the plundering, said that Captain Frisbie had very unwisely
informed Captain Maffit of its origin, and that when
it was about to be taken into the boat in order to
be transferred, Captain Maffit forbade it, remarking,
that it could not be taken off the *Jacob Bell*.   I had,
however, been very intent upon saving an article so
sacred by reason of its associations, and had asked
a subordinate officer of the *Florida* — who went on

board the *Jacob Bell* at about the time his captain left her — if he would be so kind as to see the chair sent on board. Not knowing the order of his superior in regard to the matter, he did so ; and being on deck when it was handed over the side of the steamer, I gladly pressed forward to receive it; to which no one objecting, (I think Captain Maffit was present,) it was deposited with other articles in our cabin. The fact that, during the afternoon we were in pursuit of the Danish bark, Captain Maffit had informed Captain Frisbie of his hoping, at about night-fall, to get us taken on board as passengers, led us to make some little preparation towards our desired departure; and while Charlie was engaged in arranging and tying up the package, (already described as containing the chair,) Captain Maffit entered the cabin, and after looking thoughtfully at the boy for a few moments, said, — " Why, Charlie, you are beginning early to prepare for leaving." I then repeated what we understood he had said to Captain Frisbie, remarking, that we thought it the better way, in order not to cause any delay, to be partly in readiness; that the fur rug would, in my delicate state of health, be an important article of comfort in helping to shield me from the severe cold as we approached our coast; and that nearly all the articles in the package were necessary to our wants. He said nothing more, but sat some minutes longer, regarding our movements in thoughtful silence. I watched his countenance narrowly, and in spite of the mask, at other times so effectually worn, read his thoughts so completely to my satisfaction, that the moment he went on deck I said to my young friend, — "Captain Maffit does not mean we shall have these things." We did not, however, allow ourselves to think that he could be so cruelly contemptible as to retain them by stealth. All the articles, except the chair, were doubtless appropriated to his own use; and the latter, if not destroyed, was probably kept as a trophy, which, in connection with the loyal people of the North, will be made a subject of abuse and wanton ridicule.

The fact that the following incidents, which occurred during the first two or three days of our capture, did not really open my eyes to the character of the man with whom we had to deal, may seem extraordinary ; but fright and anxiety, together with my unprotected and helpless position, had rendered me very timid, and strangely stupefied my faculties.

In giving Master Charlie's description of the plundering scene, I have spoken of the articles discarded and thrown on the deck of the *Jacob Bell* by the marauders. Some few of these articles were picked up by the boy, and Captain Maffit being near, told him that anything thus procured could be presented to me, and be accepted, without injuring my insurance. On returning to the *Florida*, he repeated the same thing to me; and just then seeing a new table-cloth, with a dozen napkins to match, — (which I recognized as belonging to my trunk of table and bed linen,) — hanging over the rail, or side of the companion-way, I said, — "And are these, also, for me?" "No, those belong to the ship," Captain Maffit quickly replied, and soon after they were taken to his cabin. Captain Maffit's table, where we were entertained, was also found ornamented, at every meal, with my very nice and rare Oriental table-mats. There were two sets, each of a different style; and both kinds were indiscriminately used at the same meal. The silver taken from the *Jacob Bell* was also used at our table, while mine, as I shall show presently, was kept in the ward-room. Some who admire and sympathize with the self-styled gentlemen and polished officers commanding the rebel piratical vessels, may perhaps regard the placing so many familiar objects before us as only an evidence of their high breeding and kind desire to make our surroundings as pleasant and home-like as possible!

One day, when speaking of our losses and remarking on the pillaging, Captain Maffit, after saying that he could not control his officers nor prevent it, related how, at the time, one officer came to him, after a package of Oriental articles had been broken open, and told him that " now was the time for him to get a beautiful present for his daughter"; and how he replied to him, — " When I want to make my daughter a present I'll pay for it." To appreciate these incidents one should have seen the fine acting, and the very proper emotion to suit the sentiment, expressed in the captain's face. A few days after our arrival in New York, an old Southern friend — a native of Charleston, and a branch of a family in high position in that city — informed us that Captain Maffit married a widow, Mrs. Reed, of Charleston, who was a Laurens, and of one of the most opulent families of that city. Lieutenant Reed is her son, and therefore Captain Maffit's step-son.[1] This young Lieutenant Reed superintended the officers who broke open and plundered our property. After seeing a part of our silver carried into the ward-room, and mentioning the fact to Captain Maffit's steward that some of the spoons were very valuable to me from family associations, and that I should like to get them, he told some one of the officers our

[1] Lieutenant Reed was finally commander of the pirate *Tacony*, and was captured near Portland. He is now in Fort Lafayette.

wishes, but quickly returned, merely remarking, that Lieutenant Reed had ordered our silver taken into the ward-room, and from his manner we readily understood that it was useless to beg further for anything. Captain Maffit was undoubtedly in collusion with Lieutenant Reed, and not only ordered him how to proceed in the plundering, but directed that all the valuables should be taken into the ward-room, where they remained until we left the steamer. There is no question in my mind that the box, containing the valuable article from Peking, — which Captain Maffit coolly told me could not be found, — was at that time in Lieutenant Reed's possession, and being safely kept for the captain, who was thus enabled to present his daughter not only with a beautiful, but a magnificent gift. The fact, also, that my small hand-trunk was well secured with two locks, and that I was careful to take it with me into the boat which conveyed us from the *Jacob Bell* to the pirate, probably inclined Captain Maffit and his officers to fancy that it might contain costly articles of jewelry; and the former, led by his cupidity, ordered it not to be delivered on board the Danish bark.

Had Captain Maffit, instead of masking his designs under this cowardly hypocrisy, at once told us that all the property on board the *Jacob Bell* was his

prize, and that the most desirable and valuable things
we had he and his officers wanted and *would* have, he
would have commanded our respect as a straight-
forward, out-spoken, fearless enemy, — a sort of
honorable freebooter, — who, although a traitor to
the best of Governments, had not yet fallen so low
as to be beneath either pity or contempt.

The captain of the *Morning Star* said that we
were about two hundred miles north of the island
of Sombrero when he took us on board; and as we
had a fair breeze during the 18th and 19th, on the
morning of the 20th we passed this island, together
with that of St. Johns, entering the harbor of the
island of St. Thomas a little after noon of the same
day.   The scenery in the vicinity of the harbor is
attractive and lovely; and the little town — which
is most picturesquely situated — consists chiefly of
one long street lined with buildings, with an occasional dwelling perched on the bold hill-side or distant mountain-slope.   The houses are mostly of
brick, of one story, and are built and tiled in the
Dutch fashion.   I had neither heart nor strength to
go on shore, to view and enjoy the scenery to better
advantage; nor did I, in all my travels, visit any
other place with such painful indifference.   The desire and hope of being spared to get safely out of
the tropics, and to reach home and friends, absorbed

every other thought; and having entire possession of my being was the burden of all my reflections. Therefore, waiting only to learn how and when we could proceed on our journey to New York, we remained on the bark.

Although annoyed at the necessity, it seemed highly imprudent in Master Charlie and I — unprotected as we were — to risk sailing further under any but a neutral flag; and learning that the *Delta* — an English mail-steamer of the Cunard line, plying between St. Thomas and Halifax — was in port, and would leave on her return voyage, *via* the island of Bermuda, the next day at twelve o'clock, we hoped to take passage in her. Although this was a circuitous route, and the winter passage from Bermuda to Halifax was usually very tempestuous, if not perilous, it nevertheless seemed to be the most direct and safe way for us to get home, unless we chose to remain in the tropics a month or two longer.

On the morning of the 21st, Mr. Edgar, our consul at St. Thomas, a gentleman of pleasing address and refined manners, came on board to see if any of the crew of the *Jacob Bell* would ship for a year's cruise in the United States man-of-war *Alabama*, which, together with two other of our vessels of war, was then lying in the harbor. The *Alabama* left at noon of that day, and steamed off in pursuit of the *Florida*. An opportunity presenting itself, I informed Mr. Edgar of our situation and wishes; whereupon he kindly advised us to take the Bermuda and Halifax route, — it being our best course, — and kindly begging me not to be anxious, nor to trouble myself any further as to our arrangements, said he would see that our passage was promptly secured.

Our few preparations were immediately made, and Captain Frisbie, who had gone on shore with Mr. Edgar, returning with our tickets, accompanied us to the steamer. Our shabbily forlorn and *bizarre* personal appearance, as we went on board the *Delta*, would have struck strangers as irresistibly amusing, had not the tale of our misfortunes preceded us. Our trunks were much soiled and marred, — one so much so as to render it necessary to be lashed together with a rope; and not having had an opportunity to pack away the contents of our counterpane bundle, nor the little bag of books, but taking them as originally tied up in our state-room into the boat with us, it may be safely said that we made up a picture, the *tout ensemble* of which must have been painfully ludicrous, and as thoroughly emigrant-like as any one could desire.

Through the humane and thoughtful kindness oj Mr. Edgar, we were put in charge of Captain T. W.

Walker, who, being on his return from India to his home in Boston, had also taken passage in the *Delta*. It was a gracious Providence that placed us in the care of one so kind and gentlemanly, and who did so much to change the current of our thoughts, then so sadly perturbed by the perils and anxieties through which we had passed. We shall ever hold him in grateful remembrance for his inestimable services and unfailing attention throughout the voyage, with its numerous detentions, until he had placed us safely in the hands of friends who met us at the Boston wharf. We also found Captain Hunter — the commander of the *Delta* — to be a noble specimen of the generous and polite English sailor, and indefatigable in his efforts to make us comfortable and happy. This kind interest in our welfare continued after our arrival in Halifax; and we shall not forget his active exertions in regard to our comfort on board the *Arabia*, nor his thoughtful message in relation to us, which we learned after leaving for Boston, he had sent to Captain Anderson and his officers.

I have spoken in another place of not having been able, while on board the friendly bark, to make any change in my clothing ; nor was that luxury enjoyed until we went on board the *Delta*. We were there provided with a large state-room, where our luggage, bundles, and all, were deposited and examined; and for the first time (it being the ninth day after our capture) I made a thorough change of toilette.

We had a fine run, and were soon out of the withering heat of the tropics, and beginning to feel the life-renewing and bracing influence of a more northern atmosphere. With a change of climate our courage also revived, and we dared to look once more towards the dear home-land with grateful hope; losing our thoughts in the fond expectation of again meeting those from whom we had so long been severed, and to whom, it at one time seemed, we never should return.

The morning of the 24th of February found us within sight of the island of Bermuda. When a few miles out a pilot came alongside, and an old colored man was soon piloting us into the beautifully picturesque harbor of St. George. The keen, vigilant eye of this man seemed to pierce beyond the narrow, but lovely passage, we were entering; and when standing upon the upper deck, — his tall and straight figure, with head thrown back, and his dexter-finger pointing, now to the right and then to the left, — strongly reminded us of an oracular seer. The water of St. George's harbor is very pellucid, and the beautiful coral formations at the bottom

can be distinctly seen as you pass to the shore.
Our stay at this island — which is a gem of the sea
— was only for twenty-four hours, but long enough
for us to visit the beautiful scenes in the vicinity of
St. George, and to be charmed with the mere *coup
d'œil* we took of them. Under more auspicious circumstances we should have been glad to remain
there a month, as one of its opulent citizens kindly
proposed we should do, in order to recruit for our
further voyage to Halifax. Carrying wherever we
went, with the story of our misfortunes, the first
news of the destruction of the richest prize that had
been taken by the rebel pirates, we naturally became
objects of peculiar interest, and while on our little
sight-seeing excursion to the settlement and vicinity
of St. George, met with acts of civility and delicate
kindness that deeply touched our hearts.

There were two long, low, lead-colored, side-
wheeled English steamers, designed for running the
blockade, lying in the port when we arrived; one of
which was already loaded with merchandise, and
was getting up steam to leave for Charleston as we
sailed for Halifax. There was a rumor that she had
caused a great dearth in the article of ladies' gloves,
her owners having purchased the entire stock of the
little town of St. George to take to the ladies of
Charleston.

Our passage from Bermuda to Halifax — especially through the Gulf Stream — was very boisterous, and attended with some peril. During our entire voyage from China — with the exception of the gale we encountered at the Cape of Good Hope — we experienced nothing comparable to it, and sometimes it seemed as though our little steamer must be engulfed. But Captain Hunter was an experienced and ready officer, evidently possessing, even to the uninitiated in nautical matters, that *savoir-faire* in his profession, which, united to his calm self-reliance and frank, gentlemanly bearing, banished anxiety, and gave us the greatest confidence in his ability and skill. The winter is too severe and stormy on this route for women, unless compelled by necessity, to incur the hazards of the season ; hence I was the only female among the passengers. Our fellow-travellers were few, and mostly English gentlemen. Some of them were in Her Majesty's service, and seemed amazed at the pirate-like treatment which we had received from such brave and high-minded *gentlemen* as, they supposed, were to be found among the officers of the " Confederate privateers ! " Captain Walker had formerly been in our naval service, and between him and our English friends there was every day more or less earnest, but calm and reasonable, conversation in regard to the unhappy state of our country, as well as to the position and relative merits of the controversy between the North and South; but no unkind remarks were made, nor did I hear even so much as a bit of pleasantry repeated, at the expense of our Government, in my presence.

One officer, after questioning us somewhat closely and hearing our story, expressed surprise, remarking that he, as well as most of his countrymen, had got the impression that the " privateers" — as the English persist in calling them — *never* destroyed private property, and were always careful not only to protect the passengers themselves, but also their luggage. He also said that if our property was insured in such a way that, by taking any part of it, the policy would be invalidated, Captain Maffit — had he wished to do the upright and noble thing — could have taken my silver, and some other articles which were valuable from family and other associations, and presented them to me. He considered that the conduct of Captain Maffit and his officers was very unlike that of the noble English sailor; and that all the particulars in relation to the destruction of our property, together with the final stealing of a part of the remnant of what Captain Maffit had given us, and promised should be sent on board the bark, ought to be made known, as it would tend greatly to correct the impression entertained by many abroad, and which had been gathered from the public prints, respecting the character of the officers of these vessels. At that time I was not aware of the deceit which Captain Maffit had practised upon me in relation to my policy of insurance, and my right to take what I could of the insured packages ; and consequently could not, as I do now, present the case in all its enormity.   Nor did I know, until I reached Boston, that the face of the document which I gave Captain Maffit to read showed no war risk ; and that had it been so, instead of leaving what I might conveniently have had, it was my duty to save all I could, and account for it to the insurers.

We found the weather extremely cold on nearing the coast of Nova Scotia, but reached Halifax on the 1st of March, just in time to get nicely housed in a comfortable hotel before the region was visited with the severest snow-storm of the season.   Here we were detained five days, waiting for the *Arabia*, which, on her voyage from England, had met with much bad weather, and was somewhat behind her time.   Meanwhile our consul, Mr. Jackson, and family, becoming acquainted with our case, sought us out, and together with some of their pleasant English friends did all they could to make our stay agreeable.   We soon learned that Mr. Jackson was very popular, and it was remarked to us by an Englishman that he filled the office with credit and dignity, being all that the position required, — and was not only a man of ability, but also a gentleman of cultivated taste and refinement.

Mr. Jackson's kind attentions to us ceased not until, following us on board the *Arabia* the morning of the 5th, he bade us good-by and wished us a safe and speedy passage home. The *Arabia* had a large number of passengers, and for a little time the news of our misfortunes, and the loss of the *Jacob Bell* created quite a sensation, and I was informed gave rise, on one or two occasions, to some spicy conversation in relation to the rebellion, between a few of our countrymen and some English gentlemen. But, as on board the *Delta*, English army officers and gentlemen were surprised at what we had experienced, and thought that ours must be an extreme case, until informed that it was the opinion of one of the officers of the *Florida* that we might be thankful for having fallen into the hands of Captain Maffit instead of the captain of the *Alabama;* as in the latter case we would not have been allowed any of our luggage, but merely the clothes we were wearing. On learning this, they had nothing more to say in favor of such out-and-out pirates, but remarked that the particulars in our case ought to be made known.

On the night of the 7th (Saturday) we were nearing Boston, but, encountering a severe snow-storm,
were obliged to stand off and blow the whistle most
of the night.   Sunday morning, however, found us
at the entrance to the harbor.   We could not have
chosen a more inhospitable morning to greet, for
the first time, our home-land; yet, on going upon
deck, the view of the coast, though bearing an aspect cold, bleak, and uninviting, brought joy and
warmth to the heart, and words of thankful gratitude to the lips.

We hoped to reach the wharf soon after breakfast, but on entering the harbor a succession of *con-
tretemps* seemed to follow us.   From some cause we
grounded, and it was not until noon that our friends
— who since early morning had been awaiting our
arrival — could step on board to greet and welcome us.

FINIS.

Bayard Taylor's Writings.

John Godfrey's Fortunes:
Related by himself. A Story of American Life. 12mo. Price $2.25.

Hannah Thurston:
A Story of American Life. 12mo. Price $1.75.

Eldorado:
Or, Adventures in the Path of Empire (Mexico and California). 12mo. Price $1.75.

Central Africa:
Life and Landscape from Cairo to the White Nile. 12mo. Price $1.75.

Greece and Russia:
With an Excursion to Crete. 12mo. Price $1.75.

Home and Abroad:
A Sketch-Book of Life, Scenery, and Men. 12mo. Price $1.75.

Home and Abroad. (SECOND SERIES.)
A new volume. 12mo. Price $1.75.

India, China, and Japan.
12mo. Price $1.75.

Lands of the Saracen:
Or, Pictures of Palestine, Asia Minor, Sicily, and Spain. 12mo. Price $1.75.

Northern Travel:
Summer and Winter Pictures of Sweden, Denmark, and Lapland. 12mo. Price $1.75.

Views A-Foot:
Or, Europe seen with Knapsack and Staff. 12mo. Price $1.75.

Standard Juvenile Books.

The History of Sandford and Merton. By THOMAS DAY. Corrected and revised by CECIL HARTLEY, M. A. Eight illustrations by Herrick and others. 1 vol. 16mo. Price $1.50.

The Swiss Family Robinson : or, Adventures in a Desert Island. A New and Complete Edition. Eight illustrations by John Gilbert. 1 vol. 16mo. Price $1.50.

Evenings at Home: or, The Juvenile Budget Opened. By DR. AIKIN and MRS. BARBAULD. Newly revised and corrected by CECIL HARTLEY, M. A. Eight illustrations. 1 vol. 16mo. Price $1.50.

Tales from Shakspere. For the use of Young Persons. By CHARLES AND MARY LAMB. Thirty illustrations. 1 vol. 16mo. Price $1.50.

Notices of the Press.

" THE HISTORY OF SANDFORD AND MERTON. — This is one of the books that never go out of date, and never lose their popularity. It charmed our grandfathers when they were boys, and it is equally charming to the boys and girls of to-day ; and there is every reason to believe that it will be equally as great a favorite with the reading youth of future generations. Its important teachings are appropriate to all times, but especially so to the present. The present edition is as attractive as the superior typography, paper, and illustrations of the famous Riverside Press can make a book, and worthy of the admirable contents." — *New Hampshire Patriot.*

" A CHARMING BOOK. — Hurd and Houghton, of 401 Broadway, New York, have published a beautiful edition of ' Swiss Family Robinson,' of four hundred pages, with eight illustrations. There is no book that has followed in the train of ' Robinson Crusoe ' that is so deservedly popular as this, or so permanently popular. The author has shown so much originality and so thorough a knowledge of natural science, and has so admirably woven into the narrative the sweet and graceful influences of Christian womanhood, that the story can never cease to charm. The present edition, like all the issues of the Riverside Press, leaves nothing to be desired in typography, paper, illustrations, or binding. Knowledge and amusement are here combined in the most fascinating form." — *Boston Traveller.*

" SANDFORD AND MERTON. — ' Among the pleasantest recollections of our boyish days,' says a contemporary, ' is that of the hours spent with this charming volume. Next to " Robinson Crusoe " in interest, and only about a half century later in the time of its publication, it is, and will remain for centuries to come, a great favorite with boys, and its important teachings were never more appropriate than now. The present edition, in the exquisite typography, paper, and illustrations which characterize the issues of the Riverside Press, is so attractive and desirable, that the book cannot fail to be a prime favorite with the juveniles in the coming holidays.' The same house have also nearly ready, uniform with ' Sandford and Merton,' the ' Swiss Family Robinson,' ' Evenings at Home,' of Mrs. Barbauld and Dr. Aikin, edited by Cecil Hartley, and ' Tales from Shakspere,' by Charles and Mary Lamb, both finely illustrated. Messrs. Hurd and Houghton seem to be aware of the high reputation they have gained for fine books, and guard it carefully. Their latest publications (some of which we shall refer to particularly, hereafter,) are among the best that have issued from the press." — *Home Journal.*

The Death and Burial of Poor Cock Robin. With 16 Lithographed Illustrations from original designs by H. L. STEPHENS. Printed with a tint. One volume, demy quarto. Price in boards, $1.25.

A Frog he would a Wooing Go. With 16 Lithographed Illustrations from original designs by H. L. STEPHENS. Printed with a tint. One volume, demy quarto. Price in boards, $1.25.

"Hurd and Houghton, of New York, have published two illustrated books, in a quarto form, which will be sure to have a great run among the children during the approaching holidays. The first is the 'Death and Burial of Cock Robin,' and the second, 'A Frog he would a Wooing Go.' Both are illustrated from original designs by H. L. Stephens, and in spirit, vigor, humor, and expressiveness excel anything of the kind we have heretofore seen in American juvenile literature. While they will delight the young, they are so full of meaning and character, and put so much human expression on animal faces, that they will well repay the study of older eyes. Everybody should go and see these deliciously humorous volumes."— *Boston Transcript.*

John Gay; or, Work for Boys. By JACOB ABBOTT, author of the Rollo Books. A Series of Juvenile Books, in four volumes, viz: Work for Winter, Work for Spring, Work for Summer, Work for Autumn. 18mo. Price in extra cloth, per set, $3.00.

Good Little Hearts; or, Stories about Children who tried to be Good and do Good. By Aunt Fanny, author of the "Nightcap Stories," &c. &c. With numerous Illustrations. In 4 volumes, 16mo. Price per set, $3.60.

A Treasury of Pleasure Books for Young People. With elegant Illustrations printed in oil colors. 8vo. Price in extra cloth, gilt side and edges, $2.00.

Standard Works.

BACON.

THE WORKS OF FRANCIS BACON, Baron of Verulam, Viscount St. Albans, and Lord High Chancellor of England. Collected and edited by JAMES SPEDDING, M. A., ROBERT LESLIE ELLIS, M. A., and DOUGLAS DENON HEATH, with two Steel Portraits of Lord Bacon, and a complete Index. In fifteen volumes, crown 8vo. Price in extra cloth, uncut, $33.75 ; half calf, gilt or antique, $63.75.

CARLYLE.

CRITICAL AND MISCELLANEOUS ESSAYS. Collected and republished by THOMAS CARLYLE, with a new Portrait of the Author and a copious Index. In four vols., crown 8vo. Price in extra cloth, uncut, $8.00 ; half calf, gilt or antique, $16.00.

DE STAEL.

GERMANY. By Madame the Baroness DE STAEL HOLSTEIN, with Notes and Appendices by O. W. WIGHT, A. M. In two volumes, crown 8vo. Price in extra cloth, uncut, $4.00 ; half calf, gilt or antique, $8.00.

FENELON.

ADVENTURES OF TELEMACHUS. By FENELON; translated by DR. HAWKESWORTH, with a Life of Fenelon by LAMARTINE; Biographical Notices, &c. &c. Edited by O. W. WIGHT, A. M. In one volume, crown 8vo. Price in extra cloth, uncut, $2.00 ; half calf, gilt or antique, $4.00.

MONTAIGNE.

WORKS OF MICHAEL DE MONTAIGNE. Comprising his Essays, Journey into Italy, and Letters; with Notes from all the Commentators, Biographical and Bibliographical Notices, &c. By W. HAZLITT. With a portrait of Montaigne. A new and carefully revised edition, edited by O. W. WIGHT. In four volumes, crown 8vo. Price in extra cloth, uncut, $8.00 ; half calf, gilt or antique, $16.00.

The Two Legacies. Printed at the Riverside Press. In one volume, 16mo. Price in cloth, gilt tops, 75 cents.

Dix. Lectures on the Pantheistic Idea of an Impersonal-Substance-Deity as contrasted with the Christian Faith concerning Almighty God. By the Rev. MORGAN DIX, S. T. D., Rector of Trinity Church, N. Y. In one volume, 12mo. Price in cloth, $1.00.

Williams. A Year in China; with an Account of the Voyage, the Capture of the Vessel by a Confederate Cruiser, &c. By Mrs. H. DWIGHT WILLIAMS. With an Introduction by WM. CULLEN BRYANT. One volume, crown 8vo. Price in cloth, $2.00.

Redden. Idyls of Battle and Poems of the Rebellion; a book for Home-places and the Camp. By HOWARD GLYNDON (Laura C. Redden). In one volume, 12mo. Price in extra cloth, $1.50.

Scott. The Poetical Works of Sir Walter Scott, with the Author's latest corrections, and all his Introductions and Notes. In six volumes, 16mo., uniform with TICKNOR AND FIELDS's edition of the Waverley Novels. Price in cloth, $9.00.

Scudder. Life and Letters of David Coit Scudder. By his Brother, HORACE E. SCUDDER. In one volume, crown 8vo. Price in extra cloth, $2.00.

Gardner. Autumn Leaves. By SAMUEL J. GARDNER. One volume, crown 8vo. (In press.) Price in cloth, $2.00.

Hopper. Fire on the Hearth. A Christmas Story. By Rev. EDWARD HOPPER. One volume. (In press.) Price in cloth, $1.25.

NEW EDITION OF IRVING.

THE COMPLETE WORKS OF WASHINGTON IRVING, now issuing in portable 16mo. volumes, with appropriate Vignettes and Ornaments, under the title of the "Riverside Edition." Each volume sold separately.

Now ready.

SKETCH-BOOK,

           KNICKERBOCKER,

                 GOLDSMITH.

In press.

THE TRAVELLER,

         BRACEBRIDGE HALL,

              ALHAMBRA, &c. &c.

16mo. vellum cloth, gilt tops, each $1.75.

Irving's Works. Sunnyside Edition, including the Life of Irving by his Nephew, PIERRE M. IRVING. Printed on tinted paper, and with numerous illustrations. 26 vols. 12mo. Price each $2.00. Half calf, each $3.50.

Irving's Life of Washington. Sunnyside Edition. Printed on tinted paper, and with numerous steel engravings. 5 vols. 12mo. Price $10.00. Half calf, $17.50.

Irving's Life and Letters. Edited by his Nephew, PIERRE M. IRVING. Sunnyside Edition. Printed on tinted paper, and with numerous illustrations. 4 vols. 12mo. Price $8.00. Half calf, $14.00.

The Complete Works of Thomas Hood. With Illustrations from his own Designs. Printed on tinted paper. 6 vols. Crown 8vo. Price $13.50. Half calf, $24.00.

www.ingramcontent.com/pod-product-compliance
Lightning Source LLC
Chambersburg PA
CBHW030902270326
41929CB00008B/540